Working the Field

WORKING THE FIELD

Accounts from French Louisiana

Edited by

Jacques Henry and Sara Le Menestrel

University Press of Mississippi / Jackson

www.upress.state.ms.us

The University Press of Mississippi is a member
of the Association of American University Presses.

Originally published in hardcover by Praeger Publishers,
an imprint of Greenwood Publishing Group, Inc., 2003.
Copyright © 2003 by Jacques Henry and Sara Le Menestrel.

Photographs courtesy of the authors unless otherwise noted.

First paperback printing 2009
∞
Library of Congress Cataloging-in-Publication Data

Working the field : accounts from French Louisiana / Edited by
Jacques Henry and Sara Le Menestrel.
    p. cm.
  Includes bibliographical references and index.
  ISBN 978-1-60473-223-8 (pbk. : alk. paper) 1. Cajuns—
Louisiana—Folklore. 2. Cajuns—Louisiana—Social life and
customs. 3. Creoles—Louisiana—Folklore. 4. Creoles—
Louisiana—Social life and customs. 5. Ethnology—Fieldwork—
Louisiana. 6. Folklore—Fieldwork—Louisiana. 7. Louisiana—
Social life and customs. I. Henry, Jacques. II. Le Menestrel,
Sara.
  GR111.F73W67 2009
  398.2'089410763—dc22   2009006578

British Library Cataloging-in-Publication Data available

CONTENTS

ACKNOWLEDGMENTS

We are grateful to our colleagues, collaborators, and friends for the assistance and helpful suggestions they generously extended to us during our fieldwork and preparation of this volume.

We are particularly appreciative of the authors' willingness to tackle emotional, sometimes sensitive and even painful, issues in reflecting on their fieldwork.

This book is also a tribute to the people who give sense to our profession and make our work possible in tolerating our persistent presence and requests.

We are indebted to Craig W. Gill for offering us the opportunity to publish this revised edition and for believing in our work, and to Mary Cicora for her meticulous and thoughtful work in editing it.

In September 2008, Jacques Henry (left) and Sara Le Menestrel (right) ponder the protean meaning of home amid moving crates. Her Louisiana fieldwork completed, she returns to Paris. He remains in Louisiana.

INTRODUCTION

The State of the Louisiana Field and Fieldwork
(with a post-Katrina and Rita postscript)

—Jacques Henry and Sara Le Menestrel

This book proposes an examination of the practice of fieldwork by social scientists interested in Louisiana's Cajun and Creole cultures. It presents a collective reflection on the methodological issues faced by social scientists doing qualitative research in a modern complex society among large groups of people deemed to share a common heritage. We give particular attention to the concept of field and the complex relationship between researchers, informants, and other participants in the cultural environment. In addition, the authors of this book cast an in-depth and a critical look at the social implications and possible applications of the knowledge acquired through the research they have undertaken.

We argue for the continued relevance of fieldwork as a tool to acquire knowledge of culture and to inform actions of social change. Contributing to the ongoing debate on qualitative methodology in the social sciences, the scholars who have contributed to this collection examine the changes researchers make to adjust to the new conditions faced by anthropology in a postcolonial and postmodern world. We do so by empirically illustrating how the debated issues (location of field, exercise of power, applied anthropology) are intertwined in our experience of fieldwork in French Louisiana. In presenting our findings here, we discuss how the methods used and the conditions of the research in the field have shaped theoretical choices and our findings. Instead of the traditional presentation of results focusing on the "what we found," we approach the process from a "how we found it" perspective. How have the physical characteristics of the territory, the location and locating of informants, the perceptions of all involved, and our personal profiles contributed to frame and influence the research? How do the global and local, the physical and virtual, meet and collide? Despite the physicality of the terrain, how discrete is the Louisiana field? Is there one field or a plurality of fields? In addition, we have various degrees of attachment to Southwest Louisiana: some of us were born there and stayed or left; others visited and returned home or lingered on. The area became field or home or both. The contributors examine how the shifting definitions of the locale impacted their work.

At the other end of the research process, we address the utilization of knowledge derived from study. The relationship between cultural anthropology and its applications is assuredly complex. The involvement of European anthropologists with their colonial administrations in Africa, that of American scholars in the Pacific after World War II, and the complicated perspective on Native American cultures are some historical cases in point. The relationship between social science and development in the postcolonial era is no less convoluted. The Louisiana field does not fall neatly into world system categories: it is both center and periphery, elite and exploited, powerful and disenfranchised. Within this context, we examine the pivotal relationship of knowledge, power, and action. In this collection we present and assess the utilization of our research findings by individuals and groups on issues as diverse as rights of minority groups, tourism, and language policy.

The authors realize that a book solely dedicated to a discussion of research methods in a rather unassuming location is a challenging proposition. After all, Louisiana is neither a remote paradise nor a hotbed of human misery and its cultural features do not appear to call for a novel methodology. Yet we believe that our approach is original because it is focused, diversified, and integrated. First, we confront and analyze our collective experience of fieldwork in a single area. Most examinations of fieldwork tend to either present the personal experience of a single researcher in its field or gather individual accounts from large and complex areas. The publication of field journals by Leiris (1934), Malinowski (1967), and Dumont (1978), to name a few, provide powerful examples of the first kind (see Stocking 1983; Tedlock 1991 for detailed accounts). In these, anthropologists reveal how they dealt with time, dislocation, living conditions, relationships, and feelings while leaving scientific reflections aside. Collective works tend to focus on large diversified areas such as the Pacific (DeVita 1990; Terrell, Hunt, & Gosden 1997), North America (Desdouits & Turgeon 1997), Latin America (Krotz 1993; Yelvington 2001), or complex entities such as the United States (Messerschmidt 1981), modern France (Bromberger 1997; Rogers 2001; Terrio 1998), or New Guinea (Gewertz & Errington 1997). Other collections assemble texts sharing an ideological perspective or belonging to a particular anthropological "school" such as a compilation of fieldwork accounts by British researchers (Dresch, James, & Parkin 2000). In contrast, this book gathers a plurality of individual perspectives on a single well-delineated field, an approach that has since been emulated by others (*Egypte-Monde arabe* 2006).

Moreover, it is also diversified. Our collection of accounts offers an assortment of periods of study (from the 1970s to the 2000s), of fields of expertise (geographer, folklorist, ethnologist, anthropologist), of methods of inquiry, of personal profiles (insider, outsider; native French- or English-speaker; Louisiana-born, foreign), and of depth of involvement in the milieu (from the active participant to the distant academic). We believe that the presentation of these crisscrossing views of the same field has a heuristic value. The dialogue between different specialists, the conjugation of reflexive and reciprocal gazes contribute to sharpening our reflection and expanding the limits of the ethnographic experience (Rogers 1991).

Finally, our approach is integrated. It encompasses all the steps of research and beyond, from the moment of entry to the evaluation of policy measures. In doing so, it presents how methods, theory, findings, and their application are combined. While neither a theoretical treatise, a methods manual, a behind-the-scenes look, a critique of ethnography, or a policy memo, our collection assembles all of these dimensions. The usual segmentation of the research process in the social sciences fits the inherent demands of logic and responds to external constraints of pedagogical presentation and task specialization. This in turn is reflected in the organization of scholarly articles, publishers' collections, and college curricula: methods, data, topics, proposals, and comments are often presented separately. But this modus operandi tends to marginalize the discussion of methodological issues. It is often restricted to the obligatory section in journal articles, relegated to an appendix (a revealing term!) or force-fed to college students by means of required courses. This is quite paradoxical considering that science is but a method of inquiry and that the emergence of the social sciences primarily results from methodological breakthroughs.

Before presenting the fieldwork narratives, we will briefly review the main features of the ongoing debate about methods in anthropology. Furthermore, in doing so we will also examine how it has shaped recent research in French Louisiana.

THE STATE OF THE METHODOLOGICAL DEBATE

We aim to avoid two pitfalls common to discussions of methodological issues. At times, they appear to obscure the purpose at hand, which is to explain a situation, not to confuse the reader with a minutiae of statistical procedures as some quantitative studies seem intent on doing. Or, as has been the case in some anthropological circles, they tend to be a tad self-centered and focus more on the researcher than on the researched. Yet, a sound and multifaceted methodology seems to be a primary condition for comprehensive and valid research. Indeed social sciences have, by and large, resolved the debate on the dichotomy between quantitative and qualitative approaches (they are both useful, and compatible) and anthropology has outgrown the distinction of emic-etic perspectives (none are pristine or superior, and they constantly interact).

Developments over the past decade suggest that the critical examination of the anthropological project ongoing since the 1970s may finally be yielding some answers to the grand question of "what's an anthropologist to do in the postcolonial world?" Prompted by the Geertzian reassessment of culture (Geertz 1973, 1983) and the critical examination of the politics of ethnography (Clifford & Marcus 1986), the central tenets, both methodological and epistemological, of cultural anthropology have been placed under close scrutiny (Bouvier 1995). The validity of anthropological knowledge has been examined in the light of its colonial past (Appadurai 1988; Trouillot 1991). Thus the objectivation of non-Western cultures as the "Other" has been challenged by a fast-growing body of "native" and "at home" anthropology (Cerroni-Long 1995; Narayan 1993; Peirano 1998). The pivotal concepts of field and fieldwork have also been critically discussed (Gupta & Ferguson 1997a, 1997b; Hirschkind 1991; Marcus 1995; Watson 1999).

As a result, discussions of research methods and field experiences have now become an integral part of anthropology if not a full-fledged branch of the discipline. Relations of field entry, dealings with informants, fortunate or dramatic happenstance, personal emotions, and even taboo topics like sexual behavior once relegated to forewords, passing mentions, or exposing memoirs now make up stand-alone texts (see Tedlock 1991). The breadth and depth of the ongoing debate are reflected in numerous publications such as the table of contents of the *Journal of Contemporary Ethnography*, the recent introduction of a permanent section dedicated to the practical aspects of the craft in the journal *Sociétés contemporaines*, dossiers in other journals (*Current Anthropology* 2000; *Journal des Anthropologues* 2000; *Social Anthropology* 2000; *Ethnologie Française* 2001; *Ethnographiques.org* 2006), as well as vigorous defenses of anthropological orthodoxy (Kuper 1994; Lewis 1999).

Apparently no field is exempt, as research in both dominant and minority groups and cultures is questioned by anthropologists of all kinds. Accounts of methodological quandaries come from the barrio, the *banlieue*, and corporate boardrooms; they deal with Uzbek national culture, Arab women, or London youth; they reflect on how to most appropriately approach the bourgeoisie, refugees, or an elite group. The discussion involves researchers from a variety of theoretical perspectives including nonanthropologists, and with vastly different personal itineraries, say a tenured Brahmin, a lesbian, or a *crioula* graduate student. It takes many forms and is found in a variety of texts ranging from epistemological arguments to pragmatic how-to manuals.

The operation is not risk-free. One general concern is that the trend of self-centeredness removes anthropology from the pursuit of its central objective, the scientific understanding of human behavior. It is true that while readers are provided with revealing "behind the scenes" looks at the making of anthropology, they learn little of the culture or people studied. But as Anthony P. Cohen (1994:135) clearly puts it "anthropologists need to think about themselves in order to think about how people think about themselves." Besides, the impressive output of anthropological publications on all types of groups and cultures constantly coming from all over the world should allay any fear that anthropologists are only interested in themselves.

Concerned researchers also fear that the critical assessment of anthropology's methods may jeopardize the whole anthropological project. Some wonder if the postmodern reassessment in social sciences may reduce the ethnographic field to just "reading texts and writing critiques," thus leaving the field fallow (Vidich & Lyman 1994:42; see also Englund & Leach 2000). In an enlightening article, Aaron Mintz (2000) deplored the "partial dismemberment of ethnography" brought about by the recent deconstruction of fieldwork and asserted its continued centrality to anthropological research. Sharing a similar concern, George Marcus attributed the waning of fieldwork accounts to the fact that traditional ethnographic research may no longer be at the "center of gravity" of the anthropological experience (the pessimistic scenario) or, more optimistically, "that fieldwork engagements and collaborations in new arenas of research are far deeper and more complex than envisioned by the traditional Malinowskian paradigm" (Marcus 2006:116).

If we are to optimistically interpret such a set of disjointed clues, then concerned researchers seem to have already decided that anthropology remains a valid method of investigating human behavior. It does not appear that it will join alchemy and Ptolemean astronomy on the heap of discarded paradigms for the near future. Now that anthropology has fessed up to its colonial heritage, reassessed its prime instrument of investigation, and questioned its relevance, it is time to digest the challenge and move on. The vote of confidence apparently given to fieldwork as a tool to understand Others and Self, the facing down of, or accommodation with, the "postmodern challenge" (Ortner 1999), and the urgent calls for an involved anthropology in the face of incomprehensible situations of human misery suggest that the moment for an informed anthropology is now or at least nearing. We believe that there is now a wide consensus on the necessity of making explicit the contexts of production and reception of anthropological work.

It is not our purpose to review in detail the history of this probing interrogation of anthropological practice and knowledge, nor is it our purpose to discuss its theoretical underpinning (for general treatments see Ahmed & Shore 1995; Hubinger 1996; Moore 1996). As researchers and teachers, we are nonetheless interested in assessing the impact of this reflexive examination on our practice. We have been confronted with most of the epistemological and methodological questions raised by the aforementioned debate. Still, a review of fieldwork-based researches on Louisiana in the past twenty years shows that very little attention has been paid to methodological, and moreover, epistemological issues.

Most authors tend to remain quite discreet on the conditions and implications of their research. In some instances, writers toe the traditional line of removing themselves from the study. They do not take into account their status of insider (Comeaux 1996; M. David 1996; Bernard 2003; Brasseaux & Fontenot 2006) or outsider (Gutierrez 1992; Ware 1994) and maintain complete silence on their relationships with informants and personal experiences. Mentions of methods are likely to be limited to a brief and traditional presentation of fieldwork (when, where, how many informants, interview style, extent of observation and participation).

Those who make references to their situation in the field typically limit mentions to brief statements placed in footnotes or forewords. They present the personal profile of the investigator and reactions of informants whose positive attitude (Dubois & Mélançon 2000; Trépanier 1989), shame to speak "bad French" (Brown 1993), or racist comments (Sexton 2000) are noted. For instance, while Maguire (1989:12) considers the "francophone commonalities" to be an advantage for Canadian researchers working in Louisiana, Henry (1997) mentions the problems he and other researchers had to overcome as both actors and observers of the cultural movement aimed at fostering Louisiana's French heritage. In an issue of the *Journal of American Folklore* (2001), researchers on Cajun Mardi Gras—many of whom contribute chapters to this book—address the challenges, frustrations, and satisfactions brought about by their situation as outsiders to the crews of riders. Several authors have also noted the impact of scholarly writings—although not their own—on the presentation and local perceptions of Cajun culture. Clifton (2000) is a rare one to express a concern about the application of her work—a better treatment of diabetes among minority groups—beyond the generic "contribution to a broader understanding."

A few writers have nonetheless looked in some depth at themselves and their role as an object of research. In line with Favret Saada's (1977) approach to witchcraft in Western France, Dana A. David (2000) makes a point at looking at the effects of her personal position as a native when researching Cajun folk-healing practices; she emphasizes the inescapability of her implication as a *traiteuse* for an accurate insight and analysis of the social network in which she and *traiteurs* are participants. Sara Le Menestrel (1999) describes how the perception of her work on cultural tourism became, while in progress, an integral part of a process of cultural validation of the manifestations she was describing. Barry Jean Ancelet (1994) gives the most explicit and detailed account of the personal dimension of his collecting folktales in the field. He lists his relationship with some of his informants (kin, friends, referrals by students and colleagues); he tells how an old friend from high school was reluctant to tell stories to somebody he knew and discloses the sometimes lucky turns of events that pushed his work forward. However, true to the pattern, a third party reveals in the preface the implications of it all. Carl Lindahl acknowledges Ancelet as "a leading figure in the Cajun musical renaissance which has deeply affected musicians and music lovers throughout South Louisiana as well as beyond the borders of the state" (Lindahl 1994:ix). He also tells of the "human warmth and artistic energy"

(Lindahl 1994:xi-xiii) exuding from the meetings between Ancelet and his informants.

Such statements capture the issues at play when conducting fieldwork in a complex culture. The overlap between research and participation, between home and field, and between friends and informants raises the questions anthropologists now have to consider: Where is the field? What exactly is fieldwork? What is the relationship between anthropologists and informants really made of? Who knows what? How is the knowledge utilized? For all their plain enunciation, these important questions are, as Sherry Ortner (1999) puts it, a "challenge to both the representation and relevance of anthropology."

WHAT IS THE FIELD?

Traditionally, the field of anthropology has paradoxically been viewed as a locus of rupture (total displacement) and a locus of contact (immersion in host culture). Colonization, postcolonialism, and globalization have increased contacts between people and various social entities, thus transforming the premise of both strangeness and purity of cultures. Anthropology, itself a scion of these processes, had to adapt. As a result, both the realities of displacement and isolation became doubtful and the relevance of these concepts faced a challenge. Consequently, the construction of the field as the place where others are and as being different from home has been questioned. For instance, in the United States, work by the American Bureau of Ethnology and the Chicago School involved American fields. But it was not until the 1950s that researchers expanded their investigations beyond Native American or ethnic cultures to features of mainstream America. As Rogers noted as late as 1991, native research in North America was still not considered as legitimate as European studies. This evolution tested the relevance of the discipline beyond exotic fields. But what kind of field is home? Can home be the field? An anthropologist working in her hometown of New York City was asked: "Can you take the subway to the field?" (Passaro 1997). Thus the question, "where is the field?" and its correlate, "what is the field?"

We can start answering the question by turning to the most empirical dimension of the field, the physicality of the space. If the field is no longer necessarily "somewhere else," it may at least be "somewhere." This minimal dimension is universally acknowledged; anthropologists typically account for the space they work in and "place" is listed as a "primary element" of the ethnographic endeavor along with actors and actions (Spradley 1980:40; see also Stocking 1992).

The French Louisiana field can be viewed as a topographical entity. It has physical boundaries: the Mississippi River to the east, the Sabine River to the west, and the Gulf of Mexico to the south. It also has political boundaries: squarely confined within the state of Louisiana, it is composed of twenty-two parishes, the Louisiana equivalent of counties. This definition has historically evolved though; over the years French Louisiana has been a colonial territory, a state, an ethnic enclave, an "official" area recognized by the Legislature as Acadiana, and a tourist region known as Cajun Country. Road signs tell drivers when they enter or leave the area, which is regularly identified on maps. The apparent discreteness and physicality of the Louisiana field is not sufficient. Louisiana's clear-cut physical and political boundaries are but a frame within which researchers have had to define their field. Over the years, the locating of French Louisiana has been a problematic and well-documented enterprise (Estaville 1986; Oukada 1978). Various techniques have been used by researchers to bound their field.

There is a preponderance of studies where the field is physically defined by environmental features, political boundaries, or a combination of both. Such is the case of "village" ethnographies dealing with a single community (M. David 1996; Esman 1985; Maguire 1989) or sometimes several of them (Dubois & Mélançon 1996; Trépanier 1989). Often the field of research is a larger physical entity: one parish (Dorais 1980) or several (Gold 1980; Maguire 1979), a larger region such as the Bayou Lafourche area (Larouche 1982), the Atchafalaya Basin (Gibson 1982), the "prairie" (Brasseaux, Fontenot, & Oubre 1994; Gold 1982), "Cajun Country" (Ancelet, Edwards, & Pitre 1991), and even more broadly, the Gulf South (Dormon 1996). In this case, the definition of the physical field often includes a combination of environmental, historical, cultural, and political markers which largely overlap. For instance, the central flat fertile prairies and the watery region along the Gulf Coast have been settled at slightly different periods by different groups of Acadian and French immigrants. During the nineteenth century, political divisions were superimposed on these environmental and historical distinctions. By and large language has been the cultural marker most often used. From the 1930s on, the concentration of French speakers has been the trait utilized to separate French and Anglo Louisiana and locate the ethnic core. French Louisiana was, and largely remains construed as, French-speaking Louisiana despite the fact that this approach is notoriously based on vague, approximative, and increasingly irrelevant criteria. Figure 1 proposes yet another

French Louisiana according to fieldwork accounts.

representation of our field, a sum of the fields worked by the contributors to this volume; by showing only the places mentioned in the texts, it attempts to integrate the physicality of the terrain with its varying conceptualization.

Indeed, it is clear that the anthropological field becomes increasingly deterritorialized. The physicality of the field is subsumed when people are not attached to a discrete location. Such is the case of the ubiquitous bourgeoisie in Western society (Pinçon & Pinçon-Charlot 1997), of transcontinental migrants (Appadurai 1992), and of itinerant groups and refugees temporarily inhabiting marginal or disputed areas and political "no man's land" (Bizeul 1999; Williams 1987). The ultimate case of deterritorialization is the virtual world where the field consists only of digital symbols traveling through cyberspace and of the network of people on the sending and receiving ends (Green 1999). The Louisiana field displays some of these features which have been used as bases for definition in addition to or in conjunction with physicality (Webre 1998).

Some researchers have defined their field as events or actions. This is the case of research on Mardi Gras (M. David 1996; *Journal of American*

Folklore 2001; Spitzer 1986; Ware 1994), folktales (Ancelet 1994), festivals and celebrations (Esman 1981; Le Menestrel 1999), and the various actions promoting Louisiana's French heritage commonly referred to as the French Movement (Ancelet 1988; Brown 1993; Henry 1997). Obviously these activities take place somewhere. However, researchers are not bounded by a locale; rather, they follow actions and participants wherever and whenever they engage in the event. The field is then comprised of, among others, festival sites, parade routes, organization headquarters, meeting halls, entertainment venues, media facilities, offices, and people's homes.

The French Louisiana field is situational because it is construed as a basis for self-identification. There appear to be two major guises of Louisiana as an identity marker. First, research has shown that people from Louisiana claiming a Cajun identity consider residence in the Southwestern part of the state as a central criterion (Dubois & Mélançon 1996; Henry & Bankston 1999; Trépanier 1989; Sexton & Guidry 2000). The proximity of family residences in rural areas, often concentrated on a road named after a lineage, signals attachment to a locality. It is embodied in the concept of *voisinage* (neighborhood), which carries a dual meaning of place bounded by physical markers such as roads or bodies of water, and networks of social interaction. This territorial sense of belonging also includes parish affiliations (to be from "Saint Martin," "Lafourche," or "the Avoyelles"), regional distinctions (the prairies, the basin, the coastal marshes), as well as differentiation between rural and urban communities. To go "*en ville*" (i.e., New Orleans) or "*au village*" (into town), to live "in the country" are powerful and meaningful statements. Census figures show that residents of Southwestern parishes tend to be more homebound than other Louisianians and Americans. In 1990, over 90 percent of residents in heavily Cajun parishes were Louisiana-born whereas the state average was 80.6 percent; the figure dropped to 78.4 percent in 2000 but it was still enough for Louisiana to have the most stable population in the United States ("La. Natives Reluctant to Leave Home" 2001; U.S. Bureau of Census 1993). Anecdotally, it is not rare to meet older and not-so-old Cajuns who have never or only rarely traveled out of state or even to New Orleans, a two-hour drive from Lafayette, the major metropolitan area in French Louisiana.

The topographical identification is also largely symbolic. The value system built around rural virtues and activities, a part of the Cajun ethnic identification, coexists with an increasingly urban residence and lifestyle. Not only do 70 percent of Cajuns live in metropolitan areas but most rural dwellers tend to have very urbanized living arrangements, occupations, and activities, when their environment itself resembles more of an expanded subdivision than a pastoral "*campagne*" (Henry & Bankston 2002). Similarly many Cajuns who have lived abroad or out of state, often for professional reasons, express longing for home. Some arrange to reconstruct a home away from home through associations, importing of food items, or organizations of celebrations. Those who are permanently established outside of Louisiana are assiduous visitors to their native state on weekends, for festivals, religious holidays, and family events. Others choose to come back to the area where they were raised, even if the move carries a cost (often in terms of jobs or comfort). "Home" and "coming home" are assuredly common themes in American culture beyond the borders of the Bayou State. However, Louisiana remains a salient referent as the homeland for resident Cajuns and Creoles and for those who are displaced. Thus, the field may be whatever it is thought to be and wherever French Louisianians may happen to be.

In addition to the physical, active, and symbolic dimensions, the French Louisiana field is also transnational. The existence of Louisiana, indeed its very name, owes much to nonnative entities. Historically global, Louisiana today maintains multifaceted relations with the French-speaking world through international cultural agreements, twinning of cities, and membership in francophone organizations. Recently, cultural links have been established with Senegal on the basis of both French culture and the slavery connection. Beyond political boundaries, Louisiana forms with the Canadian maritime provinces the symbolic territory of Acadia, the space of the Acadian diaspora. The sense of belonging to an Acadian community appears through the enhancement of a "blood" filiation, of a common historic memory based on the *Grand Dérangement* experience (the expulsion of the Acadians by the British in 1755), and of the survival theme. It is also based on the perception of common values (such as the Catholic religion), a common language (even to Cajuns who do not speak French, nowadays a majority), and, moreover, includes the perception of physical resemblance (Maillet 1984). The bond felt within the diaspora has grown tremendously these past decades with the Louisiana French Movement and the organization of the World Acadian Congress. The meetings in Moncton (1994), Lafayette (1999), and Nova Scotia (2004) were marked by highly emotional meetings between "cousins" and other long-lost kin. This convergence between what activists call "North Acadia" (New Brunswick, Nova Scotia, Prince Edward Island) and "South Acadia" (Louisiana) has had practical consequences. An Acadian Memorial has been built in Saint Martinville, Louisiana, genealogical societies and queries are on the rise, exhibits on Acadian history are being set up, and the development of an "Acadian" tourism is actively sought (Le Menestrel 1999).

Finally, one more step removed from physicality, some scholars construe French Louisiana, and more specifically Cajun culture, as virtual. It is comprised of the items, meanings, images, and statements created by and/ or broadcast through the media including printed material, radio and television programs, movies and documentaries, and websites. The field thus becomes the economy of commercial ethnic items proposed to residents and tourists alike, the corpus of representations of French Louisiana in books, films, conferences, and travel writings (Allain 1989; Ancelet 1990; Gaudet 1989), as well as the accumulation of meanings associated with Cajunness (Henry & Bankston 2002). The creation of Internet sites by Cajun individuals, businesses, and organizations displaying or touting Cajun culture has introduced Cajunness into cyberspace. The field thus is where and what the "CyberCajun" is (Sexton & Guidry 2000; Webre 1998).

Most of these dimensions, along with their inherent problems and their functional usefulness, are addressed in the following chapters. This collective discussion illustrates how the disparateness of our field—its features and our various approaches—can somehow coalesce in a unified and coherent notion. For all its dimensions, its varying meanings, and the different practices it supports, the French Louisiana field exists.

ACTORS IN THE FIELD

Concomitant to the discussion of the field is a reassessment of the relationship between the participants and the field. The debate originated in the 1970s with the discussion of indigenous anthropology in non-Western countries (*Current Anthropology* 1980) and the "frustration and dissatisfaction with social-class and racial bias of anthropology" in Western culture (Jones 1970, 1995:58). For decades, anthropology had been intent—and quite efficient—at discovering the Other. The time had come to question this conceptualization and ponder the nature of otherness and inevitably that of the Western self. Among the issues that have been raised, several are particularly relevant to our fieldwork experience.

One is the debate on home or native anthropology. Can one conduct the anthropology of his or her own culture and society? On one hand, native anthropologists benefit from deep socialization and resultant familiarity with the native paradigm, and thus they have easier access to the potential "inside scoop." The native anthropologist benefits from a unique vantage point, one that outsiders will never gain. In addition to the problems faced in the processes of entry and enculturation, the outsider anthropologist can never experience total assimilation even if it is actively sought. Frank Hamilton Cushing failed at it among the Zuni and more recently so acknowledged Klausner (1994), whose forty years in Thailand did not make him a native after all. On the other hand, the blurred boundaries between the researcher's private and professional spaces, between field and home, between what is tacit and explicit cultural knowledge, limit the distance and objectivity associated with the anthropological enterprise. The anthropologist can enjoy a strong and intimate relationship with the society but must redouble efforts to preserve a "distanced gaze." Empathy is essential to communicate with the people studied, but it must remain as a part of a process of understanding, not of identification.

Actually, our goal should be less of a search for an illusory "appropriate distance" than a constant effort to compare our reactions, representations, and experiences with those of the people we study. "The research is constructed in the interplay of differences and similarities," writes La Soudière (1988:101). Even the native anthropologist cannot escape the inherent ambivalence of his or her position. The detachment of the researcher may not be understood or accepted by his or her own group, and the issue of identity may itself become problematic. For instance, Beoku-Betts (1994), an African anthropologist, discovers that her sharing race, gender, family structure, and rural background is not sufficient when doing research among Gullah women in South Carolina. Srinivas (1997) shows that one's own society is both familiar and strange, especially when an Indian anthropologist is studying a different caste. Abu-Lughod (1991) coined the term "halfies" to describe those anthropologists with a multicultural heritage or upbringing. She recounts how she had to straddle the obstacles of her own Arab American identity when working in the Middle East. To solve this identification quagmire, Narayan's (1993:682) concept of a "multiplex identity" is useful. She proposes "to focus on shifting identities" of insiders and outsiders rather than to accept polarizing definitions thus allowing for a "multiply centered anthropology" suggested by Clifford (1997:218). In a recent account, Halstead (2001) documents how this process works; an indigenous fieldworker in Guyana, she discusses how her participants and informants—not herself—positioned her both as an insider and as an outsider and how the shifting boundaries depended on changing contexts of identification.

The French Louisiana field is remarkable by such a widespread and seemingly unavoidable meshing of roles. It has been and continues to be studied by insiders and outsiders and in-between types. To begin with, the very definition of what is inside and outside is problematic and hedges on the boundaries retained. If nationality is retained, French and Canadian scholars are outsiders; then, in this case, what to do with anthropologists hailing from California or Illinois? If language is retained, French-speaking researchers will appear to be more insiders than non-French-speakers would; in this case, however, the kind of French spoken is likely to become the relevant boundary. And then what to do with a native Cajun scholar whose French speech has been formed abroad and by academia? In addition to these critical traits, it is our experience that sex, age, race, kinship ties, marital status, level of education, and local place of residence, as well as association with particular people and organizations, are categories used by informants to situate the researcher. In addition, many scholars who have conducted research in French Louisiana have at some point been involved as participants in the cultural scene. This implication may have been more or less voluntary and may have taken place prior to, during, or after the field experience. In fact some of us have been both researchers and informants, raising the issue of the research being truly value-free. The chapters of this collection describe in detail the ballet of shifting identities and the complex—and occasionally conflicting—role playing that researchers have engaged in irrespective of their personal profiles.

Finally, we must consider the issue of power in the relationship between the anthropologist and the other participants in the fieldwork experience. While classical anthropology was characterized by an unbalanced relationship between anthropologists and informants, today's subjects are clearly empowered. Whether at home or away, people studied are likely to be aware of social research, its goals, and its political context. They are also likely to be cognizant of the scholarship on their culture either through direct readings, media accounts, or the general knowledge of past contacts with researchers (Brettell 1993). Anthropologists are now keenly aware of the impact of informants on the framing and condition of research through several strategies. Gary Larson's caricatures of modern "Others" hurriedly dressing up as preindustrial natives for pith-helmeted anthropologists on the way nicely capture the evolution of the rapport. Informants can assert control of their own image (Pinçon & Pinçon-Charlot 1997; Williams 1987) and do act as powerful gatekeepers of their own and favored interpretation of their circumstances. The issue of access is particularly relevant when working with informants in a prominent and exposed position such as popular artists, public officials, or local elites. The separation between the public and private personae can be extreme. The anthropologist "at home" can then be kept away from the inside domain by the informant. Limited to the outside and public image, the researcher thus has no access to the knowledge "from the inside" (Althabe 1990).

Management of the research can also be exercised by the assignment of an identity to the anthropologist and control of the work in progress. The researcher's identity is achieved more than automatically ascribed. The anthropologist may be viewed by insiders as a tourist, a journalist, an ally, or a foe. The researcher may even become him/herself an object of derision for those under study. Beyond the irresistible irony of Nigel Barley's narrative (1983), his disappointments with Dowayos illustrate with perspicacity the way the ethnologist can be used. Changed in turn into a nurse, a banker, or a taxi driver, he happens to be caught up in his own game, becoming himself an object of observation. There are numerous other accounts of informants turning the tables on anthropologists by using their superior resources or teaching them cultural norms (Chagnon 1992; Lee 1969; Stack 1974).

It is an understatement to say that Cajuns are wary of the perception of their culture by outsiders. Long ridiculed and still stereotyped, modern Cajuns are acutely aware of the role and impact of outsiders asking questions and conducting observations. Researchers have reported several reactions: surprise, especially when inquiries deal with everyday life; flattered interest; liberal cooperation often accompanied by informal tests to "provide evidence of good intentions"; and competence (Esman 1985:4), refusal to cooperate, a stance occasionally chosen by cultural elites but overall quite rare. They have also noted how informants, the media, organizations, or communities attempted to co-opt or shape their work. Le Menestrel (1999) has reported how tourism officials and the local media utilized her research in progress to validate and publicize their endeavors. In a brief commentary, Lindahl (2001) gingerly discussed the presence of blackfaced participants in Cajun Mardi Gras and their representation by scholars and journalists, both quite problematic. Organizers, riders, and researchers struggle to account for and analyze this race-based component of the celebration which takes place within a culture and in communities where race remains a profoundly divisive and emotionally charged issue. All those involved employ different tactics to frame the presentation and understanding of the practice they believe to be correct. Among both anthropologists and their informants, some deny, others condemn the racist content, and in between, some are wary of what to ask and how to answer.

In addition to recognizing such dicey circumstances, the chapters of this collection also illustrate how the boundless generosity and enthusiastic participation of our collaborators in the field carried our research further than we thought of going. They helped us "get it" by allowing us into their lives and minds and by doing so they informed and transformed our work beyond its original frame. Intentions and outcomes may vary, but we cannot ignore the fact that fieldwork is an exercise of power in which we are mere participants.

KNOWLEDGE AND ITS USE

We construe knowledge as the product of the interaction between researchers and insiders. In that sense, there is no monopoly on knowledge by either social scientists or informants (Augé 1994; Ghasarian 1994). As an interesting aside, there appears to be no monopoly on errors either. Notwithstanding legitimate debates dealing with differences of opinions and interpretations, factual errors and cases of plain misinformation are found in statements by scholars and informants alike. To give a few examples, a French linguist has been taken to task for his erratic transcriptions of Cajun songs (Griolet 1986), ethnic organizations have been known to fudge reality, and accounts of Acadian history by Cajun informants sometimes offer puzzling twists.

Once knowledge has been gathered, the question of its use by scientists and lay society arises. One issue deals with the perception of anthropological writings by the host culture. The traditional set of obligations of anthropologists is toward research sponsors, peers, and the people studied. The main ethical consideration toward the latter is that no harm be brought onto them during or as a result of the research (Haviland 1999). For a long time, anthropologists did not have to consider how the "natives" would react to their published works; indeed, instances of revisionism occurred decades after the original fieldwork had been completed (Freeman 1983). The context changed drastically when anthropologists started to work at home both in Western and non-Western societies. Now "they read what we write" (Brettell 1993). Furthermore, anthropologists now have to account for the fact that they "have little control over the process by which our work is publicly presented" (Linnekin 1991:447). And, could we add, received. A tool to limit if not eliminate misunderstanding both across and within cultures, anthropology may sometimes foster it. The publication of Vidich and Bensman's (1958) *Small Town in Mass Society* caused an early stir: the inhabitants of the village they studied accused them of dishonesty, twisted vision, and commercial exploitation. Hanson's (1989) approach of the Maori culture in terms of cultural invention was seen by local laypersons and scholars as an undue challenge to its authenticity. Some anthropologists recount the inextricable difficulties of delivering the results of their research to their peers when they are implicated in the problems under study (Ginsburg 1992; Winkin 1996). Recently, Hüwelmeier (2000) contemplated with some anguish the very divided and very publicized response of the "recipients" to her work on competing men's choirs in a German village. It could also be pointed out that all works of anthropology do not necessarily generate enlightenment or critique. Miner's (1956) classical text on the Naciremas's body ritual remains puzzling to many American college students who often fail to recognize their own bathroom routines described in ethnographic style. Reversely, Mahmood was surprised by the "studied neglect" displayed by the highly literate and ethnic-minded Frisians whose identity she had written about (Mahmood & Armstrong 1992).

In the case of Louisiana studies, researchers and their audience have many efficient ways to communicate and use them liberally. Language is hardly an obstacle, since most scholars work and publish in English, and occasionally in French, both vernacular languages. Access to printed material and media outlets is boundless. Local newspapers and regional television stations are on the constant lookout for stories. Public interest in what outsiders have to say about the area and its people is high, a combination of popular concern, scholarly curiosity, or media coverage. Scholars' comments on Louisiana's cultural situation are routinely broadcast with or without the consent or participation of the author, and with more or less accuracy. As scholars, we have all become adept at or wary of "the quote" requested or extracted from our work. Similarly, people let us know in person or via letters to the editor how they receive our research. The question is even more acute for the insider anthropologist (Cerroni-Long 1995). After all, he or she is also one "of them," remains within the group, and most likely has to deal with the social implications and stake of the research. In this case, informants and collaborators, neighbors, relatives, and friends do share their opinions on the work. It can be exhilarating or devastating. A recent illustration is the virulent debate that erupted following Ryan Brasseaux's article in his anthology on music scholarship in which he discussed the "authenticity" of the music of Steve Riley and the Mamou Playboys, one of the premier Cajun bands (Brasseaux & Fontenot 2006). One member of the band reacted to Brasseaux's ambiguous use of the notion of authenticity, which he presents as a "criterion" (487) as opposed to a concept to be interrogated. He expressed his surprise and anger in a highly public forum, taking serious issue with Brasseaux's seeming value judgment of his art.

The chapters in this collection illustrate the extent of our collective awareness of this situation, the consequences this knowledge has on our work, as well as the depth and complexity of emotions that sometimes our detached selves cannot help but experience.

Another question deals with the applications of our work. Issues surrounding applied anthropology or more recently the relationship between development and anthropology are too broad to be discussed here (see Gardner & Lewis 1996). Yet they are central and complex. Since the discipline has stopped perpetuating the illusion of the neutrality of its method and purpose, our implication is no longer perceived as optional and external to our work. Since the early 1990s, anthropologists have insisted on the need to see it as an integral part of our work (Althabe, Fabre, & Lenclud 1992; *Journal des Anthropologues* 1992–1993, Agier 1997b; Burawoy 2003; Leservoisier 2005).

While anthropologists may feel more committed to implication in situations of conflict and economic inequality, we all have to deal with a demand related to the value attributed to our status and expertise. Indeed, this request seems quite legitimate and fair. We cannot decline it to stay in the comfortable position of the observer. Since the group fulfills our research interest, we have to balance the exchange in the name of reciprocity. Still we must keep our independence. Hence we find ourselves in a sometimes uncomfortable position, faced with the challenge of dealing with our own ambivalence and negotiating with our informants, striving for a "reasoned engagement" (Agier 1997a). A discussion of the representation of culture by folklorists and of the exercise of power in shaping a language policy illustrates how the confrontation between anthropological knowledge and social action play out in French Louisiana.

Folklorists have engaged in a critical reflection on their involvement in the public presentation of a culture. They are warning their peers that they are an integral part of a cultural change process extending beyond the claim of preservation (Feintuch 1988). In that sense, the dichotomy maintained by academic folklore programs between "pure" and "applied" folklore no longer seems relevant. Performance-centered folklore theory and folk arts

programming in the public sector both testify to the intricate and productive relationships that can be developed between scholars and performers.

Folklorists and anthropologists, whether they are insiders or outsiders
in French Louisiana and elsewhere, have a direct impact on traditions when
they participate in their description and presentation. Their intervention
not only impacts the way a local culture is presented, it also shapes the way
the group looks at its own culture. The capturing of a performance involves
more than its contemplation and analysis. There is for instance the question
of the legitimacy of interpreters. The perception of tradition bearers viewed
as being legitimate because they belong to a proper line of descent has long
been adopted in American folklore studies; on that basis, cultural institutions such as Folk Art Programs oppose "folk artists" viewed as authentic
interpreters to "revivalists" who perform traditions which do not "belong"
to them (Kirshenblatt-Gimblett 1988). In our case, to what extent can Cajuns
be considered as the only legitimate interpreters of and contributors to
Cajun culture? Is the front porch, the festival, or the museum the adequate
locale for its presentation? Far from being irreverent or polemic, such questions address the core issue of cultural integrity, ethnic identity, and power;
although Cajunness is now widely accepted as being the result of numerous contributions, its empirical definition is still a matter of debate and the
control of its image remains contested along with the social and economic
benefits attached to it.

Heeding David Whisnant's (1983, 1988) advice, we must also question
the elitism of cultural preservation actors, their often-idealized vision of
tradition, and the watered-down image of the local society they may give.
Anthropology as well as folkloristic enterprises can no longer claim to be
beyond ideology, power relations, and the politics of culture (Feintuch 1997;
Kirshenblatt-Gimblett 1988). The study of a group's culture should not con-
ceal the paradoxes, tensions, hostilities, contradictions, and negotiations
that are integral parts of the group's traditions and identity. In the context
of Louisiana studies, simply put, should research on aspects of manifestations such as Mardi Gras rituals, which detract from contemporary norms,
be oblivious of the fracture? Communities and organizers struggle with the
options of whether to accommodate an invited audience, market a toned-
down family entertainment, or maintain disputed practices in the name
of an assumed authenticity. Researchers certainly would be remiss of their
obligations if they did not reflect this state of things by discussing it. However, if the mandate is clear, the manner in which it is to be fulfilled is left
uncharted.

Similar issues pervade the language question. "What language to teach?" has been a point of contention since French language programs were launched in Louisiana's elementary schools in the early 1970s. Advocates of Standard French have clashed with proponents of Cajun French and both have liberally drawn from scholars to buttress their arguments. The discussion took place in the Legislature, at school board meetings, in the classroom, at scientific gatherings, and in the media. It addressed political and constitutional questions such as the legal status of French and the recognition of Cajuns as a statutory minority group, points of pedagogy (what methods best ensure fluency? whom to teach?), and technical issues (the writing of Cajun French). Intense interaction between the participants framed and moved the discussion toward various stages of resolution. Activists failed to obtain the designation of French as an official language and the teaching of Cajun French but successfully negotiated a compromise to transcribe Cajun speech and include it in textbooks. The reflection on the language and its name continues. The relevance of the "Cajun French" label is being questioned, as illustrated by the recent work of linguist Thomas Klingler (2003), who introduces "Louisiana Regional French," and by the title of the forthcoming *Dictionary of French As Spoken in Louisiana*.

Such endeavors reveal the complexity of our possible engagement. For one, the colonial paradigm appears to be quite ill-adapted to guide our involvement. Not only do we work in the wealthiest and most powerful society in the world, but we deal with a group of white ethnics, a powerful group compared to subjugated minorities. Still, Cajuns encountered discrimination and prejudice and continue to experience socioeconomic disadvantage. Who then is the dominant power? Anglo conformity? The state apparatus in Washington, DC, or Baton Rouge? The *Académie française*? Business and industry leaders? The local urban elite? Can Cajuns be viewed as victims and dominated when their historical ability to assimilate others is well documented and as the "Cajunization" (Trépanier 1991) of South Louisiana proceeds evidenced by the ubiquity and commercial appeal of the ethnic label?

The very notion of an applied anthropology is perilous, given the disinterested and subversive nature of our knowledge. The production of knowledge in response to an external request faces us with difficult choices or compromises, since our vision is fundamentally critical and is not intended to "please" the people who come to us or depend on our findings. Independence is even more difficult to hold when our studies are funded by external sources, for "we risk being caught in our own trap if we ask funding from those we study" (Pétonnet & Pouchelle 1989). Since the group fulfills our research interest, we have to balance the exchange in the name of reciprocity. Actually, anthropologists themselves deliberately contribute to the redefinition of their work by claiming new roles, as for example *"porteur de mémoire"* (bearers of memory) or *"accompagnateur social"* (social traveling companion) (Monjaret 2001:113). Still we must keep our independence. Yet with these warnings in mind, application of anthropological knowledge is possible and desirable. From our Louisiana-bound perspective, the possibilities include economic benefits, especially in the field of tourism; a tool of social policy to define and protect minority groups as well as addressing issues of public health; calls to ethnic activism; definition and implementation of educational programs; and, Louisiana being the state it is, the political use of Cajun identity as an electoral argument. While our implication is a necessity, we must be careful to preserve the distance and lucidity that frame our scientific gaze. To maintain an appropriate balance between these two methodological devices is probably one of the greatest challenges of our work.

A POST-KATRINA AND RITA POSTSCRIPT

Little did we know that the issues discussed above would be put to a dramatic test after hurricanes Katrina and Rita struck in August and September 2005. In addition to the trail of death and devastation they left along the Gulf Coast, the storms impacted our practice. The field has been severely bruised. The physical terrain, both the natural and man-made environment, has endured flooding, wind damage, and a slow rehabilitation. For some of the researchers who contributed to this volume, the anthropological field—interestingly, *terrain* in French—has also changed. Our work had been dominated by cultural issues and consisted mostly of research on language, ethnic identity, or folk practices. The 2005 hurricanes prompted us to become involved in disaster studies, a field new to us. To be sure, Louisiana-based social scientists have long been involved in this and related fields such as environmental sociology and the sociology of risk (Beggs, Haines, & Hulbert 1996; Gramling 1996; Laska et al. 2005). As we watched the flooding of New Orleans, the forced exile of evacuees, and the ineptitude of governmental response, our feelings of helplessness, anger, obligation, and shame provoked our entry into disaster research. Within a couple of weeks, and especially after Rita hit the coastal parishes of Louisiana, it became clear that volunteering, hosting evacuees, and giving money were but first and insufficient steps. In the long run, we could be more useful utilizing the skills of our trade, anthropology. Access to this new field was facilitated by familiarity with the terrain, the culture, and the people that were impacted. We had conducted fieldwork in some of the urban and rural neighborhoods whose names appeared in news reports. Treme, Gentilly, Bywater, Cameron, and Vermilion were places where we had spent time, where we knew people whose lives had been abruptly disrupted.

We devised a project to analyze the factors at play in the decision to return to impacted areas or to relocate. Faced with an unfamiliar situation, we started our unexpected fieldwork without any theoretical background on disaster studies, and rushed by the necessity of meeting Katrina evacuees in Lafayette while they were still in town. As we were driving around the New Orleans area or Vermilion Parish, we were entering a *terrain sensible*, a sensitive field. Far from studying the mundane routine of everyday cultural patterns, we were working amidst disruption and destruction. Some of our past informants—musicians, cultural activists—were now victims. Our current informants shared the same circumstances, those of evacuees flushed out of their homes. In the case of Carl Lindahl's ongoing project, *Surviving Katrina and Rita in Houston,* victims, informants, and investigators are indissociable. The project's goal "to voice, as intimately as possible, the experiences and reflections of those displaced to Houston" arranges for survivors to "receive training and pay to record fellow survivors' storm stories, their memories of lost neighborhoods, and their ongoing struggles to build new communities in exile" (University of Houston, 2008).

The methodology we were most familiar with therefore felt inadequate. We needed to adjust it as we were conducting our fieldwork, a common, but in this case most uncomfortable, strategy. Indeed, dangerous fields exacerbate the illusionary image of ideal field circumstances with regard to interactions with informants (i.e., stability, trust, quietude, security, freedom from fear) and the ethnographer's position of control. As Kovats-Bernat argues, "These conditions rarely exist, forcing anthropologists to innovate new tactics and techniques for getting needed data while at the same time minimizing attendant risks to life and limb . . . . If we are to work in dangerous fields, we must begin with a fundamental shift in how methodology is defined— not as a rigid or fixed framework for the research but, rather, as an elastic, incorporative, integrative, and malleable practice" (2002:210).

Strangely enough, and fortuitously, there were continuities. People we spoke with for the next months were just as eager to cooperate as victims as they previously had been as musicians, storytellers, or educators. The

rhythm of fieldwork was also comforting: find contacts, approach and establish rapport, conduct interviews, take notes, transcribe, keep a journal, all
were familiar steps even if the topic was quite somber. Most comforting were
the occasional thanks extended after interviews and curiosity expressed at
our future findings.

Our informants themselves brought a sense of continuity. The risk of
hurricanes is inherent to life in South Louisiana. The ability to survive and
their self-definition as "survivors" were systematically claimed by interviewees. Hurricanes are incorporated into Louisianians' collective memory.
Indeed, in the case of French Louisiana, disasters are an integral part of
Cajun and Creole identity, defined by the struggle against adversity through
forced exile and stigmatization. Many Cajuns reasserted their resistance
and referred to Katrina as a "second Grand Derangement." The solidarity
and mutual assistance throughout the disaster and its aftermath were also
emphasized, reiterating Cajuns' generosity and therefore their autonomy
and independence, often mentioned as constitutive of their identity. This
is how hundreds of boat owners in Acadiana gathered in Lake Charles and
Lafayette and convoyed to flooded New Orleans as the "Cajun Navy" (Hennessy 2007). Katrina, as many disasters (Hoffman 2002), was recast as an
episode of a much larger narrative.

These elements of continuity in the content of our research—how people made sense of the event, our initial methodological intent—did not make
us any less uncomfortable. The intensity of some of the issues discussed in
this introduction turned them into disconcerting challenges. The necessity
of implication, for example, is more acute in the contexts of war and disaster, where interviewees obviously have expectations that are commensurate
with what they have endured. In our case, their level of suffering was such
that empathy, a critical feature of anthropological fieldwork, inevitably led
to an unsettling sense of vulnerability, even causing us to question the very
meaning of our research. How could we keep visiting skeletal, naked homes
without feeling that we were violating their owners' intimacy, as they were
holding back their tears? How could we feel confident about the legitimacy
of our work while the interviewees were desperate for basic practical support with immediate benefits? In what way could we reconcile our project
with an enduring feeling of our own powerlessness? This feeling was particularly acute with victims who nearly died because they lacked the means
to leave, while our own status would likely protect us from finding ourselves
in so dire a situation. It was a morbid confirmation of social injustice almost
mirrored in our own practice.

The dilemma faced by anthropologists under such circumstances is best expressed by Ruth Behar (1996:2): "In the midst of a massacre, in the face of torture, in the eye of a hurricane, in the aftermath of an earthquake, or even, say, when horror looms apparently more gently in memories that won't recede and so come pouring forth in the late night quiet of a kitchen, . . . do you, the observer, stay behind the lens of the camera, switch on the tape recorder, keep pen in hand? Are there limits—of respect, piety, pathos—that should not be crossed, even to leave a record? But if you can't stop the horror, shouldn't you at least document it?"

However we justify our fieldwork on "sensitive fields," they necessarily cause some epistemological, ethical, political, even existential anxiety, which Didier Fassin (2005:100-101) suggests is a characteristic of our practice at large: "A disquieting thought, such could be our posture, at once the most creative and the most honest, a posture far from the certainties of an anthropology that has often believed that it speaks both for itself and for others."

Since its inception, the social science of disaster has contributed to the better understanding of human and organizational behavior under catastrophic circumstances. It has dispelled some myths (post-disaster situations do not generate anarchy) and revealed patterns of temporary adaptation, continuing vulnerability, and persistence of pre-disaster inequalities. Despite the discomfort and ambiguities, we would like to think that our work will contribute to a better understanding of the way Louisianians cope with and make sense of hurricanes. We started to do so by exploring the meanings of "home" and "community," and by analyzing the networks of relationships at play, the political use of risk, and the production of locality (Le Menestrel & Henry, forthcoming). In a broader perspective, we are investigating through this case study the reconstruction phase, starting with the return of people, a topic that has not received much attention within the anthropology of disaster. By happenstance yet not quite unpredictably, Katrina and Rita transformed our French Louisiana field into a disaster zone. We made it our field again. And it appears the field will continue to make us too.

AN OUTLINE OF CONTRIBUTIONS

The meaning of an event is hardly accessible through observation only, regardless of how repeated, detailed, or extensive it might be. Carl Lindahl's twenty-year-long study of rural Mardi Gras reveals the importance of broadening fieldwork through prolonged and extensive personal interrelations with the festive actors in order to bridge the gap between what the outsider sees and what the players feel. His long-term experience has enabled him to adjust his methodology throughout the years and discover how the comprehension of self could be used as a tool for the comprehension of the Other. His choice to emphasize intensive exposure to a few individuals—"saturation fieldwork"—has led him to an understanding of the personal meanings of the ritual as the extension of the lives of his informants and the expression of their values. While solid friendships have led to inevitable biases he explicitly identifies, the strength of his relationships enabled him to capture the intensity of the participants' emotional involvement, an essential dimension of Mardi Gras.

The study of Cajun faith healing, practiced by *traiteurs*, extends the reflection on relationships as devices of crucial significance for the understanding of a cultural practice. Dana A. David grew up on a Cajun farm. This context allowed for an easy access to a social network of family and friends as informants, as well as a useful knowledge of the rhythm of life in a rural environment. In addition, speaking Cajun French facilitated communication. Whereas she expected a more visible expression of this mysterious practice, she discovered that treating is embedded in familiar daily-life relationships. She did not immediately identify the power of the spoken word and the informal non-explicit exchange that constitutes treatment. David realized the ambiguity of her position: neither seeking a treatment nor seeking to treat, she transgressed the ritualized means of transmission. Her research and membership in the social unit of *voisinage* activated cultural expectations. Since the exchange in a treatment is a manifestation of a network of reciprocity, she was expected to use her knowledge. In highlighting the multiple layers of meanings involved in relationships, David reveals the subtleties and depth of experience as a means of knowledge.

In some contexts, the political stakes are so high that they unavoidably condition the researcher's itinerary and practice. Such is the case for Deborah J. Clifton, whose work begun in 1968 was closely intertwined with the social struggle of her community. Her Creole identity provided her with no advantage at first. Her attraction to an academic career challenged the traditionalism of her family and of the Creole culture at large. Departing from role expectations, her studies and work were not only disapproved of but suspected of further stigmatizing her community. The quest of her friends and relatives for new strategies to improve social justice led to a reconsideration of her status. This change of attitude marked a turning point in Clifton's work. From then on perceived as the defender of her people, she chose to orient her fieldwork toward applied goals. Her involvement in community health (diabetes research) as well as cultural and linguistic conservation has led her to act as teacher of Creole, instructor of fieldwork techniques, museum curator, and poet.

The necessary correlation between theory and practice is precisely the subject of Barry Jean Ancelet's chapter. His long experience as an activist folklorist led him to explore the reciprocal influence of folklore fieldwork and festival programming in such fields as storytelling, music, and foodways. His concept of "cultural recycling" points to the circular process involved in the use of archives in public programming and educational settings, which in return contribute to theory building. Sites and audiences are renegotiated depending on the views of powerful actors—scholars from national institutions like the Smithsonian as well as native experts. He shows how the performance then appears as a battleground where competing views about what is "authentic" or "natural" are revealed.

Indeed, the vision of Cajun social practices as homogeneous and unified comes from a romantic and consensual perception that Marc David invites us to reconsider. His study of the relationship between the rise of agrarian capitalism and Mardi Gras in a rural community led to the brutal discovery of a fragmented collectivity. His effort to locate in his own trajectory the position from which he poses his ethnographic questions emphasizes the irreducibly political character of fieldwork, as an "inherently agonistic undertaking." Participant observation in Mardi Gras encouraged him to partake in a passionate public debate about the use of racial stereotypes in the ritual. His account exemplifies the challenge of articulating our relationships in the field with our academic work.

Sara Le Menestrel also questions the nexus of power, representation, and personal involvement, but from the outside. She discusses the shifting of roles imposed by and during her fieldwork experience. Some roles arise from her own choices, such as being an anthropologist, deciding to study cultural touristic endeavors, or playing Cajun music; other roles are ascribed to her by informants, friends, and acquaintances, who view her as potential resource, almost-kin, valued or contested scholar. This inherently ambivalent position must also be reconciled with the professional obligations of researchers toward their peers and the field of work. She explores the ethical and personal ramifications of the process.

Jacques Henry questions the practice of participant observation from yet another angle. His position as a communication specialist, then executive director, of the Council for the Development of French in Louisiana (CODOFIL) ironically resulted from lassitude toward ethnographic fieldwork and academia. After an initial study of the Louisiana French Movement as an anthropology student in France, he decided to establish himself as a bilingual consultant in Louisiana. The lack of job opportunities encouraged him to accept an unexpected offer from CODOFIL. The transition from being a critical evaluator of the agency's mission to acting as its employee put him in an awkward position. His eagerness to provide a scientific assessment of the Louisiana French situation conflicted with the one-sided position of his chairman, whose use of unreliable data served propaganda objectives and helped gain political support. Once hired director against all expectations, he was overwhelmed by the weight of politics and bureaucracy that interfered with his plans. Returning to academia after ten years to resume his study of the French Movement from the outside, he long struggled to avoid the biases of ethnic advocacy in his analysis. His experience and his status as foreigner yet involved resident shed a light on the complexity of combining knowledge and action.

Cécyle Trépanier and Dean Louder widen the perspective by setting Louisiana in the context of *Franco-Amérique*. Studying French Louisiana strikes a particular chord with them, offering the unique position of Québec as the paradigm of the struggle for Francophonie in America. Their chronological account of a series of fieldwork experiences starting in the late 1970s underlines the evolution of their perception and the ambiguity of their feelings: from the excitement of discovery, they went through years of doubt concerning the future of French. Finally, in the past ten years, they have come to combine these two contradictory stances: dismay regarding the importance French Louisianians attach to outside validation, and hope for a renewed solidarity which they see as central to the future of French speakers in North America. Their collective work with and around the *Projet Louisiane* has significantly impacted the reflection on French American identity in Québec. It has offered French Louisiana a better visibility while contributing to moderate the explosive relations between Québec and Canada's other French-speaking communities. The inclusion of the Louisiana field in the Laval University curriculum shows an awareness of its role and specific profile—a common heritage combined with a unique *créolité*—within French America.

REFERENCES

Abu-Lughod, Lila. 1991. "Writing Against Culture." In *Recapturing Anthropology: Working in the Present*. Richard Fox, ed. Santa Fe, NM: School of American Research Press, pp. 137–162.

Agier, Michel. 1997a. *Anthropologues en danger. L'engagement sur le terrain*. Paris: Jean-Michel Place.

———. 1997b. "Ni trop près ni trop loin. De l'implication ethnographique à l'engagement intellectuel." *Gradhiva* 21, pp. 69–76.

Ahmed, Akbad, & Cris Shore, eds. 1995. *The Future of Anthropology: Its Relevance to the Contemporary World*. London: Athlone Press.

Allain, Mathé. 1989. "'They Don't Even Talk Like Us': Cajun Violence in Film and Fiction." *Journal of Popular Culture* 23(1), pp. 65–76.

Althabe, Gérard. 1990. "Ethnologie du contemporain et enquête de terrain." *Terrain* 14 (mars), pp. 126–131.

Ancelet, Barry. 1988. "A Perspective on Teaching the 'Problem Language' in Louisiana." *The French Review* 61(3), pp. 345–356.

———. 1990. "Cajuns in Film." Paper presented at the meeting of the American Association of Teachers of French, July.

———. 1994. *Cajun and Creole Folktales: The French Oral Tradition of South Louisiana*. New York: Garland Publishers.

Ancelet, Barry, Jay Edwards, & Glen Pitre, eds. 1991. *Cajun Country*. Jackson: University Press of Mississippi.

Appadurai, Arjun. 1988. "Putting Hierarchy in its Place." *Cultural Anthropology* 3(1), pp. 36–49.

———. 1992. "Global Ethnoscapes: Notes and Queries for a Transnational Anthropology." In *Recapturing Anthropology: Working in the Present*. Richard Fox, ed. Santa Fe, NM: School of American Research Press, pp. 191–210.

Augé, Marc. 1994. *Pour une anthropologie des mondes contemporains*. Paris: Aubier.

Barley, Nigel. 1983. *Adventures in a Mud Hut: An Innocent Anthropologist Abroad*. New York: Vanguard Press.

Behar, Ruth. 1996. *The Vulnerable Observer: Anthropology That Breaks Your Heart*. Boston: Beacon Press.

Beggs, John, Valerie Haines, & Jeanne Hulbert. 1996. "Effects of Personal Network and Local Community Contexts on the Receipt of Formal Assistance in Disaster Recovery." *International Journal of Mass Emergencies and Disasters* 14, pp. 57-78.

Beoku-Betts, Josephine. 1994. "When Black is Not Enough: Doing Fieldwork among Gullah Women." *NWSA Journal* 6, pp. 413–433.

Bernard, Shane. 2003. *The Cajuns. Americanization of a People*. Jackson: University Press of Mississippi.

Bernard, Russell H., ed. 1998. *Handbook of Methods in Cultural Anthropology*. Walnut Creek, CA: AltaMira Press.

Bizeul, Daniel. 1999. "Faire avec les déconvenues: Une enquête en milieu nomade." *Sociétes contemporaines* 33-34, pp. 11-137.

Bouillon, Florence, Marion Fresa, & Virginie Tallio, eds. 2005. *Terrain sensibles. Expériences actuelles de l'anthropologie*. Paris: Centre d'études africaines, EHESS.

Bouvier, Pierre. 1995. *Socio-anthropologie du contemporain*. Paris: Galilée.

Brasseaux, Carl, Keith Fontenot, & Claude Oubre. 1994. *Creoles of Color in the Bayou Country*. Jackson: University Press of Mississippi.

Brasseaux, Ryan, & Kevin Fontenot, eds. 2006. *Accordions, Fiddles, Two-Step and Swing: A Cajun Music Reader*. Lafayette: Center for Louisiana Studies.

Brettell, Caroline, ed. 1993. *When They Read What We Write: The Politics of Ethnography*. Westport, CT: Bergin & Garvey.

Bromberger, Christian. 1997. "L'ethnologie de la France et ses nouveaux objets. Crise, tâtonnement et jouvence d'une discipline dérangeante." *Ethnologie française* 27(3), pp. 294–313.

Brown, Becky. 1993. "The Social Consequences of Writing Louisiana French." *Language in Society* 22, pp. 67–101.

Burawoy, Michael. 2003. "Revisits: An Outline of a Theory of Reflexive Ethnography." *American Sociological Review* 68 (October), pp. 645–679.

Cerroni-Long, E. L. 1995. Introduction in *Insider Anthropology*. E. L. Cerroni-Long, ed. NAPA Bulletin 16. Arlington, VA: American Anthropological Association.

Chagnon, Napoleon. 1992. *Yanomamo: The Fierce People*. 4th ed. New York: Holt, Rinehart & Winston.

Clifford, James. 1997. "Spatial Practices: Fieldwork, Travel and the Disciplining of Anthropology." In *Anthropological Locations: Boundaries and Grounds of a Field Science*. Akhil Gupta & James Ferguson, eds. Berkeley: University of California Press, pp. 185–222.

Clifford, James, & George Marcus. 1986. *Writing Cultures. The Poetics and Politics of Ethnography*. Berkeley: University of California Press.

Clifton, Deborah J. 2000. "N'avait cauchemar té gain nom: Stress Transformers and Diabetes among North Americans of Native and French Descent." Dissertation. Lafayette: University of Louisiana at Lafayette.

Cohen, Anthony P. 1994. *Self-Consciousness: An Alternative Anthropology of Identity*. London: Routledge.

Comeaux, Malcolm. 1996. "Cajuns and their Adaptations to a Modern World." In *Human Geography in North America: New Perspectives and Trends in Research*. Klaus Frantz, ed. Innsbruck: Geographical Institute.

Current Anthropology. 1980. 20(5).

Current Anthropology. 2000. 41(2).

David, Dana. 2000. "Parole, pratique et pouvoir: Le rôle des traiteurs dans la société cadienne." Dissertation. Lafayette: University of Louisiana at Lafayette.

David, Marc. 1996. *Riziculture et Mardi Gras: L'organisation du travail et le carnaval rural dans la petite production marchande en Louisiane*. Mémoire de maitrise. Montréal: Université Laval.

Desdouits, Anne-Marie, & Laurier Turgeon, eds. 1997. *Ethnologies francophones de l'Amérique et d'ailleurs*. Sainte Foy: PUL.

DeVita, Philip, ed. 1990. *The Humbled Anthropologist: Tales from the Pacific*. Belmont, CA: Wadsworth.

Dorais, Jean-Louis. 1980. "Les Avoyelles." *Vie Française* 34 (7, 8, 9), pp. 52–53.

Dormon, James, ed. 1996. *Creoles of Color of the Gulf South*. Knoxville: University of Tennessee Press.

Dresch, Paul, Wendy James, & David Parkin, eds. 2000. *Anthropologists in a Wider World: Essays on Field Research*. New York: Berghahn Books.

Dubois, Sylvie, & Megan Mélançon. 1996. "Cajun is Dead: Long Live Cajun. Shifting from a Linguistic to a Cultural Community." *Journal of Sociolinguistics* 1(1), pp. 63–93.

———. 2000. "Creole Is, Creole Ain't: Diachronic and Synchronic Attitudes toward Creole Identity in Southern Louisiana." *Language in Society* 29, pp. 237–258.

Dumont, Jean Paul. 1978. *The Headman and I: Ambiguity and Ambivalence in the Fieldworking Experience*. Austin: University of Texas Press.

Egypte-Monde Arabe. 2006. "Terrains d'Egypte, anthropologies contemporaines" 3, série 3.

Englund, Harri, & James Leach. 2000. "Ethnography and the Meta-Narrative of Modernity." *Current Anthropology* 41(2), pp. 225–248.

Esman, Marjorie. 1981. "The Celebration of Cajun Identity: Ethnic Unity and the Crawfish Festival." Dissertation. New Orleans: Tulane University.

———. 1985. *Henderson, Louisiana: Cultural Adaptation in a Cajun Community*. New York: Holt, Rinehart and Winston.

Estaville, Lawrence. 1986. "Mapping the Cajuns." *Southern Studies* 25(2), pp. 163–171.

Ethnographiques.org. 2006. "Ethnographie réflexive, nouveaux enjeux" 11. Octobre.

Ethnologie française. 2001. Numéro spécial, "Terrains minés en ethnologie" (janvier–mars).

Fassin, Didier. 2005. "L'innocence perdue de l'anthropologie: remarques sur les terrains sensibles." In *Terrain sensibles. Expériences actuelles de l'anthropologie*. Florence Bouillon, Marion Fresa, Virginie Tallio (dir.). Dossiers africains, Paris, Centre d'études africaines, EHESS, pp. 97–103.

Favret-Saada, Jeanne. 1977. *Les mots, la mort, les sorts*. Paris: Gallimard.

Feintuch, Burt, ed. 1988. *The Conservation of Culture: Folklorists and the Public Sector*. Lexington: University Press of Kentucky.

———. 1997. "Les écueils de l'ethnologie appliquée." In *Ethnologies francophones de l'Amérique et d'ailleurs*. Anne-Marie Desdouits & Laurier Turgeon, eds. Sainte Foy: PUL, pp. 317–328.

Freeman, Derek. 1983. *Margaret Mead and Samoa: The Making and Unmaking of an Anthropological Myth*. Cambridge: Harvard University Press.

Gardner, Katy, & David Lewis. 1996. *Anthropology, Development, and the Post-Modern Challenge*. London: Pluto Press.

Gaudet, Marcia. 1989. "The Image of the Cajun in Literature." *Journal of Popular Culture* 23(1), pp. 77–88.

Geertz, Clifford. 1973. *The Interpretation of Cultures; Selected Essays*. New York: Basic Books.

———. 1983. *Local Knowledge: Further Essays in Interpretive Anthropology*. New York: Basic Books.

Gewertz, Deborah, & Frederick Errington. 1997. "Why We Return to Papua New Guinea." *Anthropological Quarterly* 70, pp. 127–136.

Ghasarian, Christian. 1994. "L'anthropologie américaine en son miroir." *L'Homme* 34(131), pp. 137–144.

Gibson, Jon, ed. 1982. *Archeology and Ethnology on the Edges of the Atchafalaya Basin, South Central Louisiana*. Lafayette: University of Southwestern Louisiana.

Ginsburg, Faye. 1992. "Quand les indigènes sont nos voisins." *L'Homme* 32(121), pp. 129–143.

Gold, Gerald. 1980. "Les Prairies." *Vie Française* 34(7, 8, 9), pp. 47–51.

———. 1982. "Language and Ethnic Identity in South Louisiana: Implications of Data from Mamou Prairie." In *The Quebec and Acadian Diaspora in North America*. Roland Breton & Pierre Savard, eds. Toronto: Multicultural History Society of Ontario.

Gramling, Robert. 1996. *Oil on the Edge: Offshore Development, Conflict, Gridlock*. New York: State University of New York Press.

Green, Nicola. 1999. "Disrupting the Field: Virtual Reality Technologies and 'Multisited' Ethnographic Methods." *The American Behavioral Scientist* 43(3), pp. 409–421.

Griolet, Patrick. 1986. *Cadjins et Créoles en Louisiane*. Paris: Payot.

Gupta, Akhil, & James Ferguson. 1997a. "Discipline and Practice: 'The Field' as Site, Method, and Location in Anthropology." In *Anthropological Locations: Boundaries and Grounds of a Field Science*. Akhil Gupta & James Ferguson, eds. Berkeley: University of California Press, pp. 1–46.

——. 1997b. "Beyond 'Culture': Space, Identity, and the Politics of Difference." In *Culture, Power, Place: Explorations in Critical Anthropology*. Akhil Gupta & James Ferguson, eds. Durham, NC: Duke University Press, pp. 33–51.

Gutierrez, C. Paige. 1992. *Cajun Foodways*. Jackson: University Press of Mississippi.

Halstead, Narmala. 2001. "Ethnographic Encounters: Positioning within and outside the Insider Frame." *Social Anthropology* 9(3), pp. 307–321.

Hanson, A. 1989. "The Making of the Maori: Culture Invention and its Logic." *American Anthropologist* 91, pp. 890–902.

Haviland, William A. 1999. *Cultural Anthropology*. 9th ed. Fort Worth, TX: Harcourt Brace.

Hennessy, Jefferson. 2007. "The Cajun Navy: Heroic Louisiana Volunteers Saved Thousands of Hurricane Katrina Evacuees," September 5.http://www.associatedcontent.com/article/340031/the_cajun_navy_heroic_louisiana_volunteers.html.

Henry, Jacques. 1997. "The Louisiana French Movement: Actors and Actions in Social Change." In *French and Creole in Louisiana*. Albert Valdman, ed. New York: Plenum, pp. 183–213.

Henry, Jacques, & Carl Bankston. 1999. "Louisiana Cajun Ethnicity: Symbolic or Structural?" *Sociological Spectrum* 19(2), pp. 223–248.

——. 2002. *Blue Collar Bayou: Louisiana Cajuns in the New Economy of Ethnicity*. Westport, CT: Praeger.

Hirschkind, Lynn. 1991. "Redefining The 'Field' in Fieldwork." *Ethnology* 30(3), pp. 237–249.

Hoffman, Susanna M. 2002. "The Monster and the Mother. The Symbolism of Disaster." In *Catastrophe and Culture: The Anthropology of Disaster*. Susanna M. Hoffman & Anthony Oliver-Smith, eds. Santa Fe, NM: School of American Research Press, pp. 113-141.

Hubinger, Vaclav, ed. 1996. *Grasping the Changing World: Anthropological Concepts in the Postmodern Era*. New York: Routledge.

Hüwelmeier, Gertrud. 2000. "When People Are Broadcast Their Ethnographies. Text, Mass Media and Voices from the Field." *Social Anthropology* 8(1), pp. 45–49.

Jones, Delmos. 1970. "Toward a Native Anthropology." *Human Organization* 29, pp. 251–259.

——. 1995. "Anthropology and the Oppressed: A Reflection on 'Native' Anthropology." In *Insider Anthropology*. E. L. Cerroni-Long, ed. Arlington, VA: American Anthropological Association, pp. 58–70.

Journal des anthropologues. 2000. "Ethiques professionnelles et expériences de Terrain." Numéro spécial, 50–51 (hiver-printemps).

Journal of American Folklore. 2001. Special Issue, "Southwestern Louisiana Mardi Gras Traditions" 114(452), Spring.

Kemper, Robert V., & Anya Peterson Royce, eds. 2002. *Chronicling Cultures: Long-Term Field Research in Anthropology*. Walnut Creek, CA: AltaMira Press.

Kirshenblatt-Gimblett, Barbara. 1988. "Mistaken Dichotomies." *Journal of American Folklore* 101, pp. 140–155.

Klausner, William. 1994. "Going Native." *Anthropology Today* 10(3), pp. 18–19.

Klingler, Thomas. 2003. *If I could turn my tongue like that: The Creole Language of Pointe Coupee Parish, Louisiana*. Baton Rouge: Louisiana State University Press.

Kovats-Bernat, Christopher. 2002. "Negotiating Dangerous Fields: Pragmatic Strategies for Fieldwork amid Violence and Terror." *American Anthropologist* 104(1), pp. 208-222.

Krotz, E. 1993. "The Production of Anthropology in the South: Characteristics, Perspectives, Lines of Thought." *Alteridades* 3(6), pp. 5–11.

Kuper, Adam. 1994. "Culture, Identity and the Project of a Cosmopolitan Anthropology." *Man* 29, pp. 537–554.

"La. Natives Reluctant to Leave Home." 2001. *The New York Times on the Web*, August 29. www .nytimes.com.

Larouche, Alain. 1982. *Ethnicité, pêche et pétrole: Les Cadjins du Bayou Lafourche en Louisiane francophone*. Projet Louisiane, Monograph 1. Toronto: York University.

Laska, Shirley, George Wooddell, Ronald Hagelman, Robert Gramling, & Monica Teets Farris. 2005. "At Risk: The Human, Community and Infrastructure Resources of Coastal Louisiana." *Journal of Coastal Research* 44, pp. 90-111.

Lee, Richard B. 1969. "Eating Christmas in the Kalahari." *Natural History* (December).

Leiris, Michel. 1934. *L'Afrique fantôme*. Paris: Plon.

Le Menestrel, Sara. 1999. *La Voie des Cadiens. Tourisme et identité en Louisiane*. Paris: Belin.

Le Menestrel, Sara, & Jacques Henry. Forthcoming. "Sing Us Back Home: Music, Place, and the Production of Locality in Post-Katrina New Orleans." *Popular Music and Society*.

Leservoisier, Olivier. 2005. *Terrains ethnographiques et hiérarchies sociales. Retour réflexif sur la situation d'enquête*. Paris: Karthala.

Lewis, Herbert. 1999. "The Misrepresentation of Anthropology and its Consequences." *American Anthropologist* 100(3), pp. 716–731.

Lindahl, Carl. 1994. Series Editor's Preface in *Cajun and Creole Folktales: The French Oral Tradition of South Louisiana*. Barry Ancelet, ed. New York: Garland Publishers, pp. ix-xv.

———. 2001. "A Note on Blackface." *Journal of American Folklore* 114(452), pp. 248–254.

Linnekin, Jocelyn. 1991. "Cultural Invention and the Dilemma of Authenticity." *American Anthropologist* 93, pp. 446–449.

Maguire, Robert. 1979. "Creoles and Creole Language in St Martin Parish, Louisiana." *Cahiers de Géographie du Québec* 23(59), pp. 281–302.

———. 1989. *Hustling to Survive: Social and Economic Change in a South Louisiana Black Creole Community*. Projet Louisiane, Monograph 3. Québec: Université Laval.

Mahmood, Cynthia, & Sharon Armstrong. 1992. "Do Ethnic Groups Exist: A Cognitive Perspective on the Concept of Cultures." *Ethnology* 31(1), pp. 1–14.

Maillet, Antonine. 1984. *Les Acadiens, piétons de l'Atlantique*. Paris: A.C.E.

Malinowski, Bronislaw. 1967. *A Diary in the Strict Sense of the Term*. New York: Harcourt, Brace and World.

Marcus, George. 1995. "Ethnography in/of the World System: The Emergence of Multi-Sited Ethnography." *Annual Review of Anthropology* 24, pp. 95–117.

Messerschmidt, Donald, ed. 1981. *Anthropologists at Home in North America: Methods and Issues in the Study of One's Own Society*. Cambridge: Cambridge University Press.

Miner, Horace. 1956. "Body Ritual among the Nacirema." *American Anthropologist* (June), pp. 503–507.

Mintz, Sidney. 2000. "Sows' Ears and Silver Linings: A Backward Look at Ethnography." *Current Anthropology* 41(2), pp. 169–189.

Monjaret, Anne. 2001, "Fermeture et transfert de trois hôpitaux parisiens. L'ethnologue, accompagnateur social." *Ethnologie française* 31(1), pp. 103–115.

Moore, Henrietta, ed. 1996. *The Future of Anthropological Knowledge*. New York: Routledge.

Narayan, Kirin. 1993. "How Native Is a 'Native' Anthropologist?" *American Anthropologist* 95, pp. 671–686.

Ortner, Sherry. 1999. "The Future of Anthropology: Its Relevance to the Contemporary World/ Grasping the Changing World: Anthropological Concepts in the Postmodern Era/The Future of Anthropological Knowledge." Book review, *American Ethnologist* 26(4), pp. 984–991.

Oukada, Larbi. 1978. "The Territory and Population of French-Speaking Louisiana." *Revue de Louisiane/Louisiana Review* 7(1), pp. 5–34.

Passaro, Joanne. 1997. "You Can't Take the Subway to the Field." In *Anthropological Locations: Boundaries and Grounds of a Field Science*. Akhil Gupta & James Ferguson, eds. Berkeley: University of California Press, pp. 147–162.

Pétonnet, Colette, & Marie-Christine Pouchelle. 1989. "Le rôle de l'ethnologue dans sa société." In *L'Autre et le semblable*. Martine Segalen, ed. Paris: Presses du CNRS, pp. 183–191.

Pinçon, Michel, & Monique Pinçon-Charlot. 1997. *Voyage en grande bourgeoisie, Journal d'enquête*. Paris: PUF.

Rogers, Susan Carol. 1991. "L'ethnologie nord-américaine en France." *Ethnologie française* 21, pp. 5–12.

———. 2001. "Anthropology in France." *Annual Review of Anthropology* 30, pp. 481–505.

Sexton, Rocky. 2000. "Zydeco Music and Race Relations in French Louisiana." In *Multiculturalism in the United States: Current Issues, Contemporary Voices*. Peter Kivisto & Georganne Rundblad, eds. Thousand Oaks, CA: Pine Forge Press, pp. 175–184.

Sexton, Rocky, & John Guidry. 2000. "'You might be a Cajun if': The Tenacity of Place in a Changing World." In *Worldview Flux: Perplexed Values among Postmodern People*. Jim Norvine & Jonathan M. Smith, eds. Lanham, MD: Lexington Books, pp. 111–132.

Social Anthropology. 2000. Dossier, "The Future of Ethnography: Visions from the Field," 8(1), February.

Soudière, Martin de la. 1988. "L'inconfort du terrain. 'Faire' la Creuse, le Maroc, la Lozère." *Terrain* 11, pp. 94–106.

Spitzer, Nicholas. 1986. "Zydeco and Mardi Gras: Creole Identity and Performance Genre in Rural French Louisiana." Dissertation. Austin: University of Texas.

Spradley, James. 1980. *Participant Observation*. New York: Holt, Rinehart and Winston.

Srinivas, M. N. 1997. "Practicing Social Anthropology in India." *Annual Review of Anthropology* 26, pp. 1–24.

Stack, Carol. 1974. *All Our Kin: Strategies for Survival in a Black Community*. New York: Harper and Row.

Stocking, George W., Jr. 1992. "The Ethnographer's Magic Fieldwork in British Anthropology from Tylor to Malinowski." In *The Ethnographer's Magic and Other Essays in the History of Anthropology*. George W. Stocking Jr., ed. Madison: University of Wisconsin Press, pp. 12–60.

———, ed. 1983. *Observers Observed: Essays on Ethnographic Fieldwork*. Madison: University of Wisconsin Press.

Tedlock, Barbara. 1991. "From Participant Observation to the Observation of Participation: The Emergence of Narrative Ethnography." *Journal of Anthropological Research* 47(1), pp. 69–94.

Terrell, John Edward, Terry L. Hunt, & Chris Gosden. 1997. "The Dimensions of Social Life in the Pacific: Human Diversity and the Myth of the Primitive Isolate." *Current Anthropology* 38(3), pp. 155–195.

Terrio, Susan. 1998. "Deconstructing Fieldwork in Contemporary Urban France." *Anthropological Quarterly* 71, pp. 18–31.

Trépanier, Cécyle. 1989. *French Louisiana at the Threshold of the 21st Century*. Projet Louisiane, Monograph 2. Quebec: Laval University.

———. 1991. "The Cajunization of French Louisiana: Forging a Regional Identity." *The Geographical Journal* 157, pp. 161–171.

Trouillot, Michel-Ropl. 1991. "Anthropology and the Savage Slot: The Poetics and Politics of Otherness." In *Recapturing Anthropology: Working in the Present*. Richard Fox, ed. Santa Fe, NM: School of American Research Press, pp. 17–44.

University of Houston. 2008. "Folklorist Researches Stories of Hurricane Survivors," http://www
.class.uh.edu/newsandevents_newsletter.html. Consulted September 12, 2008.

U.S. Bureau of the Census. 1993. *Census of Population—1990. Social and Economic Characteristics,
Louisiana*. Washington, DC: Bureau of the Census.

Vidich, Arthur, & Joseph Bensman. 1958. *Small Town in Mass Society*. Princeton: Princeton
University Press.

Vidich, Arthur, & Stanford Lyman. 1994. "Qualitative Methods: Their History in Sociology and
Anthropology." In *Handbook of Qualitative Research*. Norman Denzin & Yvonna Lincoln, eds.
Thousand Oaks, CA: Sage Publications, pp. 23–59.

Ware, Carolyn. 1994. "Reading the Rules Backward: Women and the Rural Cajun Mardi Gras."
Dissertation. Philadelphia: University of Pennsylvania.

Watson, C. W., ed. 1999. *Fieldwork in Anthropology*. Herndon, VA: Pluto Press.

Webre, Stephen. 1998. "Among the CyberCajuns: Constructing Identity in the Virtual Diaspora."
Louisiana History 39(4), pp. 443–456.

Whisnant, David E. 1983. *All that is Native and Fine: The Politics of Culture in an American Region*.
Chapel Hill: University of North Carolina Press.

———. 1988. "Public Sector as Intervention: Lessons from the Past, Prospects for the Future." In *The
Conservation of Culture: Folklorists and the Public Sector*. Burt Feintuch, ed. Lexington: University
Press of Kentucky, pp. 233–251.

Williams, Patrick. 1987. "Les couleurs de l'invisible. Tsiganes dans la banlieue parisienne." In
Chemins de la ville. Enquêtes ethnologiques. Jacques Gutwirth & Colette Petonnet, eds. Paris:
Editions du CTHS, pp. 53–72.

Winkin, Yves. 1996. *Anthropologie de la communication. De la théorie au terrain*. Bruxelles: De Boeck
Université.

Yelvington, Kevin A. 2001. "The Anthropology of Afro-Latin America and the Caribbean: Diasporic
Dimensions." *Annual Review of Anthropology* 30(1), pp. 227-260.

Working the Field

Carl Lindahl (left) with Vories Moreau at Basile's Mardi Gras street dance, 1999. (Photograph by Theadocia Austen)

1. FINDING THE FIELD THROUGH THE DISCOVERY OF THE SELF

—Carl Lindahl

I am a folklorist whose chosen "field" is largely submerged. I study personal dimensions of public performance—here, specifically, ways in which the Cajun Courir de Mardi Gras is internalized as memory and as value system and interpreted through narrative. The festive surface of this holiday is stunningly accessible to outsiders: costumed revelers go out of their way to draw strangers into their game through dancing, begging, and other means of direct engagement. Yet the personal meanings that Mardi Gras carries for its core participants are often elusive in the extreme even to the most observant. Such meanings will not reveal themselves fully in the course of play alone: they must also be sought in the events that frame the festival—the processes of preparation and recollection—as well as in the intimate moments of daily life, to which Mardi Gras holds up a carnival mirror often at least as subtly accurate as it is crazily distorted. Therefore, in addition to the detailed, objective observation required of all folklore fieldwork—techniques well suited for documenting the public face of this celebration—my research focus requires prolonged and extensive personal interrelations with the festive actors whose traditional arts and values I study. Unless I can achieve intimacy with people whose backgrounds and daily life experiences differ deeply from my own, it would be only by accident that I could say anything worthwhile about them.

One of the problems in Mardi Gras literature is that none of the earlier publications attempted to depict how the festival is experienced, either by outsiders or insiders. This is the gap that I have tried to narrow with my own research, a goal I regard as necessary to pursue, even if impossible to achieve: understanding and representing the Mardi Gras community on the players' own terms.

THE SCHOLARLY FIELD AS I FOUND IT

My fieldwork experiences in Cajun country grew from an unlikely combination of professional accident and personal good fortune. When I first visited the prairies, in the spring of 1981, less than a year had passed since I'd earned my Ph.D. in folklore. The degree itself was based largely on approaches dismissed by many of my contemporaries as already out of date. When I entered the field, I was the product of a discipline that was thoroughly divided against itself. The most old-fashioned of such studies took the objectification process to extremes, by asserting that we should study the "primitive" people of today to learn about our own cultural past. Arriving in Louisiana, I found that folkloric studies of Cajuns tended toward objectification and that the "folk" themselves were treated as anachronistic relics of an ancient and simple world. For example, Cajun traitement (a tradition of faith-based folk healing) was characterized as the product of people who had "preserved one of the purest examples of a 17th century folk culture to be found in the United States" (Brandon 1964:261, quoting Smith & Hitt 1952:107).

Not surprisingly, early studies of Mardi Gras portray it as a "survival" from a much earlier time, as if so describing it were sufficient to explain its meanings. In 1964, Harry Oster pronounced the Cajun festival older, "more traditional and more folk" than the New Orleans celebration, and claimed (without offering evidence) that preparations for the twentieth-century rural Mardi Gras were essentially the same as that practiced by the earliest Cajuns in the 1780s (274). Decades later, speculation concerning origins remains a major theme in Mardi Gras scholarship (Mire 1993). The early Mardi Gras literature is remarkable for its failure to draw upon the interpretations of the participants. It is then perhaps understandable—if not justifiable—that my earliest work on Mardi Gras (Lindahl 1992) was based almost entirely on observation and speculation, and relatively little upon my interaction with the people who practiced Mardi Gras.

THE SURFACE AND THE DEPTHS OF MY FIELD

The festival to which I have devoted almost twenty years of research is a model of structural simplicity—or at least, so it would seem to anyone who has read early scholarly descriptions:

Preliminaries. In the predawn hours of Mardi Gras Day, men and women—aged 16 to 80, but most in their teens and twenties—begin to assemble at a central location in Basile. A group of unmasked, whip-bearing capitaines herd the costumed players into two large truck-drawn trailers. The full company numbers between 60 and 150 guisers. These are the Mardi Gras: in Cajun country, "Mardi Gras" names not only a date and a festival, but more importantly the festive actors who carry the holiday with them right into their neighbors' yards, transforming everything they touch into more Mardi Gras.

House Visit. By 7:00 a.m., the Mardi Gras is on the road, with a capitaine in the lead truck. Within a few minutes he halts the procession and steps from his truck into a neighbor's yard. After obtaining the host's permission, the capitaine gestures to his troupe to enter the yard. The Mardi Gras cluster around the capitaine to sing a begging song in French, in which they seek ingredients for a giant gumbo that the entire town will share. Then the players dance with each other and the unmasked spectators. The job is to put on a good show; the capitaines use their whips like lion tamers to lash those players who fail to perform their parts. The host eventually rewards the beggars' call for "charity" by offering food, or occasionally money. The most cherished gift is a chicken, even though it is offered with strings attached: the Mardi Gras must catch it first. The capitaine throws the chicken in the air and the guisers tear after it. Once the chicken is captured, the group celebrates its victory and devotes itself to a period of free-form play—which ends when the capitaines summon the players back to their trucks, in order to travel to other houses to repeat this ritual game, as many as forty times by day's end.

Street Dance. After tracing a twisting path through their small town (population 1700) to visit the focal homes and family businesses, the Mardi Gras reassemble in the heart of town for a march down Main Street, where a street fair is in progress. A band plays and as many as 200 people look on. Again, the Mardi Gras sing, dance, and beg—but this time they linger to mix and dance with their spouses, family members, and boy- and girlfriends.

Gumbo. While the Mardi Gras has pursued its route through town, a group of women has stayed behind preparing the gumbo that will feed the Mardi Gras—as well as all those whom they have invited during their day's travels to share the feast. The gumbo is consumed by 5:30.

Bal. There is a break in the action, allowing revelers to rest, re-costume, and prepare for their final festive act: the procession and dance that begin the evening bal. About 6 p.m., townspeople congregate for the dance; at 7, the band strikes up the Chanson de Mardi Gras as players march two-by-two on to the dance floor. One last time, they sing and dance as a group. Then the whole crowd, masked and unmasked, joins in the bal. Most Mardi Gras, exhausted from their day's play, leave the dance well before midnight, when Ash Wednesday begins, and most will be in church early the next morning to receive the penitential ashes that mark the beginning of Lent.

Folklorists' accounts suggest a structure transparent to any outside observer, tidy even to a fault, but such descriptions do not come close to portraying a first-timer's experience of the festival, which is so vivid that it obscures the more abstract understandings of Mardi Gras. Rather than a structure and a goal, the initiate will experience an immediate, seductive, perhaps even terrifying, intimacy with a group of wild, drunken players intent on demolishing all obstacles between them and their newfound prey. The newcomer will remember best the maskers who begged from her, untied her shoelaces, forced her to dance, and picked her up and started running with her in their arms, as if to abduct her.

"THE COMPREHENSION OF THE OTHER BY THE DETOUR OF THE COMPREHENSION OF SELF"

In 1980, when I received my Ph.D. in folklore, I did not define my work and my interests as I do today. Who I have become as a folklorist and what I see as my strengths and goals were transformed by my fieldwork experience in Cajun Louisiana, through a two-decade-long process of dual discovery: discovery of a community's culture and discovery of myself.

Although positivistic approaches dominated folklore study in Louisiana, the trend among my contemporaries was to undercut them. According to these younger theorists, the objectification of culture was both undesirable and impossible: attempts at objectivity simply substitute the collector's subjectivity for the subjectivity of the culture under study. The most articulate expression of this new perspective was Paul Rabinow's *Reflections on Fieldwork in Morocco* (1977), which asserted that the only valid response to omnipresence of subjectivity is to surrender to it: Stop pretending that you can know anything other than yourself; make fieldwork one more means of measuring your own subjectivity. The goal of fieldwork becomes "the comprehension of the self by the detour of the comprehension of the other" (1977:5–7). Although I instinctively rejected Rabinow's message, I found myself attracted by part of it.

As a stranger timidly facing a foreign culture, I could conceivably take comfort from this Self-centered perspective: the idea that I was embarking upon a cultural journey whose ultimate destination was home again. All I had to do was learn more about myself, and all those Cajuns that I met in the field would simply become the supporting actors in my own intellectual autobiography.

I knew that such a construction was extraordinarily arrogant. I couldn't bring myself to attempt it. Instead, I retreated to my earlier training and assumed an objectifying stance. I reverted to the old cultural catalog approach: noting details and patterns and deriving knowledge exclusively from a watchful distance. During my first ten years of Mardi Gras research, I attended over thirty different celebrations, talked to some leading participants, and took part in three enactments as a costumed player, but I conducted no lengthy interviews. My social distance from the Mardi Gras communities ensured that Cajun studies would not become a major part of my scholarly life. I already possessed a few specialties, and was at work on a book and several articles—all devoted to non-Cajun subjects. Intensive Cajun fieldwork could easily become a detour rather than a boost for my career. Cajun folk tradition could conceivably do me almost as much disservice as I could do it, a frightening thought indeed.

Prior commitments, combined with a hesitation to immerse myself in a culture so alien to my own, worked together to create a long gestation. Fourteen years would pass between my first Mardi Gras and the publication of my first scholarly essay on Mardi Gras. The opportunity to witness the festival without having to write about it was a luxury that all sincere fieldworkers deserve, but few of us experience (thanks to the institutional imperative to publish or perish). In a less squalid world, this opportunity would be a simple right: the right *not* to misrepresent the people one studies.

During this lengthy dormancy, my research underwent a dual motion: a long process of self-discovery, complemented by an equally long and ultimately rewarding process of attempting to understand the Mardi Gras players. In effect, I found myself practicing Rabinow's philosophy in reverse: instead of "the comprehension of the self by the detour of the comprehension of the other," I embarked upon the "comprehension of the other by the detour of the comprehension of self." Experience led me to embrace much of what Rabinow proposed, as long as I could use self-knowledge as a tool rather than as an end.

These are some of the things about myself that I half-knew before beginning fieldwork and that became progressively and painfully obvious as I moved further into it: my background and predispositions were so different from those of the Cajuns that it still remains something of a mystery to me that contact ever occurred. My knowledge of Cajun culture was sparse and clichéd, resting on such cultural stereotypes as Hank Williams's song "Jumbalaya" and the sentimental film *Louisiana Story*. I had "learned" French in seven years of schooling, but the French I knew, though adequate for getting me through any written text I attempted, was not oral and did nothing to prepare me for the Cajun I heard spoken in Louisiana.

Beyond these drawbacks were more imposing cultural factors. My father was the son of Swedish immigrants, born in Chicago; my mother grew up in Kansas, but left it behind for good to marry my father. My experience of the world had been limited almost entirely to urban, suburban, and campus life. I had lived almost all my life in the Midwest. My first fieldwork was conducted among people whose backgrounds did not differ remarkably from my own: for example, suburban legend tellers, whose middle-class backgrounds and interests in a secularized supernatural world paralleled those prevailing in suburbs where I had lived. Even when studying a millennial cult in Indianapolis, I found that, their unique religious dogma notwithstanding, we shared a virtually identical cultural vocabulary.

More personally, I discovered that my own talents as a fieldworker lay almost exclusively in one-on-one situations. I was an excellent listener under such circumstances, and soon found—much to my surprise—that I functioned almost as a confessor for some of my informants. Narrators shared with me, a stranger, stories and beliefs that they had never previously shared with outsiders—or, in certain cases, anyone before. Yet this one undeniable skill seemed seriously out of place in Cajun country, where very nearly the only person I have ever interviewed one-on-one was a widow who lived alone. Nearly all the tangible traditions connected with Mardi Gras were highly public phenomena.

Most disconcerting, while my past successes in fieldwork involved older informants, the great majority of participants in Cajun Mardi Gras were ten to fifteen years younger than I was (I began fieldwork at age thirty-three). Hunting was a mainstay of their lifestyle; I, on the other hand, came from a family in which it was forbidden to possess or use guns. I lacked knowledge of, interest in, and experience with fishing, outdoor cooking, and cars, among other things—all of which made it seem impossible for me to communicate with these men. I saw the Cajun Mardi Gras culture as so alien to my own that I did not trust myself to act even as a distant observer of it.

During my long transition from cultural alien to community member, I maintained a strong relationship with one Cajun insider. I would probably never have gotten to know anything about Cajun culture were it not in the context of this close personal friendship. I met Barry Jean Ancelet as we were both studying toward graduate degrees in folklore, and I knew him for six years before I ever visited Cajun Louisiana. When I moved from Bloomington, Indiana, to Houston, Texas, to accept a professorship in folklore, Barry suddenly became my closest friend, geographically, though our homes were separated by two hundred miles.

Barry was as different from me as any friend I had ever had. When we met, I was on my home turf, and he was the cultural outsider; the extent of our differences was immediately obvious. Barry sorely missed his home and family. Although I considered myself deeply attached to my own family, the intensity of Barry's attachment seemed much stronger. He found Midwestern cuisine inedibly bland. He thought his fellow students almost suicidally impractical; though he admired their scholarship, he was perpetually (if politely) amused by their difficulties in living in the everyday world. He often told me about his encounter with another student on the banks of a creek that flows through the Indiana University campus. She had just trapped a crawfish in a glass jar. Barry—who had never before seen a crawfish in Indiana, nor anyone eat a crawfish there—was delighted. He was preparing to join her in catching, boiling, and eating a home-style meal when the woman told him that she was going to take the crawfish home and put it in her aquarium. This got to Barry: no Cajun would have a crawfish for a pet. Midwesterners did not know enough about the world to understand its gifts.

As hungry as he was for Cajun food, Barry was at least as hungry for someone with whom to share Cajun traditions. I was more than willing to fill this role. Barry cooked Cajun food in my apartment, played recorded Cajun music for me, entertained me with Cajun folk narratives, and introduced me to the great musicians and storytellers whom he knew. The excitement that he always carries to discussions of Cajun culture was intensified by his physical distance from it. He couldn't stop talking about it, and I couldn't stop listening.

In 1981, when I first came to Cajun country, our circumstances were reversed. I was now the cultural alien and Barry was on his home turf. Even at age thirty, he was probably the country's best-known specialist in Cajun folklore. Cajun ethnicity, stigmatized just a few years earlier, had recently become fashionable among outsiders and a point of public pride for insiders. There was no shortage of people eager to hear what Barry had to say about his culture. Even in the midst of a crush of attention that daily invaded his privacy, Barry never tired of sharing his culture with me.

Vis-à-vis that culture, I saw myself as the archetypal outsider, playing a role of little value, yet Barry valorized that role. He told me that I had given him perspectives difficult or impossible for insiders to find. He took me with him to interview musicians and storytellers. Although my ineptness with Cajun French kept me silent for hours on end, and although I often understood no more than half of the dialogue, I reached a vicarious rapport with storytellers, who perceived my interest and respect even when we communicated only in the most limited ways.

It was Barry who introduced me to the Cajun Mardi Gras. Since 1982 I have attended at least one Mardi Gras enactment a year in his presence and benefited enormously from his experience and skills as an observer. All the while, I recorded my own observations, which I regarded as only part of the story: Barry and other Cajuns would supply the better half. After ten years of joint fieldwork, Barry and I decided to collaborate on a book on Mardi Gras, and we began more systematically planning our fieldwork, so that we would be able to survey all the active Mardi Gras communities.

FINDING MY CHOSEN FIELD

In 1991, I stumbled into the community that was to become the focus of my serious Mardi Gras research. After a decade of observing Mardi Gras, I still viewed the festival essentially as one day's play and had not given serious thought to the ways in which it permeated the lives of its core practitioners. My fieldwork had been confined almost exclusively to the mini-dramas of the house visits. In 1991, however, I witnessed the "afterlife" of one particularly intense Mardi Gras: the Basile bal. By 8:00 p.m., their revelry presumably finished for the year, the Mardi Gras were already re-creating the festival orally, with stories about the day's activities, about past Mardi Gras, and about great Mardi Gras tricksters, past and present. These interchanges were as dramatic as anything I had witnessed during the festival, and they forced me to begin to see Mardi Gras as a complex story that is told, "pre-lived," and relived in the days preceding and following the masked quest itself. For its core participants, this story engages memories, expectations, and emotions more powerful than those attending Christmas in my own community.

For me, the distance between what the outsider sees and what the players feel was brought home most dramatically in 1993, when—after following the Basile Mardi Gras all day—I stood listening to a group of young men talking, with an almost masochistic cheerfulness, about what they had sacrificed just to secure their opportunity to go crazy for this one day:

> Their employers told them that if they didn't come to work on Tuesday morning, they would not be coming back. And that's exactly what happened. [Another player] had just been released from the hospital with a serious knee injury. By the end of a day of chicken chasing, begging, and trickery, his pants were red with the blood of his injured leg. Another man, . . . who had been scheduled for neck surgery, instead chased chickens, climbed trees, ran through fields for eight hours— and was chosen best all-around Mardi Gras at the bal that night. Some of these men sacrificed their livelihoods, others arguably risked their lives, for one day of calculated madness. (Lindahl 1996b:128)

Mardi Gras, then, is not merely a game or even a drama, but a passion for its core players. No matter how much pleasure they give and get from their play, there is a deeper, almost gravely serious dimension to their game which transforms it from a simple day of play to a Day of Obligation. As Mardi Gras evening 1993 wore on, the passion behind the game grew more intense and obvious. At the bal that concludes the day's celebrations, after the Mardi Gras had performed its last act of group play, some of the guisers danced on with their spouses and friends, and capitaine Hoover Landreneaux stood in their midst with his whip finally relaxed in his hand and a faraway smile on his face. His eyes were watering. Before I could say a word to him, he explained: "This is just the same as being in church. This is just the same as Ash Wednesday. This is part of it. You can't have Mardi Gras without Lent, or Lent without Mardi Gras. They're part of each other."

Later that same night, Potic Rider found stronger words for how players live their Mardi Gras passion than any I've heard before or since:

> At the end of seventeen hours of songs, dances, processionals, and after revelers half his age had been carried home, Potic Rider . . . stood in the dance hall, the last of the Mardi Gras remaining at the bal. His fortieth Mardi Gras was over. He was surely feeling the old wounds—the broken back, the knee and neck injuries—that ensured he would be walking with a cane tomorrow morning. He was drinking the last of the day's many beers—the last beer he would drink before Easter, for Lent was just minutes away. No one asked him for an explanation, but he wanted to talk about feelings that words cannot name: "I can't explain it. Mardi Gras doesn't come from the head; it comes from the heart. It's in you. You can take anyone off the street and make him a clown, but you can't make him a good clown. You can't make him a Mardi Gras. You have to live it. It's like Moses going to the mountain-top and seeing the burning bush. And the burning bush said, 'I am that I am.' Well, 'I am that I am': Potic. I run Mardi Gras." (Lindahl 1996b:134)

Looking back, I feel as if it was planned. I had been preparing for it, more or less unconsciously, for a decade, and training in earnest the past two years. That night revealed a dimension of Mardi Gras that nothing I had read so much as hinted at.

Listening to these two, it did not take me long to realize that Mardi Gras meant so much to them because it meant so many things that extended beyond the boundary of the day itself: things about family, community, loyalty, work, friendship, and survival. The new goal of my fieldwork was to understand everything in the experience of such devoted players that contributed to their passion for that one day. When they said they lived for Mardi Gras, they were challenging me to learn everything about their lives.

So I began fieldwork in earnest, attempting to measure the dimensions of the field beyond the confines of Mardi Gras day. My plan included the requisite call upon the official leader: in this case, Potic Rider, President of the Basile Mardi Gras Riders Association. Potic had another guest, a man who "knows more about Mardi Gras than anyone else alive," Vories Moreau. Vories and Potic soon overwhelmed me with their intense eloquence; by their account, they "lived" for Mardi Gras.

SATURATION FIELDWORK

I had seen enough of the varied faces of Mardi Gras to acquire a strong sense of its most public structures and meanings. My new goal was saturation fieldwork, continued lengthy exposure to a few people willing and able to share with me. With a full-time job and a family two hundred miles away, I could not move to Basile to immerse myself for months or years. But I could commit myself to getting to know some of the players well. Rather than the more orthodox ideal of immersion—total absorption into the community—I strove for saturation: filling myself with the experiences of the few whom I had a real opportunity to know. I characterize the traits, strengths, and weaknesses of this approach as follows:

> Saturation fieldwork by definition leads to partial representation. It is geared to sounding the depth rather than spanning the breadth of the play and the players. If my research was crippled by the necessity of slighting most community members in order to know a few, I compensated in part for my lack of breadth by concentrating on those festive actors recognized as integral Mardi Gras within the community.

If intensive exposure to a few individuals might distort the public nature of this festival, such an approach was perfectly consonant with my greatest strengths as a fieldworker. First, it allowed me to draw upon my success with long, one-on-one interviews. Second, it enabled me to exploit my greatest skills as a listener and my deepest experience as a traditional being: my rapport with old people. My two grandmothers were great storytellers and my greatest teachers; they had taught me how to listen. As I began to study the personal dimensions of Mardi Gras, I played to my strength, seeking out the oldest players—aged sixty-five to seventy-three when I first met them. All were still extremely active in Mardi Gras, not as masked beggars, but as musicians, cooks, and capitaines. And all had passionate feelings about the holiday, which they were delighted to share.

Immediately, they taught me something that had not emerged in earlier research: that they considered themselves as vital to the festival as the young boys who chase the chickens. There was evidence that the community shared their opinion: their neighbors demonstrated obvious respect of these elders and their Mardi Gras roles. Whatever the shortcomings of my method, it had already opened up a realm of Mardi Gras experience untouched in previous study.

Saturation fieldwork requires seeking Mardi Gras everywhere that it might appear, but most intensively where it has not been sought before. Listening to Basile's oldest Mardi Gras, I quickly learned that what had seemed focal in my earlier, more superficial examinations of Mardi Gras was not necessarily focal for them. For example, in the extant literature, the chicken chase is regarded as the single most important facet of the celebration—and in certain communities and among certain factions (especially the younger males) the chicken chase indeed is, effectively, Mardi Gras. Yet, for Basile's elders, the playful and sometimes threatening begging games assumed far greater weight than chicken chasing. Begging in turn complemented the ideals of generosity, redistribution, and charity, ideals expressed in the gumbo served free of charge to all comers. Basilians take great pride in distinguishing themselves from those communities that put a price tag on the Mardi Gras gumbo. Begging and the communal gumbo assume greater importance in Basile than in any other Mardi Gras community I have visited.

I sought out deeply committed players who were nevertheless marginal to the official power structure. I tried to situate myself as a "personal" insider/friend, but not as an "official Mardi Gras insider." I tried, for example, to minimize my contact with the leaders of the Mardi Gras Association, and to concentrate instead on dedicated revelers regarded unofficially as leaders and models by the rest of the group.

As important as the older generation was to me, and as important as my favorite informants were to Basile's Mardi Gras, I nevertheless sensed the danger that my study could develop into an exercise in memory culture, to the harmful neglect of the younger participants. It would be too easy for me to unwittingly create an idealized reconstruction of former times and to shut my eyes to the Mardi Gras of here and now. Yet I was most interested in the ways in which the old affects the new, in which past players and their memories influence its current practice.

At this crux, the unconscious wisdom of my choice to seek out the oldest players paid off in unexpected ways. Once I had sought out senior community members, junior members sought me out. When younger Cajuns sensed how much I respected their parents and grandparents, they became accepting of me. Among the people I got to know first and best were the sons and daughters of the older Mardi Gras whom I had interviewed. In ten years of fieldwork in Basile, I have never had to solicit an interview with a younger Mardi Gras; they all came to me. I had not foreseen how the approval of older Cajuns would earn me the approval of the young.

In saturation fieldwork, the informants create the agenda. My approach was doubly risky: I was concentrating not only on a fraction of the community, but particularly on those people to whom I felt closest. The danger was great that my interviews would simply mirror my own values rather than Basile's. I sought to open a space in which the town's vieux monde could speak for themselves.

I was most apprehensive of what I call "conspiratorial interpretations" (Lindahl 1997:54–55). These are as follows. The very fact that an older man from a foreign culture has given me days of his time is an indication that he is willing to please me. If I offer him an interpretation, it is likely that I will simultaneously signal to him, consciously or otherwise, the degree of my investment in that interpretation. His innocent desire to please me—sometimes mixed with a sense of courtesy—often leads him to agree with my interpretation, even if in other circumstances he would not accept it.

To counteract this risk, I tried to refrain from offering interpretations. I always had questions in mind and tentative answers formulated, but I strove to induce fieldwork contexts in which my preconceptions would be "outnumbered," that is, liable to be overridden. My ideal was for the informant to control the conversation, so that his or her values would surface with as little direction as possible from me. The best situation was one in which I was physically outnumbered by my informants, so that what emerged on the tape recorder was less a performance solicited by me and rather, as much as possible, an interaction controlled by the Mardi Gras community.

Saturation fieldwork engages and acknowledges the "folk" as cocreators of the research. It was essential that those quoted at greatest length have the right to delete, expand, or alter any words about them ultimately published under my name. I am aware that a community's self-representations are often notably biased, but would they be less accurate than my representations of them? In all of academe, I find no discipline more willing than folklore to characterize the "soul" or "essence" of a group, but less willing than folklore to produce evidence that such characterizations indeed reflect the perceptions of the group itself, rather than those imposed by the author.

A common objection to my practice is that insiders are likely to exaggerate their own most positive personal qualities or to gloss over the troubles of their communities. My first answer, based on moral conviction: my colleagues in the humanities and social scientists accept it as given that all authors idealize to some extent in constructing self-portraits. Why should those who tell their stories orally, those whom folklorists are committed to attempt to represent, be the only ones who are denied the right to edit themselves?

My second answer, based on experience: most of my informants have been more modest in describing themselves than I have been in describing them. They have also been frank about their relationships with other people or groups in their communities, particularly figures and institutions of authority. They have sometimes been so open in describing conflicts and rivalries that I have felt impelled to edit out some of the more negative remarks. Thus, it is I, and not my informants, who has "prettied up" the picture of Basile's Mardi Gras community.

Folklore (whose very name invokes a "folk") demands a responsibility not only to the individual, but also to the community. Folklorists consider every individual both in and for himself and as a representative of at least one social group. This stance faithfully reflects the self-images of the members of Basile's Mardi Gras. Every player who has spoken to me at length considers himself to have at least three Mardi Gras identities: as an individual, he may judge himself the best beggar in his group; as a member of the Basile Mardi Gras, he will contrast his festival to that of, say, Mamou, and invariably conclude that Basile has the best Mardi Gras in the world; as a member of the Cajun community, he will see the country Mardi Gras as a marker of Cajun pride, and in comparison, find the New Orleans Mardi Gras to be a mindless, soulless waste of time.

In my experience, extending informants the "right" to edit themselves seldom results in a truly collaborative creation. Typically, by the time I have written up my research clearly enough for others to read, the informant and I have reached such a level of cordiality that he or she would not think of offering major changes. The only corrections offered by residents of Basile have been those of concrete fact: the spellings of names, for example. No deletions have been proposed. Only once have additions been proposed, and these were not interpretations, but rather lists of names. I believe that my informants viewed my efforts at collaboration less as an issue of faithful representation than as a matter of courtesy: in their eyes, I had been courteous enough to ask for their approval; they were determined to show their courtesy by granting approval.

Because my research relied on close-up views of a select few community members, I did not find it practicable or advisable to attempt to disguise their identities. I never considered pseudonyms as an option for my major informants, nor did any one of them ever request that his or her name be withheld from my published research. To a person, they were happy to be cited.

There was only one sort of situation in which I presented quotes anonymously: when dealing with statements that might cause a certain amount of social damage if attributed to a named speaker. I feel obliged to depict the more factious and inflammatory aspects of community. For example, racial tensions sometimes surface during Mardi Gras, and people make provocative statements about race relationships. At the end of the 1993 celebration, one man loudly proclaimed a connection between the Mardi Gras and the Ku Klux Klan (the most common piece of Mardi Gras headgear is a tall conical hat that resembles the pointed hats worn by Ku Klux Klan members). This remark represents an extreme point of view: I have never heard any other citizen of Basile express this opinion. Though unrepresentative of the group as a whole, this statement illustrates one pole of the group's value system. In a recent piece on Mardi Gras and race, I quoted the speaker without giving his name. I approach most other volatile issues in the same way, even when speakers are willing to have their names attached to negative opinions.

Saturation fieldwork requires that researchers do everything in their power to outnumber their subjectivity. I recognize that I could follow religiously the precepts outlined here and still produce a characterization of Mardi Gras that conforms much more closely to my predisposition than to the values, emotions, and aesthetics of the Mardi Gras community. Indeed, I believe that some of my work has suffered just such an outcome.

If there is no safe way I can ignore my subjectivity, there are few ways I can use it to my advantage unless I outnumber it. Being outnumbered by one's informants is one step toward this goal. Another means of outnumbering subjectivity is team fieldwork, a tactic familiar to me from my early Mardi Gras research with Barry Ancelet. A second observer can prove a significant check on the excesses of the first, provided the two observers fight the impulse to create their own brand of conspiratorial interpretation.

In a town the size of Basile, team fieldwork possesses more disadvantages than advantages. With each additional researcher who takes the field, prospects for being outnumbered by the host community diminish. Basile could not comfortably or profitably accommodate a large team. It is fortunate, then, that Basile has not received much outside attention. During a typical Mardi Gras day, as many as twenty "official observers"—fieldworkers, journalists, folklore students—may visit, but in my eleven years in Basile, I have witnessed only four such outsiders spend the entire day with the Mardi Gras. Folklorist Carolyn Ware is the only person besides myself who has done so more than twice. Her knowledge of Basile's Mardi Gras and her response to my observations have been extremely valuable to me.

Carolyn and I have spent at least eight years watching the Basile Mardi Gras together from start to finish. In 1995, we co-organized a folklorists' field trip to Basile, after which we were invited to collaborate on a book focusing on the Mardi Gras masking traditions (Lindahl & Ware 1997). Carolyn's specialty—the relatively young female Mardi Gras tradition in Basile—complements my focus on the older men and their memories. Our fieldwork paths overlap sufficiently to allow us to compare our views of identical events (thereby to learn about the natures of our separate subjectivities), but also diverge sufficiently to allow us to share the results of our separate experience: a range of community viewpoints that neither could have learned without the other's help.

The greatest strength of saturation fieldwork is also its greatest weakness: the intensity of the personal relationships it requires. My interviews with older players were so successful and personally gratifying that they caused me to neglect many contemporary aspects of the festival. I became much more attuned to idealized past Mardi Gras celebrations than to present-day enactments, and I began to judge Mardi Gras aesthetics more according to the values of the past than of the present. My ties to my favorite informants also led to a certain amount of partisanship, as I slowly discovered aspects of factionalism and rivalry within the Mardi Gras community. I attempted to compensate by distributing my interviews more evenly among diverse community members, but I have not succeeded. The personal focus of my work has taken its toll in terms of representation.

Over the years my primary informants became such good friends that I returned to Basile principally to see them, and not to document the Mardi Gras. In recent years, my work commitments in other realms have become so great that I have not had the time both to conduct thorough Mardi Gras research and to see my best friends in Basile. The friends won out: nearly all my time in Basile in the past three years has been spent with them.

Through saturation fieldwork, I came to see Mardi Gras as the natural extension of the lives of my older informants and the quintessential expression of their values. I learned so much about two of my informants, Vories Moreau and Mrs. Agnes Miller, that I considered writing a book based primarily on the narratives of these two extraordinary people. In the book, Mardi Gras would be important, but their daily work, their religious and supernatural beliefs, and their family relationships would prevail. Both of these people have died since I planned on writing this book, and I must admit that much of my interest in writing about Mardi Gras died with them.

PRODUCTS OF RESEARCH; COMMUNITY AND SCHOLARLY VERDICTS

By 1994, I felt that my Basile experiences had brought me closer to my goal—the comprehension of the other by the detour of the comprehension of self—than I had ever come before; in three years, I had learned more about myself and enormously more about my informants than I had in perhaps all my previous years of fieldwork combined.

It was time to begin writing what I was learning, adhering as closely as I could to the primary goal of folklore research: the representation of the community on its own terms, a goal as necessary to pursue as it is impossible to achieve. If I was persistent and lucky enough to have reached a certain comprehension of the Basile community, my job was now only half done, because I now had to present that community in such a way that it would speak for itself. The ideal published result would be both fully satisfactory to the insiders in Basile and equally comprehensible and satisfactory to any group of strangers who might want to know about the town's Mardi Gras community. I had two imperatives: to allow the Mardi Gras insiders to express themselves as often and as effectively as possible in their own words, and to provide a framing "cultural translation" that would give outsiders enough information and "feel" for the players that they could put themselves effectively in the shoes of the Mardi Gras (or at least be aware of how much distance lay between their experience as readers and the revelers' experience of their special day). Thus, to help an outsider understand the words of, say, Potic Rider, when he compares himself to the burning bush of the book of Exodus (see previous mention), it is not enough simply to quote him. No matter how eloquent, the words derive greater force from the facts that they were spoken just as Mardi Gras was becoming Ash Wednesday, spoken by someone who religiously observes both the excesses of carnival and the austerity of Lent, someone for whom Mardi Gras is the essence both of self-indulgence and self-sacrifice.

I have coauthored one book (Lindahl & Ware 1997), edited a special issue of the *Journal of American Folklore* (Lindahl 2001), appeared as a commentator in a film (Mire 1993), and written four scholarly articles (Lindahl 1996a, 1996b, 1997, [2003]) and two magazine pieces (1992; 1998) devoted to Cajun Mardi Gras. I am most proud of one article, "The Presence of the Past in the Cajun Country Mardi Gras" (Lindahl 1996b), which succeeded, I believe, because it focused directly upon ways in which older revelers' memories and narratives continue to live in today's celebrations. I attempted to present three different voices as clearly as possible: (1) my own participant-observer's voice, informed by six years of fieldwork in Basile; but outnumbered by (2) several hard-core Mardi Gras voices, words spoken during the festival itself by people intensely engaged in the day's activities; and by (3) narratives and evaluations from Vories Moreau, one of Basile's great Mardi Gras participants, whose memories stretched back to the 1930s.

After the article appeared, two of these voices received validation from crucial listeners. My scholarly voice was praised by the judges who awarded the article the Alcée Fortier Prize of the American Folklore Society (1997). Closer to the core, two of Basile's zealous active Mardi Gras celebrants told me that their voices had come through in the article. One of them wrote me, "I . . . want you to know that it's very, very powerful. I can't read, hardly any quotes without crying because they're true to the core. . . . I challenge any Mardi . . . 'Hard Core One' to read this if his blood doesn't move, if he doesn't get excited or doesn't cry." This was the highest praise I could imagine, and it came from a man who was not only a great Mardi Gras, but also the son of Vories Moreau, the hero of the piece. I was sure I had gotten it right.

But the single most important critic was Vories himself; the article was about him more than anyone else. His judgment, though polite, was damning: "It was good, but you left out the excitement." That was surely not my intention. Outsiders had told me that Vories's words had deeply excited them; one outsider had told me that reading Vories's words had made her cry. So, proud as I am of this essay, I have to regard it as failed in one major way; Vories's criticism was a sure signal that I had not outnumbered myself. (The previous three paragraphs are updated from Lindahl 1997:64–65.)

I attempted to set things right by collaborating with Vories on an article expressing his view of Mardi Gras (Lindahl 1998). I asked him what he most wanted to talk about; it seemed to me that the topics he stressed had all been treated as he wished in the previous essay, but Vories liked the new piece better. He had insisted upon adding two passages: a catalog naming great past players (all of them now dead) who had taught him to run Mardi Gras and a list of family members and neighbors who learned Mardi Gras from him. I am willing to bet that no outsider reading these lists would find them moving, but for Vories these few sentences did more than anything else to provide the excitement that had been missing from the first piece. There are ways in which insider and outsider voices cannot be fully reconciled—such a gulf will exist as long as any distinction remains between the two. Here, the folklore fieldworker's job is to narrow the gap as much as possible—and, when one essay cannot bridge all the gaps between the two sets of understandings, write a second, or a third.

Kim Moreau's praise of my article, considered in tandem with his father's cooler response, led me to a meditation on the nature of the "others" I was trying to discover. Did my work appeal more to the past-minded younger Mardi Gras than to the older men whom I was trying hardest to voice? Perhaps there was more of a younger man's hero worship than an older man's memories in the work that I had written. Perhaps I was seeing Mardi Gras more fully through the eyes of the younger players than I had imagined.

The scholarly reception of my articles has done much to bolster my sense of the value of the precepts outlined above. Yet whatever validity my writing possesses, it rests on deeply personal bonds and experiences. After eleven years in Basile, the most important tangible rewards I have received all came not from the scholars, but from the Mardi Gras community. First, was the letter from Kim Moreau. Second, was a plaque presented to me in 1999, naming me an honorary member of the Basile Mardi Gras Association. Third, were the words written to me by Joyce Moreau on April 4, 2001, the day after her husband Vories died. She was writing to thank me for agreeing to deliver his eulogy: "I feel you are the ideal person to tell us about Vories. I think you understood and knew him better than most of his lifelong friends."

The "others" that I discovered in Basile turned out to be best friends. In some regards, my work is terribly biased: biased toward them, toward a sentimentality reflecting my feelings about them, toward depicting a Mardi Gras that is as much a passion as a game, the kind of Mardi Gras perhaps most poignantly played and felt by those too old to play the way they once did. Yet I maintain that this work is faithful to one dimension of Mardi Gras as I have seen it played and heard it re-created: the passion of those who, like Vories Moreau, "live for Mardi Gras" so intensely that their love for that day outlives them:

[On Mardi Gras day 2001] Vories Moreau, one of Basile's greatest Mardi Gras, lay in a hospital in neighboring Mamou. Robbed by mortality of his hopes for running Mardi Gras in Basile, he planned instead to don his mask, suit, and capuchon inside the hospital and run the halls to entertain his fellow patients. Vories ultimately proved too sick to suit up on Mardi Gras day, and by the end of Lent he was dead. But he carried Mardi Gras with him past the threshold of death. At the funeral home, his mask and capuchon lay at his side, close to a floral arrangement sent by the Basile Mardi Gras Association. At the end of the funeral, a group of musicians played the Mardi Gras song as they walked Vories to his grave. (Lindahl [2003]:31)

REFERENCES

Brandon, Elizabeth. 1964. "Traiteurs or Folk Doctors in Southwest Louisiana." In *Buying the Wind: Regional Folklore in the United States.* Richard M. Dorson, ed. Chicago: University of Chicago Press, pp. 261–266.

Dorson, Richard M., ed. 1964. *Buying the Wind: Regional Folklore in the United States.* Chicago: University of Chicago Press.

Lindahl, Carl. 1992. "Unraveling the Mysteries of Cajun Mardi Gras." *Houston Metropolitan* (February), pp. 23–26.

———. 1996a. "Bakhtin's Carnival Laughter and the Cajun Country Mardi Gras." *Folklore* 107, pp. 57–70.

———. 1996b. "The Presence of the Past in the Cajun Country Mardi Gras." *Journal of Folklore Research* 33, pp. 125–153.

———. 1997. "The Power of Being Outnumbered." *Louisiana Folklore Miscellany* 12, pp. 43–76.

———. 1998. "One Family's Mardi Gras: The Moreaus of Basile." *Louisiana Cultural Vistas* 9(3), pp. 46–53.

———. 2001. "Ways Inside the Circle of the Cajun Country Mardi Gras." *Journal of American Folklore* 114(452), pp. 132–139.

———. [2003]. "'That's My Day': Cajun Country Mardi Gras in Basile, Louisiana." In *Carnaval!* Barbara Mauldin & John Nunley, eds. Los Angeles: Fowler Museum of Cultural History.

Lindahl, Carl, & Carolyn Ware. 1997. *Cajun Mardi Gras Masks.* Jackson: University Press of Mississippi.

Mire, Pat [Director]. 1993. *Dance for a Chicken: The Cajun Mardi Gras.* 57 min., 16 mm., color. Eunice, LA: Attakapas Productions.

Oster, Harry. 1964. "Folk Celebration: Country Mardi Gras." In *Buying the Wind: Regional Folklore in the United States.* Richard M. Dorson, ed. Chicago: University of Chicago Press, pp. 274–281.

Rabinow, Paul. 1977. *Reflections on Fieldwork in Morocco.* Berkeley: University of California Press.

Smith, T. Lynn, & Homer L. Hitt. 1952. *The People of Louisiana.* Baton Rouge: Louisiana State University Press.

2.   "ARE YOU GOING TO TREAT?"

Asking Questions about Vernacular Medicine

—Dana A. David

During one of my frequent *veillées*, or visits to my grandmother in my native Vermilion Parish while doing fieldwork on treaters and their vernacular medicine, she asked me, "Are you going to treat?" More than a little uncomfortable with the role reversal, I hesitated, trying to find the words to explain the objective distance necessary to study a cultural phenomenon like faith healing that Cadien treaters practice. While my mind raced to analyze the situation, my grandmother quickly answered, "Good, because people need it." I had not been prompt enough to identify the power of the spoken word, the basis of vernacular medicine among Cadiens. A *traiteur*, treater in English, recites a prayer as a treatment for various ailments.[1] Having these sacred words empowers an individual to heal. Treaters are a part of the belief system in Cadien culture, and through my questions I had become a part of the process of construction and negotiation of beliefs. I had discovered in the course of my fieldwork that people talked around treating, telling stories which affirmed or negated some treater's power or the tradition in general, or to negotiate their own therapeutic power. On a practical level, because I was not seeking out a treater for healing, the perception of my research was that I desired to become one. On a cultural level, as my grandmother's question implied, if I was going to ask about and for these sacred words, there was and is a cultural imperative for me to use this knowledge.

Dana David (left) with her
grandmother Ti Dai (right)
or the fieldworker with her
informant.

Of course, my objective starting out was much simpler: to describe a
cultural practice that no one had satisfactorily addressed. When the Francophone Studies Program was inaugurated at the University of Louisiana at
Lafayette, I jumped at the chance to come home and study Cadiens. I had
hesitated starting a doctoral program with a more classic formation in the
French periods of literature, culture, and history because I felt I would only
be moving further away from what interested me most: Cadiens and their
cultural practices. I was drawn to the subject of treating in part because I
was skeptical about its validity and in part because I wanted to know why
Cadiens used treaters when we had access to modern health care systems.
What was the social and historical context that permitted the two systems
of healing, biomedical and traditional, to coexist? The most obvious element
missing in the literature on belief systems was information about the setting.
Where did treaters and other traditional practitioners practice? Where could
I observe a treatment? How was I going to find treaters and their patients?

From the limited literature on the subject, I pieced together the guidelines that treaters appeared to be following. The local oral tradition stipu-
lated the following: the patient must ask for a treatment but cannot thank
the treater; a treatment is believed not to "cross" a body of water; there is no
payment but a gift is accepted; prayers are allegedly transmitted to someone
of the opposite sex; in the past, a treatment consisted of a three-prayer cycle

with a ten- to fifteen-minute interval between prayers but this sequence has evolved toward just one prayer per treatment; some treaters use herbal remedies, the most frequent being the seed from the Mamou plant which, brewed as a tea, is good for treating colds; finally some treaters say that an illness such as sunstroke will "come back" on them.

Most scholars placed treaters and their vernacular medicine under the rubric of superstition, an approach which reduces this system of beliefs and the practice it supports to a set of coincidences and empirical conditions— signs and causes that justify the event. Having grown up familiar with what a treater was, I believed that there was a better explanation waiting for me in the field.

MY MOTIVATION FOR SEEKING OUT TREATERS

My return to Louisiana for graduate studies and the conscious choice to go back to my native Vermilion/Cameron Parish was for me an effort on one level to learn more Cadien French and on another level to write about *nous autres*, Cadiens. I had left Klondike after high school and went on to pursue undergraduate and graduate degrees in French language and culture. I always sensed a certain distance between the content of what I was learning and my experience growing up in a francophone milieu. Why was it that on my frequent visits home, my standard French did not meet my grandmother Tee Dai's standard?[2] In addition to this disconnect between the variants of spoken French, my personal experiences while living and working outside of Louisiana pointed to a limited notion of Cadiens on the part of outsiders. I always insisted on the French pronunciation of my family name, explaining that I was Cadien from Louisiana to justify my preference. This inspired diverse reflections on Louisiana culture. Often people spoke of Mardi Gras in New Orleans: useless to tell them that most Cadiens immigrated through the port to areas west of the city. Others spoke of the cuisine and asked if I could cook like Justin Wilson, a Cadien cook with a syndicated show. Certain others marveled that I did not have an accent (like Justin Wilson), which was not surprising since I was educated in English. This common denominator perspective, that is, food, language, place, on Cadiens did not reflect the experience I had of growing up in a Cadien family. Occasionally even family and friends grabbed at stereotypes of the happy, "laissez le bons temps rouler" Cadien or of the dim-witted Cadien found in literature of the nineteenth century. I was enriched by a culture that was marginally represented and taught to me in an informal fashion. I wanted to understand it explicitly. I felt that Cadien culture was an unspoken side of our lives. Taking the discussion to a more formal level was an opening to understanding ourselves.

I began my field research with the individuals who had first informed me about treaters in my childhood, my mother and grandmother who lived in the western corner of Vermilion Parish. Both played an integral role in my research, the former providing me with names of treaters and the latter serving as a sounding board for what I was finding in my interviews. Beginning with my grandmother, who consulted a treater and another source in Acadia Parish, my interviews snowballed and covered the parishes of Vermilion, Jeff Davis, Acadia, and Lafayette from 1996 through 1999. Growing up in a farm family, I understood the rhythm of life in the parishes west of Lafayette: days start early and end early. Thus, when scheduling interviews, I knew the windows of opportunity operated around mealtimes. I quickly learned that calling more than two days ahead of time was futile, because I often got the response "Baby, I don't know what I'm doing yet." When I made second visits, I intuitively brought along baked goods in appreciation for our conversations. This offering was something I had learned as a child: we always exchanged goods, especially food—it was *lagniappe*.

Indeed, exchange was an integral part of social life growing up in a Cadien family. Visits to Tee-Dai's entailed a steady transfer of Tupperware dishes that were filled and refilled with extra food and circulated between our household and hers. While there, I was often enlisted to peel, cut, or chop vegetables that someone had given her. I say exchange was an integral part of social life, because the exchange was the reason for the visit. In my grandmother's house there was a constant flow of people drinking coffee after having dropped something off. My father often received similar types of goods, such as ducks or crawfish, for lending a tool or a helping hand on a labor-intensive day of work. These types of exchanges flowed into the more structured exchanges in Cadien culture. The *boucherie* and the *ramasserie* were direct exchanges establishing relations of reciprocal dependence between families and neighbors. Although of short duration, these practices contributed to build minimal links between people. The *bal de maison* and *veillée* added other layers of social relationships. Cadiens developed relationships of interdependence out of economic necessity, yet the official forms of exchange among Cadiens also demonstrate that reciprocity was valued in structuring social life. Treaters provided health care service, and still do, to their isolated rural communities by praying over those who asked for a treatment. The understood gift exchange that occurs between treater and patient is thus part of the overall social structure.

The advantage of doing field research in my own culture was that I could tap into my relationship to place and to family. Despite my career as a flight attendant that had me frequently going to foreign destinations, I had continued to cultivate ties to people and place, a common element in Cadien culture. My anchor in the culture was Klondike, the small community on the Cameron/Vermilion parish line in which I grew up, and I used this as the reference point by which people could situate me. Once at an interview, I initiated the conversation in French that led to a discussion of my genealogy: "Are you a David from Church Point?" Once we had established my position on the genealogy/geography map, a connection was established and the entry was relatively easy. The fact that I spoke Cadien French, with only a trace of standard, enabled treaters to communicate more freely in their native language. In fact, I believe this enriched my interviews by meeting them on their terms, in their language.[3]

This is not to say that the linguistic environment in doing fieldwork in Louisiana is not complex. Speaking French required persistence because of the emotional nuances, voiced or not, surrounding the language. Beginning a conversation in French often required talking, in English, about speaking French. It triggered an individual's memory of being punished at school for speaking French or being discriminated against for being francophone. Their stories communicated not only a pride in their ability to speak French, but also a pride in overcoming the social obstacles of being francophone. If we could make the transition to French, some people would ask me where I learned it. When I admitted that I learned it in Europe, the conversation turned to the negative value ascribed to Cadien French until very recently. When confronted with language attitudes, I explained that standard French was only one variety and that I enjoyed learning new Cadien words and terms. I tried as much as possible to ask questions using appropriate forms that people would understand. Some individuals chose to speak English when French was their mother tongue. Either they no longer felt comfortable speaking in French or were intimidated by the variation I spoke, or simply could not understand my vocabulary. Whatever the case, I respected their choice. In the end, negotiating language involved exchanging experiences about being francophone. By explaining how I came to speak French, that is, my relationships with family and place, I was claiming my cultural collateral as a native.

While I worked myself into relationships where I was permitted to witness treatments, I was surprised at the difference between how the practice was represented in scholarly literature and what I was encountering in the field. Scholars placed belief in cultural healing traditions such as treaters under the rubric of magico-religious practices of minority groups. Just as the representation of vernacular medicine suggests, the therapeutic power of the treater is placed in opposition to that of scientific medicine in such a way that the rubric "magic" frames any discussion of the topic (Turner 1967; Van Gennep 1966; Yoder 1972). This was also the case in reviewing the literature on Cadiens treaters, most of which outlined the general guidelines to treating, but did little more than relegate it to the category of superstition (Brandon 1962, 1965, 1976; Leyda 1961). As I looked for treaters and the space in which treating takes place, I was waiting to witness a mysterious event that never happened. What I did witness were people much like my grandparents, aunts, uncles, and cousins speaking in order to heal themselves. Because I was interviewing people who were a part of my cultural landscape, I did not perceive them to be marginal in the way the literature presented them. On the other hand, because people and place were so familiar to me, gaining a scientific understanding of the context required time and the creation of a distance that a researcher from the outside would automatically have.

TRANSGRESSING CULTURAL NORMS AND ROLES
The Ambiguity of Speaking about Treating

The part of my cultural landscape implicated in treating that I did not distinguish immediately was space and time. I was nagged by my question about place: when and where did treaters treat? One day I arrived at a scheduled interview with a treater, only to find that he and his wife had visitors. We sat in the kitchen area in a semicircle of chairs on a *veillée* nearly the whole afternoon, a similar use of space to what I saw in many of the homes I had visited. They welcomed me into their circle and we talked about the David family, duck hunting (because I am from Gueydan, the self-proclaimed duck capital of America), and whatever else. Periodically, Mr. Broussard would leave the room with a visitor, I believed, to treat them. I was anxious as the afternoon wore away, sensing that there might not be time for an interview. I realized later that I had witnessed my first treating session and more importantly that treating is embedded in relationships, old and new. The couples present had come with the objective of being treated, yet the treatment appeared to be superseded by the visit.

In my eagerness to get to the source, the treater, I almost missed the layers of relationships that make a treater effective. Vernacular medicine among Cadiens is a shy tradition for the very reason that treaters administer their treatments in the multifunctional space of the kitchen during the cycle of an illness.[4] The tradition does not follow an established community rhythm such as weekly dances, annual *boucheries*, or Mardi Gras celebrations. The tradition is "shy" also in the sense that talking about treating is ambiguous. Treating is a ritualized speech act, and the discourse around treating reveals an organic cultural process. Treaters are an element of the popular belief system among Cadiens: people know what role treaters perform even if they have never visited one. The stories I collected in formal interviews and informal encounters keyed me to the ongoing negotiation of belief: stories were used to convince the listener of the treater's power to heal. Unlike doctors in a biomedical context who display diplomas to certify their training, treaters in Cadien society build legitimacy through telling stories. For their part, by sharing their positive or negative healing experiences with treaters, people affirm the role of the treater in Cadien society.

Treaters speak in two instances: to perform a treatment and to communicate their abilities to others. When I asked them to talk about treating, I was placing them in an ambiguous situation since I was neither seeking a treatment nor seeking to treat. I was transgressing the ritualized means of transmission in two different ways. First, in order to give me their prayers, they had to reveal the entire process, which includes the demonstration of the practice as well, although I was not seeking a treatment. Second, my request also failed to match another cultural expectation since I did not receive the knowledge to become a treater myself. My grandmother was right to ask what I was going to do with the knowledge I was collecting. Doing fieldwork in a place where people could identify me as *la petite-fille à Tee-Dai* and *la fille à* Ronald and Mary, I was walking into established patterns of interaction that superseded my academic work.[5] I was receiving/taking cultural knowledge but what I was giving back was left unclear: the exchange was taking place without me acknowledging my part in the process.

I was clear about my research goals but my fieldwork experience made me aware of larger cultural expectations involved. I had been initiating a particular kind of dialogue with family, friends, and others with whom I was spending extended amounts of time. I had become familiar with older people describing their illnesses to me in the hopes that I might know a treatment for what ailed them. I recognized the reality of the process I was involved in one evening as I was having dinner with a couple, Carol, an accountant, and Cecil, a farmer, both from my hometown. Cecil and his family suffer from allergies, and Carol began talking about her nephew, who was having a particularly severe experience. In the middle of eating our pasta, she casually asked me if there was anything I could do for him. It was implicit to those in my social network that if I was talking with treaters, then I had to be one. I had to accept that my network shaped the parameters of my research, which in turn helped me to grasp the multiple layers of meaning involved in treating.

The Ambiguity of Being a Woman

Along with encountering cultural expectations, I bumped into what were for me outdated notions of appropriate female behavior. Claiming my cultural collateral came with consequences. A conversation with my grandfather indicated to me that there were yet other concerns about my doing fieldwork in my territory. My interviews were leading me to the town of Lake Arthur where I had identified a widower, my grandfather's age, as a treater. According to my grandfather, this gentleman had a certain reputation with women. I understood that he did not want me visiting this treater out of concern for how my visits could be perceived. I respected his wish and did interviews elsewhere for a time. I encountered the same concern from Mr. Duhon, a captain in the women's Mardi Gras run I was involved in, and a regular at a local bar/grocery that I frequented while doing my research. A woman ran the establishment and I felt comfortable going in alone, but I was careful to enter on the grocery side. Once on my usual stool, I knew that the older French-speaking customers would filter through and we would talk. Mr. Duhon, like my grandfather, would warn me about questionable characters. People were watching me because I was a single woman! I had heard the stories about the dances where the parents kept a watchful eye on the young people but I had never thought I would experience this surveillance firsthand.

Reflecting on the experience of being a woman researcher in rural southwest Louisiana, I became conscious of the cultural spaces occupied by Cadien women. Lauren C. Post (1962) notes that the house and surrounding courtyard were the woman's domain but there is little else about Cadien women's folkways (Ware 1995). It was not easy finding older Cadien women treaters because frequently only their husbands' names were listed in the telephone directory. Outside of their immediate social networks, these women were somehow hidden by a male identity. Yet I knew that women treaters practiced and were known for their abilities on their own terms, because my mother, grandmother, and others were talking about them. Once I found them, women of my mother and grandmother's generation, I met them in their space, in their homes. Put off initially by my own main-stream notions of equality, I came to the understanding, through watching and listening to Cadien women treaters, that their practice of vernacular medicine was empowering for themselves and for the culture. My contact with them was truly enlightening: it was through interviews with women treaters that I first understood that there was an implicit exchange in the context of a treatment (David 2000).

LISTENING FOR THE LOGIC IN A TREATMENT

Understanding the context in which treaters practice proved to be a challenge because the discourse about treating appeared contradictory. I formulated a questionnaire for them following the guidelines found in the literature along with questions about how they integrated treating into their daily life. I was interested in learning about any resistance vis-à-vis the prac-tice from officials in the religious or medical communities. My aim was to get a sense of the norms at play in treating. Most of those interviewed could cite the rules just as I had found them in the literature, but in the course of the interview, they would contradict themselves. What were people doing when they asked but did not thank a treater for a service, when they would take a payment but called it a gift? The paradoxes concerning rules pointed to the importance of verbal exchange in a treatment.

Given the ambiguity of talking about treating, observation, listening, and patience were the methods that unraveled the paradoxes. Both by vis-iting and by working my way into relationships where I could be present while treaters administered treatments, I looked at the spatial arrangement of rooms, I watched how people interacted, and I observed the verbal and nonverbal exchanges between treater and patient. By listening, I understood that the rules people recognized and could quote pointed to much larger concepts of how community in the abstract becomes community in the moment. The explicit meaning or ideology supporting treating is the notion of "*aider le monde*" or, as Tee-Dai put it, "people need it [treating]." The paradoxes I identified rest on an axis linking ideology and practice: people listen, negotiate, and synthesize the cultural meanings they learned in their social network within the *voisinage*. Then their understanding of the rules allows them to create their own meaning and shape their own practice to form a dialectical process.

The Exchange

The notion of gift intrigued me because I observed people leave money and I listened to patients and treaters describe their view of that aspect of the healing tradition. On one hand the restriction on payment and on a verbal thanks to the treater is well known to patients, as Vincent Mouton explains:

> *Si on a payé? Oh no. Euh, ça voulait pas tu les payes, ça voulait pas tu eux dis merci. Ils disent si tu payes, si tu les disais merci, le traitement travaillait pas. Je connais pas si c'est vrai ou c'est pas vrai.* . . . (If we paid? Oh no! They don't want to be paid, not even a thank you. They say that if you pay, the treatment doesn't work. I don't know if it's true or not. . . .)

On the other hand, interview after interview, the response of treaters to the question of payment was nearly formulaic: *"Ça fait, j'accepte n'importe quoi, mais je cherche pas rien"* (I accept whatever, but I don't ask for anything). Listening to what treaters were saying involved understanding what they were not saying, that is, there is an implicit payment for a treatment. What seemed to emerge was a circular pattern of exchange: something was given with the understanding that the gesture would be returned.

Through observing, listening, and questioning, I recognized treating as an exchange, much like other exchanges taking place in traditional Cadien culture such as the *boucherie*, the *échange du temps*, and even the *bal de maison* documented by historians and folklorists (Ancelet, Edwards, & Pitre 1991; Brasseaux 1992; Post 1962). The exception is that treating is offered to the community with no explicit payment and no time line. In fact, payment has to be in the form of a gift and thus is often hidden in the exchanges of extra garden vegetables, figs, or Christmas gifts among neighbors and friends. Cash can be left behind on the table, but if discovered by a third party, it can be perceived as an inappropriate form of payment.

The verbal exchange in the treatment proved to be the most subjective element of the practice because the demand for a treatment implies a cultural competence of shared community knowledge. A speech act contains a linguistic and social form (Hymes 1972:56–57), both of which can be identified within the core of healing. Because of the restrictions placed on both the treater, who cannot offer to treat, and the patient, who cannot thank the treater, the speech act between the two represents a ritualized verbal exchange. The patient voices in words the illness he/she is experiencing and invokes words from the treater: *un échange de mots pour maux* (an exchange of words for illness). The social form of the speech act translates into the implicit material exchange outlined earlier. The social form of the treatment lies in the open-ended transaction such as the one I witnessed at Louis Arceneaux's Saturday morning clinic. A man and woman from down the road came by to have the woman's shingles treated. As the couple made their way to their car, there was the usual discussion about weather and gardens, when the man asked Mr. Arcenaux if he liked green beans, explaining that he would have more than he could use. Mr. Arcenaux answered yes and they shook hands. The scene was seamless in the sense that everyone seemed to understand the linguistic and social patterns implicated in a treatment.

One of the structural patterns of Cadien society revealed by the circulation of words and goods that take place in treating is that of reciprocity. Treaters view their words (prayers) as a gift, which implies an obligation toward the community to treat, as Mrs. Eunice Duhon explains:

Il [son père] m'a dit qu'il faulait pas que je refuse à personne de les traiter. "Ça fait quand quelqu'un vient, si c'est noir ou blanc, traite-les. Parce que il dit, "ils ont le même mal que nous autres on a." Ça fait, comme ça, je traite n'import' quel. (He [his father] said I could not refuse treating anybody: "So when someone comes black or white, treat them." Because he said "they have the same illness as we do." So this way I treat anybody.)

An individual's demand for a treatment activates the latent obligation to give to the community and sets in motion the circulation of *"mots pour maux."* And, as I have earlier pointed out, Vincent Mouton has suggested that the treatment's effectiveness is itself linked to the observance of the rules of reciprocity. The ritual of exchange thus reinforces the rule: if it is broken, the treatment does not work. The gift to the treater, not a payment but an obligation of exchange, reinforces communal relationships while creating them. Thus, the norms of treating ensure that the basic principle of reciprocity will be followed: no demand of payment and no expression of gratitude; obligation to treat and obligation to give. Treating reflects an ideology of unity and continuity: the circulation of goods and services ensures that everyone has what they need.[6]

The *Voisinage*

Treating is a manifestation of a network of reciprocity much like the *bals de maisons* and *boucheries*. Like these forms of interaction, it also contributes to define the *voisinage*, a small, rural community most often located near a waterway such as a bayou. It was often named after the most predominant family in the settlement. Furthermore, it functioned as the primary economic and social unit of the Cadien prairie until recently and it remains a cultural space where people define their relationships to others and to place. The *voisinage* has been transformed with the modernization in agricultural practices, with the departure of men for oil field jobs, and with the necessity of women to work outside of the home. As subsistence farming practices disappeared, the *voisinage* system gradually entered into the free-market system, an evolution that has brought about economic differentiation and modern technology. The free-market system also impacted treating.

The changes that were brought about by this form of vernacular medicine can be viewed as a case of emergent culture: the creation of new values and meanings from old associations and relationships in the face of new conditions (Williams 1977:123). For example, treaters are adapting the old restriction, which prohibits treaters from administering a treatment across a body of water, to include family members and others who live at extended distances. The long-noted restriction on treating across a body of water is no longer a hard and fast rule among treaters. The service the treater offers is a specialized talent that he or she performs in the home. The necessity of touching the patient points to the importance of space in the therapy and helps to explain why the delivery of treatment is limited by boundaries of water. Historically, bodies of water defined the treater's community on the prairie. The exchange system of the early *voisinage* was anchored in the settlement pattern of the prairie region. Water was essential for living and agriculture, but it was also a barrier to frequent interaction with other *voisinages* (Brasseaux 1995). The urbanization of Cadien society and the development of modern means of transportation have altered this situation.

The necessary physical proximity of treater and patient is also related to the exigency of speech in an oral tradition. Treating requires listening, and this could only be achieved through face-to-face contact. But social change and modern means of communications have transformed the administration of treatment. The telephone now allows for distant treating, an interesting vernacular use of technology. Eunice Duhon's comment on patients who live far or nearby illustrates the evolution: *"Well s'ils pourront pas venir, je les traite loin. Mais eux autres, il faut . . . je touche la personne."* (Well, if they can't come, I treat them from afar. But them, I have to . . . I touch the person.) This reevaluation points to the geographical and symbolic expansion of the concept to the *voisinage* community. Its boundary expands beyond water to include all those who need treating and call into the network.

VERNACULAR MEDICINE AND CREATING COMMUNITY

Community is a felt reality.
—Dorothy Noyes

Following the arguments made by David Hufford (1985) and Raymond Massé (1995), I insist that experience is in itself a means of knowledge. Reflecting on my fieldwork, I acknowledge the many layers of experience that helped me understand the common denominator in the cultural process set in motion by an illness. I faced field research with a certain naïveté, believing that I would "see" and would not be seen. Instead, I was drawn into an organic cultural process whereby I was asked to give in return for asking in more subtle ways than my grandmother Tee-Dai's question. My experience attests to the transformation of certain aspects of community among Cadiens. Although the experience of the *voisinage* of fifty years ago has been documented by historians and folklorists alike, technology and mobility have drastically changed how Cadiens live their daily lives, but not necessarily how they structure their lives. The exchange of *"mots pour maux"* in a treatment is a manifestation of a network of reciprocity, of interaction that defines the *voisinage*. I discovered through my fieldwork experience that the *voisinage* is a network of reciprocal exchange more than a spatial community. This in turn helped me understand my place in the network. I no longer live in Klondike, yet I value deeply the network of reciprocity born in my experience and my parents' and grandparents' experiences of living in a *voisinage*. Through my field research, public presentations, and my participation in a women's Mardi Gras run, I have created a network of relationships grounded in a shared notion of community.

Will I be a treater? In my very first interview with a treater, she asked me if I wanted to be a treater. And then, very much in the same way my grandmother answered her own question, this woman said to me, "You wouldn't have come to me if you didn't want to be a treater." Although it seems I had no choice in the matter, I choose to live in such a way as to be open to healing. I struggled with the conventions of treating for some time. How could I treat if I didn't live in a place like Klondike? Would I ever take anything for a treatment? If I refused, I would mute the meaning of the treatment. How do I negotiate belief in my knowledge? When those questions arise, I remember the voices of those treaters with whom I spoke. Some would stop and say to me, "Tu connais?" (Do you understand?) I have come to understand that working with Cadiens treaters has deeply influenced my life.

Community, imagined and performed, takes place through treatments. Individuals utilize the *voisinage* matrix in which and through which means individual knowledge is elaborated: they plug into what the community knows and can provide given the situation. Treating is a venue for people to tell their stories and it demands that one be present in the moment to listen. Speaking and listening, giving and receiving, offering and accepting, all these actions are manifest in a treatment. Much like in Mardi Gras, with treating, too, in the end everyone will have what they need. Marcel Mauss (1950) evacuates the power of healers (i.e., exchange) to the culture's higher power; Maurice Godelier (1995) reclaims it for traditional people by stating that the power is their choice in structuring their society. My experience has been that treating is a cultural space where Cadiens define themselves by affirming what is meaningful to them. I am constantly reminded of the circular movement of goods and words, and I wonder if I could live outside of that motion, outside of the circle.

I gathered my knowledge on treating in an unconventional way, since my anthropological approach was inappropriate from a Cadien cultural perspective. My sense is that if I choose to practice, it will be just as unconventional. Looking to the treaters that I worked with, most did not start treating until they had reached a spiritual maturity that appears to come with age. I am still too young to be considered a treater. I appreciate the process of integrating the knowledge imparted to me into my life. I agree with scholars who argue that, given the forces of globalization, culture is no longer a homogeneous entity. But I hope that my work with treaters has demonstrated how Cadiens are redefining old associations and relationships into a coherent whole of new values and meanings.

FRENCH TERMS

Bal de maison: a house dance.

Boucherie: In the past, this was a weekly exchange of fresh meat among neighbors. The sharing of meat occurs today, but the time line has changed.

Echange du temps: a labor exchange when intensive labor is needed for a project.

Grand Dérangement: an Acadian term for the forced exile of the Acadians in 1755 from present-day Nova Scotia.

Lagniappe: goods given as a goodwill gesture.

Mardi Gras: a pre-Lenten celebration with masked celebrants begging for contributions for a communal gumbo. *Courir* is the term used for the procession that proceeds throughout a neighborhood.

Ramasserie: labor exchange during the harvest season.

Traiteur: an individual who has received prayers from an older community or family member and who is qualified to pray and lay hands on those who seek relief from various sicknesses.

Veillée: an evening visit among friends which may include cooking, playing cards, or conversation.

NOTES

1. The term *traitement*, or treatment in English, refers to the reciting of prayers that treaters use. The possession of these prayers, known only by the treater, empowers an individual to treat illnesses such as warts, shingles, heat exhaustion, bleeding, earaches, sprains, arthritis, pneumonia, and asthma.

2. Her real name and the names of the people I have worked with during my research from 1995 to 2000 have been changed.

3. Concerning treatments, I found English-speaking treaters who had learned their prayers in French, Cadiens who were reciting their prayers in Creole, and Francophones who recited prayers in Latin. Reflecting on this code alternating, I realized that, if French is a marker for identity among Cadiens, the way language is used is equally important.

4. Treaters and their traditional practice belong to the domain of vernacular belief systems linked to health, defined as the ensemble of conceptions and ideas that permit individuals to organize their perceptions and their medical experiences (Massé 1996; O'Connor 1995).

5. Sharon Sherman (1986) makes a similar point when she notes that family relationships and her participation in her family's Seder celebration were at times more important than her fieldwork on the celebration. In my case, I avoided working with treaters I had visited prior to my research.

6. An interesting recent evolution is taking place. Concerning payment, the treater's sense of obligation remains, yet that of the patient to reciprocate is becoming vague, because people, accustomed to market exchange, interpret literally the rule disallowing payment.

REFERENCES

Ancelet, Barry, Jay Edwards, & Glen Pitre, eds. 1991. *Cajun Country*. Austin: University of Texas Press.

Brandon, Elisabeth. 1976. "Folk Medicine in French Louisiana." In *Folk Medicine*. W. Hand, ed. Berkeley: University of California Press, pp. 215–234.

———. 1962. "Superstitions in Vermilion Parish." In *The Golden Log*. Mody Boatwright, Wilson Hudson, & Allen Maxwell, eds. Dallas: Southern Methodist University Press, pp. 108–118.

———. 1965. "*Traiteurs* or Folk Doctors in Southwest Louisiana." In *Buying the Wind*. Richard Dorson, ed. Chicago: University of Chicago Press, pp. 261–266.

Brasseaux, Carl. 1992. *From Acadian to Cajun: Transformation of a People, 1803–1877.* Jackson: University Press of Mississippi.

David, Dana. 2000. "La traiteuse cadienne: Pouvoir équilibré." In *L'Acadie au féminin*. Maurice Basque, Isabelle McKee-Allain, Linda Cardinal, Phyllis LeBlanc, & Janis Pallister, eds. Moncton, N.B.: Chaire d'Etudes Acadiennes, pp. 319–340.

Geertz, Hildred. 1979. "The Meaning of Family Ties." In *Meaning and Order in Moroccan Society*. Clifford Geertz, Hildred Geertz, & Lawrence Rosen. Cambridge: Cambridge University Press, pp. 315–391.

Godelier, Maurice. 1995. "L'enigme du don, I. Le legs de Mauss." *Social Anthropology* 3(1), pp. 15–47.

Gold, Gerald. 1979a. "The French Frontier of Settlement in Louisiana: Some Observations on Culture Change in Mamou Prairie." *Cahiers de Geographie du Quebec* 23, pp. 263–280.

———. 1979b. "Toward the Critical Study of French Louisiana: Views from Inside and Outside *Acadiana*." *Reviews in Anthropology* 6, pp. 57–69.

———. 1980. "The Changing Criteria of Social Networks in a Cajun Community." *Ethnos* 45, pp. 60–81.

Hufford, David. 1985. "Reason, Rhetoric, and Religion: Academic Ideology versus Folk Belief." *New York Folklore* 11, pp. 177–194.

Hymes, Dell. 1972. "Models of the Interaction of Language and Social Life." In *Directions in Sociolinguistics: The Ethnography of Communication*. John J. Gumperz & Dell Hymes, eds. New York: Holt, Rinehart and Winston, pp. 35–71.

Lançon, John 1986. "Des remèdes aux traiteurs: An Introduction to Folk Medicine in French Louisiana." Dissertation. Lafayette: University of Louisiana at Lafayette.

Leyda, Seraphia. 1961. "Les treateurs." *Louisiana Folklore Miscellany* 1, pp. 18–27.

Massé, Raymond. 1995. *Culture et santé publique*. Montréal: Gaëtan Morin.

Maus, Marcel. 1950. *L'essai sur le don*. Paris: Presses Universitaires de France.

O'Connor, Bonnie Blair. 1995. *Healing Traditions: Alternative Medicine and the Health Care Professions*. Philadelphia: University of Pennsylvania Press.

Parsons, Talcott. 1951. *The Social System*. Glenco, IL: Free Press.

Post, Lauren C. 1962. *Cajun Sketches*. Baton Rouge: Louisiana State University Press.

Ramsey, Carolyn. 1957. *Cajuns on the Bayous*. New York: Hastings House Publishers.

Sexton, Rocky. 1992. "Cajun and Creole Treaters: Magico-Religious Folk Healing in French Louisiana." *Western Folklore* 51, pp. 237–248.

Sherman, Sharon. 1986. "*That's How the Seder Looks:* A Fieldwork Account of Videotaping Family Folklore." *Journal of Folklore Research* 23, pp. 52–70.

Turner, Victor. 1967. *The Forest of Symbols: Aspects of Ndembu Ritual.* Ithaca: Cornell University Press.

Van Gennep, Arnold. 1966. *The Rites of Passage.* Chicago: University of Chicago Press.

Ware, Carolyn. 1995. "Reading the Rules Backward: Women, Symbolic Inversion, and the Cajun Mardi Gras Run." *Southern Folklore* 52, pp. 137–159.

Williams, Raymond. 1977. *Marxism and Literature.* Oxford: Oxford University Press.

Yoder, Don. 1972. "Folk Medicine." In *Folklore and Folklife.* Richard Dorson, ed. Chicago: University of Chicago Press, pp. 191–215.

3.   ARE YOU IN FOR THE LONG HAUL?

—Deborah J. Clifton

Although a 6-pound machine is easier to carry than a 12-pound machine is, any machine becomes a burden when carried over long distances. . . . Those same conditions which require foot travel will also require extreme precautions in the shipment of all equipment; therefore porters will be used.
—William J. Samarin (1967:89)

THE SAFARI

I began this chapter thinking that it would be a simple piece of technical writing. As work progressed, I found it becoming an increasingly personal confrontation with myself and some thirty years of professional life. When doing fieldwork in one's own culture, it becomes necessary every so often to reevaluate familiar and taken-for-granted places, people, and activities and try to see them through new lenses. This type of experience happened to me during the 2001 Christmas holiday.

Riding across the prairie between Lafayette and Lake Charles on Christmas morning, I found myself fretting over whether I could really afford to take time away from the pile of paperwork on my desk and some ongoing research on Prairie Creole culture to actually go and spend a couple of days participating in the Prairie Creole culture with my family.

I knew everyone would be talking about the recent unfortunate death of Anthony Charles Chavis, son of the late Zydeco musician and pride of Calcasieu Parish, Wilson "Boo Zoo" Chavis. Charles Chavis had literally dropped dead of a heart attack at a bingo game, while his horrified wife and other witnesses watched. One of those witnesses was my cousin, who is really more like a sister to me. The Chavis family are friends of my family, and even though I knew there was nothing I could do to help, it seemed especially important to go to Lake Charles.

Charles Chavis's death was all the more poignant, occurring as it did right at Christmas. Still, there was that nasty pile of paperwork. Determined to respond to the double responsibility of family-tribal-parish-town solidarity and professional paperwork, I started counting heads of cattle and horses for another research project. By the time we reached Iowa, a small town just east of Lake Charles, I was convinced that the population density of horses and livestock in Southwest Louisiana is indeed greater than the population density of humans. So I felt better, and experienced not a bit of paperwork guilt as I sat down with family to our annual Christmas feast.

Of course, the conversation eventually turned to Charles Chavis's unfortunate demise, and as the numbers of eyewitnesses—first to the actual incident, then to the condolences at the Chavis family home—increased, I realized this was folklore in the making. I realized, as I have on many other occasions, that here in the ordinary events of life, death, and celebration were the seeds of a classic oral history collection. If I could only separate myself from the plate of fried turkey in front of me in order to write it all down.

On the way back to Lafayette the next morning, I dutifully resumed my horse and cattle headcount. It was interrupted, however, because by the time we reached Crowley the bus had filled to standing room only and it was impossible to see out the windows. As I got off the bus in Lafayette, I found myself wondering what kind of article I could write that would even begin to convey the actual participation.

How does one capture a living culture on the two-dimensional medium of text? How does one draw the line between one's circle of family and friends and one's work? Nowadays in that circle, people pretty much take it for granted that I am doing work that will help to keep the culture alive. Everybody has camcorders, tape recorders, and home media centers. Now friends and relatives will actually ask me for tips on documenting our culture. It was not always this way. Every linguist, folklorist, or anthropologist has a personal image of fieldwork. Often this ideal was formulated in the early romantic phases of young adulthood and was based as much on fantasy as anything else. At least for me this was the case. My fantasy image of fieldwork began to take shape in the tenth grade when our class was given a career aptitude test. When I received my test scores, they indicated that I had a 96 percent aptitude for an adventurous, outdoor-oriented career such as forest ranger, rescue worker, medical missionary, field biologist, or general explorer. Surprised and delighted, I immediately conjured up exotic images of myself in safari clothes, leaping from fire towers in national forests to administer first aid to wild creatures.

This revelation was given to me right before Thanksgiving. So I stashed the test results away with the intention of impressing the family at our holiday get-together. They were impressed all right, but not in the way I had hoped. My mother nearly fainted. My grandmother went catatonic. My grandfather shook his head in disbelief. One of my aunts voiced her hope that I would soon grow out of whatever kind of a "phase" it was. I knew at that moment with an adolescent's infallible instincts that I had just made a major faux pas in dealing with authority figures. It would not be my last one.

The only thing that saved that dinner party for me was one of my cousin's taking advantage of the momentary speechlessness of the authorities to announce that he was planning on becoming a midwife. In the outbreak of pandemonium that followed, I slipped off to nurse the wounds to my ego. I resolved that day that I would do the adventurous career thing, and I would get one of those elusive Ph.D.'s. I also made plans, yet to be realized, to get myself a safari outfit.

With the enforced mellowing made possible by the aging process, and an ever-growing appreciation for the benefits of air-conditioning, I have revised my fantasy image of fieldwork somewhat. It no longer includes the necessity of jumping from two-hundred-foot-high fire towers. Thanks to the technology explosion, it no longer includes carrying around six- to twelve- pound tape recorders either.

My definition of fieldwork now includes any time research is taken away from one's desk into a natural social situation in order to gain a better understanding of human communicative behavior and to provide the services that facilitate communication among people. My work has also been framed by the social struggle of indigenous peoples seeking to gain access to the professions and maintain their cultural identities. Creole and Acadian Louisiana has provided the environmental and cultural matrix for this work, as well as the point of departure for fieldwork with other cultures. This chapter seeks to share a part of my story.

THE BEGINNING

My career has been worked out in the context of a struggle to balance traditional responsibilities with a personal attraction to fieldwork and scientific research. I did not start out in the late 1960s with a coherent research question or agenda. Louisiana was a wide-open research area in the sense that there was so much to be done; one could do pioneering work in almost any specialty.

Although ethnically Creole, my interest in Louisiana and North American French as areas of research resulted from working for several years as a research assistant and student of Dr. Catherine Callaghan at the Ohio State University. A specialist in California Indian languages, especially those of the Miwok family, she also had an interest in languages and cultures of the Southeastern United States, having been a student herself at Berkeley under the late Mary R. Haas. Dr. Callaghan was familiar with Mary Haas's earlier work on Louisiana languages, and she encouraged me to pursue research on Louisiana Creole.

Linguists at that time considered Louisiana to be one of the most difficult fieldwork areas. This was due to both its extreme linguistic heterogeneity—surpassed only by that of aboriginal California—and its rigorous climate and terrain. For this reason, linguists of my acquaintance believed that definitive work on Louisiana languages would require a cadre of trained linguists who were natives of Louisiana cultures.

Previous research done in Louisiana on the Chitimacha and Coushatta languages, on Cajun French, and on Louisiana Creole was considered to be exploratory and tentative. Overall, work on Louisiana's languages had been marred by theoretical problems centered on ethnic and racial diversity, as well as by methodological issues.

Because of the enduring importance of French cultural influences in Louisiana, there was and continues to be a tendency to view the state's linguistic heritage as being wholly French or Acadian. This is a gross oversimplification because there are actually several French-speaking ethnic groups here. A fully contextualized understanding of Louisiana requires an appreciation of its role in the evolution of the American South, the Southern Great Plains, the Spanish Borderlands, and the Caribbean Basin.

When I began work in this field, there were few researchers outside of Louisiana who were aware of the extent of geographic variation in Louisiana French. Investigators tended to assume that a white person should automatically speak Acadian or Cajun French, and that a black person should automatically speak Creole. Native American speakers of French were not being worked with at all. There was still a lot of denial that Louisiana even had Native American communities. So of course, if we are denying people's existence, we can't acknowledge that existence by studying their linguistic behavior. The myopia in regards to Native American cultures in Louisiana continues to this day in some quarters.

The question of whether Louisiana French still existed in three distinct varieties—Colonial French, Acadian French, and Black Creole—was a theoretical question that was just beginning to be dealt with in the late 1960s and 1970s. Continuum theory was at that time not as developed as it is now, and scholars were only beginning to discuss whether Louisiana represented three interacting codes, or a post-Creole continuum. The question is still unresolved.

My first objective was to recognize Louisiana French as the incredibly rich linguistic system that it is in its own right. I tried to find a way to represent the power of the oral language in writing and to illustrate that it is capable of expressing abstract technical subjects, such as linguistics, without the necessity of imposing a European form (Standard French) on an indigenous North American form (Louisiana French).

Also, I was one of the first researchers to suggest that race might have little to do with ethnicity or language affiliation in Louisiana. I attempted to analyze the language according to how people actually behaved linguistically, without trying to impose, or explain it in terms of, preconceived racial ideologies.

I started doing fieldwork on Louisiana in 1968. I have continued it with varying levels of activity into the present. I started before the explosion of computer technology. Portable cassette recorders were around, but weren't as sophisticated as they are now. I remember slip files and eight-track tapes. Although I have worked with French-speaking and non-French-speaking groups in a dozen western and midwestern states, as well as in Canada, Louisiana has always been my base of operations.

A CONTROVERSIAL STATUS

My formal course work in field linguistics, also with Dr. Callaghan, was to work one-on-one with key informants using William Samarin's (1967) text as a guide. William Labov's work was new and his quantitative approach was still controversial. I found, however, that the key informant approach did not work well in trying to do fieldwork on Louisiana French, while the Labovian approach was impossible. The minority status of the French-speaking communities, the long years of active persecution of the French language in Louisiana, and sexism all combined to negatively influence fieldwork.

In linguistics training, we had talked at length about the need for more native linguists and anthropologists and it seemed simple and logical in the imaginary world of the classroom. All that needed to be done was to locate talented people with the desired ethnic credentials and train them to do this work. What I actually experienced in the field, however, was that people in minority communities were suspicious of the whole endeavor. A lot of people communicated to me their fears that this kind of research would bring them negative attention from nonindigenous authorities, and they felt that the less the dominant culture knew about them the better.

At that time, people in Louisiana had been subjected to so much stigma and so much violence about their speech,[1] they just could not get used to the idea that anyone would want to collect it for any other reason than to further humiliate them. I felt like a pest going around to relatives and friends trying to get them to sit still for interviews. A few people even accused me of planning to make them look ridiculous to the outside world by portraying them as uneducated and "country." Nothing could have been further from my intentions. I wanted the world to come to know and love my community as I did. I wanted to see my people appreciated and respected for their unique knowledge, and saw fieldwork as a potential means of making that possible. But I never felt able to communicate that. The systematic suppression of Louisiana's cultures had succeeded all too well. I did manage during this initial phase to get one person, a Vietnam veteran, to sit still for the interview process. I ran into him a few years ago at a family gathering and he jokingly asked me if I was still in the human experimentation business.

My family had happily chosen to be myopic about the infamous Thanksgiving when my cousin and I had declared our future career plans for forestry and male midwifery. However, they were still politically conservative, culturally traditional, and as matrilineal as always. So the idea of a young woman of color from a respectable family roaming around unchaperoned with a tape recorder and notepad, talking to "Tom, Dick, and Harry," seemed pretty outlandish to them. My grandmother feared that people would think I had loose morals.

I remember once trying to get into a male-only gambling room in Lake Charles for some interviews, only to run into my uncle and grandfather there. They let the bouncer put me out. Later my grandfather had a lot to say to my grandmother about how that "fancy Yankee school" I had attended had me out of control and thinking I could do anything I wanted, including hanging around any old body and going to saloons.

Lake Charles has always been something of a frontier town, so in the 1960s and 1970s, before it got gentrified, saloons were just what the name implies—the Wild Wild West. So these early years were rough going. My college-girl sense of adventure, sanctioned by standardized test results, was clashing head-on with the traditionalism of my family and the Creole culture. I was simply not conforming to role expectations.

Thirty years ago, there were low levels of legal protection for human participants in research. Universities were just beginning to establish Institutional Review Boards (IRB) The Native American Graves Protection and Repatriation Act (NAGPRA) did not yet exist. The movement to protect the religious freedom, privacy, and intellectual property rights of indigenous communities was in its infancy. International laws aimed at preventing the looting of weaker countries for their cultural patrimony were either nonexistent or poorly enforced. Anthropologists, linguists, and other behavioral scientists frequently appeared to feel no obligation of accountability to groups they worked with.

It was an entirely colonial relationship in which abuses could and did occur. The mere fact that an investigator was of the same racial or ethnic background as the community in question was no guarantee of protection. On the contrary, the few minority researchers there were at that time were primarily research assistants on short-term contracts. Few had doctoral degrees. Few were project directors. So minority researchers had almost no role in setting research policy or designing protocols, and no control over the interpretation or application of their research.

Given these obstacles, few minority group members bothered to aspire to careers in research disciplines. Most of those who got an opportunity to pursue graduate education chose to go into applied fields such as education, social work, medicine, nursing, and law, and to devote their professional lives to providing basic services in underserved communities. This is of course a noble calling and more more professionals are needed in public service. But it should be the result of personal choice and not the result of limited opportunities.

Considering these conditions, it can be better understood why my desire to get a Ph.D. and go into a research-oriented discipline like anthropology was viewed by many people in my family and community as a frivolous waste of time and resources on a degree I might never be able to earn, and if earned, might never be able to use. The possibility that I could be manipulated into the perpetual research assistant trap and used against my own community in such a field was also a major, and realistic concern. I was the first person in my family to break ranks and attend an integrated land grant institution instead of a minority serving educational institution. This was already controversial. People did not know what to expect. So the family was truly taken aback when, on the point of graduation from Ohio State University, they were presented with papers to sign so I could go to Laval University and study anthropology.

Although I had applied secretly to Laval's graduate program and presented the admission papers as a fait accompli, my grandparents, much to my surprise, quickly got over the shock. They agreed that Laval was a good idea as long as I would study something practical there. My parents thought that once I got to Québec, where people could speak French all the time, I would never want to return home. They were willing, however, to help me get a doctorate in something like medicine or pharmacy, or in something like French or anthropology, if I would combine it with something people of color could find employment in—and closer to home.

THINGS TURN AROUND

What ultimately changed this whole situation for me was that my grandparents and other community elders finally became so distressed about the direction that the struggle for social justice in the South was taking, they decided some more innovative approaches were needed. The older people felt that things had been for too long cast in entirely Black and White terms, leaving the concerns of other ethnic groups unaddressed. They began to realize that the isolationism that had dominated their thinking up to that point was no longer viable and that if traditional Creoles and Cajuns were to survive as distinct indigenous peoples, we would need spokespersons. But the elders wanted to train and appoint their own spokespersons, not have token representatives elevated to the position by outsiders. They wanted young people who spoke the language and who were literate in it; people who could fit in socially with the traditionalists and yet move comfortably in the outside world; people who were strong enough to stand up for community interests, but not violent militants. I apparently fit the bill and was selected to be among those they wanted to train for leadership positions. This started in about 1971.

Overnight I went from being considered a maverick borderline delinquent with a preconceived field methodology, running around trying to get people to submit to my interviews, to being a representative for traditionalist Creoles and Cajuns. At last a traditionally acceptable role had been found for me (and for my notepads): defender of my people. Accepting this responsibility did bring me a lot of unwanted attention. With my uncanny ability for getting on the wrong side of authorities I soon found myself branded a "semi-speaker" of the language and a dangerous "revolutionary" who wanted to march on Baton Rouge. I was also accused on various occasions of politicizing the use of the French language (as though it had ever been political); abusing the apostrophe; attempting to ruin education in Louisiana by legitimizing Cajun French; and setting a bad precedent for the population of color by being educated, hardworking, and French-speaking. I admit to apostrophe abuse. However, my new role also opened the door to an extremely fulfilling life filled with wonderful friends and colleagues.

KNOWLEDGE APPLIED TO THE COMMUNITY

Taking on in-group responsibilities gave me access to a wealth of information and led to people taking me into their confidence about aspects of cultural life that would not have been shared so openly otherwise. It also meant that I now occupied a partisan position within the culture and was expected to keep silent about proprietary cultural knowledge. The result is that I can no longer make even a weak claim to be an impartial scientific observer—if one could ever be made. For me that has been mostly a positive development, but for many other researchers it might not be. It depends on where one's professional priorities are set.

Most of my research on Louisiana French has been of an applied nature. I haven't ignored theoretical questions, but much of my fieldwork has been undertaken with applied goals in mind. Although I have worked on some large-scale, theoretically oriented surveys such as *Projet Louisiane* (see Louder, Morisset, & Waddell 2001), the bulk of it has focused on issues of community health, cultural, and linguistic conservation. These interests led directly to my getting involved in diabetes research. I had worked with alcoholics and prison inmates prior to getting involved with diabetics. Numerous observers and scholars, beginning with Díaz (1963) and Las Casas (1992) in the sixteenth century and continuing down to Deloria (1988) and Matthiessen (1992) in modern times, have documented the negative impacts of colonial and postcolonial situations on indigenous cultures. These negative impacts have not been limited to the Americas, but have been reported from every continent. In recent decades, there has been a lot of research on these phenomena, especially in the fields of mental health and medical anthropology. Much of this research has focused on various stress and traumatic syndromes, such as post-traumatic stress disorder, transgenerational trauma, cognitive dissonance, spiritual distress, and various culture-bound syndromes (Clifton 2000).

Research on vernacular healing systems has suggested that chronic diseases such as Type II diabetes belong to this group of reactive syndromes (David 2000; Festinger 1957; Hufford 1974, 1982; Massé 1995; Roy 2001; Wallace 1956, 1969). In the course of my earlier work with Native substance abusers and prison inmates, I began encountering diabetics with increasing frequency. Nearly every family I knew, including my own, had its share of diabetics. Many people had cases that were proving uncontrollable in spite of adequate biomedical intervention. Finally, people began asking me to research diabetes itself. It eventually became a specialty area and I wrote my doctoral dissertation on the sociocultural dimensions of epidemic diabetes among people of mixed French and Native American descent in North America.

This research has led me more deeply into exploration of the North American French *imaginaire* (symbolic culture) and into researching the use of poetry and traditional art forms in healing dysfunctional communication patterns. The effects of transgenerational trauma in indigenous communities have been pervasive, crippling, and unyielding to Western forms of psychotherapy. Many communities have turned to traditional (i.e., vernacular) forms of healing in order to address these problems. This has led to a national revitalization of indigenous traditions.

Among the North American French, including those in Louisiana, the oral arts of storytelling, music, and poetry have long been used in various ways in healing. Best known is perhaps the work of the *traiteurs*.[2] *Traiteurs* are vernacular healers who use prayers in their work. Many of them heal exclusively through the use of prayers, not relying on herbs or any other form of material intervention. The prayers are transmitted orally from one *traiteur* to the next and are generally in the Cajun or Creole French languages. The work of the *traiteur* is both an oral and a performative folk art.

Although my fieldwork in Louisiana began with a concentration on linguistic structures, it has evolved over the years to focus on the total environmental matrix in which those structures are embedded and of which they are expressive. This has led me, in addition to the study of health problems and vernacular healing systems, into the study of material culture. Along with this shift of subject focus has come a shift of workplace. I have moved from a field-based orientation to working more with archives, museums, libraries, and historical sites. In fact I have recently served as a curator at two museums, the Lafayette Natural History Museum and Vermilionville.

The Lafayette Natural History Museum and Planetarium has a collection of approximately ten thousand artifacts, most of which are ethnographic objects pertaining to the region's indigenous cultures. The museum's collection also features biological and meteorological specimens and a teaching collection that travels to schools and other educational institutions in the area.

Vermilionville is a different facility and it presents greater challenges. It is a twenty-three-acre living history and folklife museum that interprets the Cajun and Creole cultures of the Lafayette region during the period of 1765–1890. Vermilionville, the original name of Lafayette, has a collection of more than seventeen hundred movable artifacts and twenty structures, including several original historic monuments. It is also a botanical museum, with a small farm, working blacksmith shop, boat building center, cooking school, chapel, schoolhouse, restaurant, and performance center.

As the curator at Vermilionville from 1999 to 2002, I had the responsibility for overseeing restoration and interpretation of the historic structures, the movable collections, and the archives, as well as for cataloging the entire material culture collection. I was also expected to build up the museum's collection, a challenging proposition. On one hand, I had little involvement in the active solicitation of acquisitions because Vermilionville receives most of its items from donations rather than from purchases. To be accepted, an object must meet the basic criteria of time period (between 1765 and 1890), of regional origin (Southwest Louisiana) and, more loosely, of cultural affiliation. In addition to Cajun and Creole items, the museum collects artifacts belonging to neighboring cultural groups that have had a strong influence on the evolution of both regional French-based cultures. These include the Native American, African American, Anglo-American, and German American cultures of the region. However, because the collection is built primarily on donations, it is dependent on what potential donors bring in. Since few potential donors from non-Cajun communities approach Vermilionville, there is a certain imbalance to the collection as it tends to be overstocked with objects of Cajun provenance and understocked with items from other ethnic groups.

Consequently, criticism has been publicly leveled that Vermilionville has catered more to Cajuns than to Creoles. It is certainly true that in the Lafayette area there exists an enduring legacy of racism and friction between elements of the Cajun and Creole communities. It is also true that when Vermilionville opened in 1986, the Cajun community was beloved of tourist industry marketers. This situation led to a general overemphasis on the Cajun heritage at the expense of other groups.

Museums in general are coming under increasing pressure to produce marketable programming. In the living history discipline in particular, this pressure can translate into a presentation of the past in which unpleasant historical realities like slavery, forced relocations, and ethnic cleansing are romanticized and whitewashed to make them less disturbing. So although Vermilionville urgently needs to increase its holdings of artifacts of Creole, African American, and Native American provenance, that is difficult to achieve as long as budgetary restrictions make it dependent on donations and members of the Cajun community remain the primary people willing to donate their historic artifacts to the collection.

Another problem I faced in working with Vermilionville's collection lies in the fact that many underrepresented groups, such as Creoles, have been systematically excluded from the academic research process upon which museum programming and collection building are based. This creates imbalances in the underlying database that can take many years to rectify, no matter how good intentions may be. However, because the access of minorities to doctoral degrees and research careers has greatly improved in recent decades, both the quantity and quality of information on Louisiana's Native and African heritages have increased. This is having a positive impact on the field of Creole studies, and this should result in a better representation of this culture in museums.

Another important aspect of curatorial work is the interpretation of the collections. Of course, material culture collections form part of the historical record of the human communities that produced the artifacts, so interpreting the collection is really at heart a question of interpreting a culture and its way of life. For these types of decisions I rely as much as possible on my academic background and sound research, but also it requires continuing fieldwork. While a large part of the work of an archivist and collections curator takes place in offices and conservation laboratories, the very nature of living history museums requires fieldwork. That involves interviewing people, helping clients decipher old manuscript documents, and learning to work with biological specimens, as well as less academic endeavors required by the eclectic decisions curators are called on to make on a daily basis.

Often the interpretive challenge starts with a detail that would normally appear to be insignificant, such as the necessity of replacing a set of antique outdoor benches. In a historical setting, it becomes a major decision as to how to construct the replacement benches so that they are up to modern safety standards yet aesthetically consistent with the period decor and historically accurate in terms of materials and construction techniques. Pest control and repairs in historic buildings, as well as meeting the accessibility requirements of the Americans with Disabilities Act (ADA), also involve major interpretive issues. For these types of interpretive concerns, academic scholarship in public folklore helps much less than having had a family that was in the construction business, like mine. It also calls for scrambling through poison ivy and crawling around under two-hundred-year-old houses to inspect for termite and other forms of damage.

My fieldwork activities also figure prominently in my developing teaching career. We have a shortage of trained fieldworkers in Louisiana, and there is still much work to be done. Teaching gives me an opportunity to hopefully increase the number of potential investigators by teaching fieldwork and cultural resource management skills to others. I have, for example, developed a field school for a group of community researchers involved in an educational project designed to document the remaining traditional foodways of rural St. Landry Parish.[3] I have also developed college level courses in the Louisiana Creole language and Creole culture in which students are expected to do fieldwork.[4] Additionally, I have been working with the Creole community in Lafayette Parish on the development of some long-term, comprehensive cultural preservation projects. This work involves training others to do fieldwork and also to work with museum and archival collections.

My writing and publishing have tended to address primarily French and Native American audiences. I have moments when I feel totally schizoid, since I have the beginnings of a literary career in French and Creole and the beginnings of a scientific career in English. Sometimes the two seem poles apart. This is primarily the result of a lopsided education and of not having had the opportunity to study technical subjects in French—with the exception of one year spent in Montreal. This is a source of enduring pain to me. I feel that I have been cheated out of the chance to become truly literate in French. Of course, I don't write poetry in English (Clifton 1999).

On the other hand, the work I have been doing with poetry and healing of transgenerational trauma is helping to bridge that gap. Much of the work being done in this area involves the reclaiming of ancestral languages. So I increasingly understand my mission as bringing together work to stabilize indigenous languages, protect historical sites, and improve the availability of health services to communities in Louisiana.

I suppose that in the eyes of some linguists and anthropologists I would be a classic example of what not to do in the field (i.e., of being totally immersed in a culture and losing one's objectivity). But I hope that part of what this chapter can show is that we are never truly objective. All linguists bring parts of themselves into the field and those personal factors shape the interaction that takes place with the surrounding culture. The purpose of the fieldwork ceremony is precisely to tear down the imaginary wall that separates us from the "Other" and that permits us to objectify our fellow human beings and dehumanize them. And that dehumanization can be mutual.

We should not be so naive as to presume that it is only the investigator who is capable of objectifying people. Part of the value of fieldwork is that it puts the would-be social scientist into the role of being an outsider, even in one's own community. People have to find an explanation for this strange behavior. They need to find a way to assimilate the fieldworker into their worldview. So in true fieldwork, the anthropological lens is actually a mirror. When we look into that mirror to examine the "Other," we are brought into an unavoidable confrontation with ourselves. Most people only experience that confrontation when they die. We get to experience it in the prime of life. It hopefully changes us, and we live to tell about it. Gone native, not possible, *partie marron*, definitely. Fieldwork for me is a voyage into my own cultural *imaginaire*, kind of like Alice.

NOTES

1. This phenomenon is described poignantly in Jean Arceneaux's poem, "*Schizophrénie linguistique*" (Ancelet 1980).
2. See David (2000) and Fontenot (1994) for in-depth discussions of treating and *traiteurs*.
3. Among the persons involved in that project are Judith Sylvester, a registered dietician and former public health nutritionist who conceived of the project, Agnes LeBlanc, Eugenia Veillon, John Slaughter, Dana David, and John Laudun.
4. Herbert Wiltz, a French and Spanish teacher in Lafayette Parish, has taught Creole informally for several years and developed a newspaper column, titled "La Leson Kreyol," that offered

instruction in the language. Other materials have been developed by Margaret Marshall at Southeastern Louisiana University, Thomas Klingler at Tulane University, the staff of the Creole Heritage Center at Northwestern State University in Natchitoches, and Mathé Allain at the University of Louisiana at Lafayette.

REFERENCES

Ancelet, Barry J., ed. 1980. *Cris sur le Bayou*. Montréal: Les Editions Intermède.

Clifton, Deborah J. 1999. *À cette heure, la louve*. Moncton: Perce-Neige.

———. 2000. "N'avait cauchemar té gain nom: Stress Transformers and Diabetes among North Americans of Native and French Descent." Dissertation. Lafayette: University of Louisiana at Lafayette.

David, Dana. 2000. "Parole, pratique et pouvoir: Le Rôle des traiteurs dans la société cadienne." Dissertation. Lafayette: University of Louisiana at Lafayette.

Deloria, Vine, Jr. 1988. *Custer Died for Your Sins: An Indian Manifesto*. 2nd ed. Norman: University of Oklahoma Press.

Díaz del Castillo, Bernal. 1963. *The Conquest of New Spain*. London: Penguin.

Festinger, Leon. 1957. *A Theory of Cognitive Dissonance*. Stanford, CA: Stanford University Press.

Fontenot, Wonda L. 1994. *Secret Doctors: Ethnomedicine of African Americans*. Westport, CT: Bergin & Garvey.

Hufford, David John. 1974. "Folklore Studies and Health: An Approach to Applied Folklore." Dissertation. Philadelphia: University of Pennsylvania.

———. 1982. *The Terror That Comes in the Night: An Experience-Centered Study of Supernatural Assault Traditions*. Philadelphia: University of Pennsylvania Press.

Las Casas, Bartolomé de. 1992. *A Short Account of the Destruction of the Indies*. London: Penguin.

Louder, Dean, Jean Morisset, & Eric Waddell. 2001. *Vision et visages de la Franco-Amérique*. Sillery, Québec: Septentrion.

Massé, Raymond. 1995. *Culture et santé publique: Les Contributions de l'anthropologie à la prévention et à la promotion de la santé*. Montréal: Gaëtan Morin.

Matthiessen, Peter. 1992. *In the Spirit of Crazy Horse: The Story of Leonard Peltier and the FBI's War on the American Indian Movement*. New York: Penguin.

Roy, Bernard. 2001. "Sang sucré, pouvoirs codés et médecine amère. Diabète et processus de construction identitaire: Les Dimensions socio-politiques du diabète chez les Innus de Peshamit." Dissertation. Québec: Université Laval.

Samarin, William J. 1967. *Field Linguistics: A Guide to Linguistic Field Work*. New York: Holt, Rinehart and Winston.

Wallace, Anthony F. C. 1956. "Revitalization Movements." *American Anthropologist* 58, pp. 264–281.

———. 1969. *The Death and Rebirth of the Seneca*. New York: Vintage.

4. THE THEORY AND PRACTICE OF ACTIVIST FOLKLORE

From Fieldwork to Programming

—Barry Jean Ancelet

This chapter focuses on the relationship between the theory and practice of folklore, between what folklorists think and how they convey the results of that thought to a range of audiences, from other colleagues to the general public. The practice of folklore generally starts with fieldwork, the process of gathering information from cultural sources. This fieldwork can lead directly or indirectly to a variety of possible expressions, from a paper or an article to a book, to a documentary film, to a festival presentation, to a museum exhibition, among others. Or it can lead to nothing more than a better understanding of an issue by the fieldworker. The fieldwork itself can produce a variety of documentary trappings, including field notes, audio- or videotape recordings, drawings, photographs, and maps. This documentary evidence can remain in the possession of the fieldworker or it can become part of a collection of similar materials, usually called an archive.

"WHAT I THOUGHT I WAS LOOKING FOR"

For my own part, I became involved in fieldwork quite simply because I realized that it was the only way to reach the information that was missing from the record. The most important untapped source of

A reflective Barry Jean Ancelet waits backstage at the 1989 Festivals Acadiens in Lafayette where he acts as stage announcer. One of the founders of the festival in 1974, Ancelet has continued his involvement in this endeavor and numerous other enterprises aimed at presenting, explaining, and defending Cajun and Creole cultural heritage and creation. (Photograph by Jacques Henry)

information on the Cajuns and Creoles was the Cajuns and Creoles themselves. The fieldwork-based approach of folkloristics provided a method to reach that source. The naturally interdisciplinary nature of folkloristics, necessarily integrating considerations of history and art, text and context, provided the wide range of approaches needed to understand the complexities of culture and tradition, including oral tradition, traditional music, vernacular architecture, folk art, and seasonal rituals, among other cultural expressions. Folkloristics also led to considerations of important cultural and social issues such as conservation, transmission, and innovation within the context of tradition. And folkloristics and linguistics made perfect partners in the effort to understand the context of French Louisiana.

The experience of living out of Louisiana for a year appeared to be essential to the orientation of my work. In 1972, I spent an academic year in France. Homesick after nearly a year away from my native South Louisiana, I was drawn to the announcement of Roger Mason's performance of "la musique cadienne de la Louisiane." After the concert, I met with Mason, an American folk musician who had encountered Cajun music through Cajun musician Dewey Balfa on the folk festival circuit, and who was now performing it on the Maisons de la Culture circuit in France. I told him how much I had appreciated hearing the music that I had always associated with my father's generation. Growing up in the late 1950s and 1960s, I listened to rock and roll like the rest of my generation, but we heard Cajun music on the radio, on television, and when it was Daddy's turn to choose the records. Mason said, "If you're from Louisiana, you must know the people that I learned from, Dewey Balfa, Nathan Abshire." I had to admit that I didn't know them. While I had studied French for four years in high school and three years at the university to that point, we had not been afforded the opportunity to learn about our own French culture, language, and history. Mason suggested that if I was interested in learning more, I should look up Dewey Balfa. Soon after my return to Louisiana, I went to Dewey's house just south of Basile and introduced myself, telling him about the experience I had had in France, and insisting that I needed to know him more than Roger Mason. He laughed and invited me in. We started a conversation that was to last nearly two decades. I learned at least as much from Dewey as from any professor I ever had in a formal university setting. It is then through a foreign artist, in a foreign country, that I was directed toward the most influential person in my career.

People are most aware of my work in Cajun and Creole music, perhaps because of the high visibility of the Cajun Music Festival and the Liberty Theater radio show, but what first drew me to the study of Cajun and Creole folk cultures was oral tradition. My first book project (Ancelet 1984, 1999) grew out of my work with musicians, but it was based more on them than their music. Elemore Morgan Jr. and I got the idea to visit the musicians involved in the first festival where they lived, worked, and played, to interview them about their lives and experiences, and to photograph them in their own worlds. What we were doing was indeed fieldwork, but it felt more like visiting. It was our intention to see and hear in their own terms these "barbers and bus drivers, farmers and firefighters, mechanics and masons" who "sell discount furniture, discount gas, insurance and insulation," who "work nine-to-five and seven-and-seven, onshore and offshore," because "they make art out of everyday life," and because they were also becoming important figures in this cultural self-preservation experiment (Ancelet 1984:11). Elemore and I worked for ten years on the project, collecting oral histories and taking photographs of these remarkable performers in various contexts, from their kitchens and front porches to festival stages and concert halls in Louisiana and beyond.

Around the same time, I became interested in Louisiana French fictional tales. French-speaking Cajuns and Creoles have virtually no literary tradition, since most did not have the opportunity to learn to read or write French. Yet they do have a tradition of oral poetry (in songs) and oral stories (in tales). And just because the storytellers and singers could not themselves write their own stories and songs down, this did not mean that the stories and songs could not be written down by someone who had learned to write the language of their expression. In an attempt to place these traditions on the record, I began recording folktales and folksongs and transcribing them. Lacking any formal training at the time, I improvised my own first fieldwork forays based on instinct and good intentions. I found that identifying potential singers was fairly easy; friends and family members were generally aware of those in their midst who can sing. Identifying storytellers proved to be more of a problem, at least initially. This is ironic, since everyone tells stories of one sort or another at one time or another. But in the early going, I was approaching the issue from the same direction as my predecessors, including Alcée Fortier, Calvin Claudel, Corinne Saucier, and Elizabeth Brandon. We had all looked for the animal tales and magic tales that clearly illustrated the connection between French Louisiana and its historical and cultural roots in France and Africa. Basically, we found what we were looking for, but there was not much of it. We knocked on the doors of potential informants and asked, "Do you know any animal tales or folktales?" If they said "No," we thanked them and went on to the next lead. We often found out what they did not know, but not what they did know. Sometime later, when I read Saucier's assertion that her collection of thirty-three tales was small but "representative . . . of our Southern Louisiana form of oral tradition known as folklore, a heritage that is disappearing in our mechanized age" (Saucier 1962), it occurred to me that something must be wrong. First, my activist position made me unwilling to admit that the tradition was dying. And second, I knew that there were more stories because of the thousands of stories I had heard over the years in my father's barbershop where I had spent nearly every afternoon after school. So I rethought my fieldwork strategy. I realized that it is much easier to find out about storytellers in a bar or a barbershop or a garage than in the parish rectory. An essential aspect of my change in methodology involved being open to any context and form of story*telling* rather than focusing only on identified story*tellers*. I found that the first method had exposed the tradition of memory, the stories that a few people remembered from long ago, but no longer really told actively, while the second exposed the active tradition, the stories that people were telling each other on their own, unprompted by a folklorist's questions.

My fieldwork interests have also been driven by my interest in and commitment to preserving the French language in Louisiana. At the turn of this century, several successive generations of young Cajun and Creole children found themselves in classrooms for the first time. They also found themselves forbidden to speak their native French language in those classrooms. Among the results of this language repression was a rip in the social fabric. Parents who had learned to be ashamed of their language and culture, of their parents and of themselves, avoided inflicting what they considered a social liability on their own children. A major current in the natural flow of cultural transmission was of course severely disrupted. The language struggled to survive, due to remarkably well-organized efforts to eradicate it. Given this situation, that storytelling in French would persist in the South Louisiana context to this day might reasonably be considered nothing short of a miracle. Yet I have been able to record thousands of stories in French since 1974. What is often described as a fragile tradition seems instead to be remarkably resilient because of the nature of its transmission.

It quickly became clear to me that the stories were not ends in themselves. The storytellers themselves were the real treasures. My aim was to enhance their ability to adapt, innovate, create new forms of stories through their talent and charisma. Their willingness to share their knowledge was essential to the progress of my research. The first time I met Mrs. Evelia Boudreaux, she told me four stories, including an animal tale and a version of Petit Poucet, responding to my request for such tales. By the time I visited her one year later, I had had my epiphany and opened my consideration of tales to include anything she wanted to tell. She told me seven more stories. When I returned home that night, I found a message that Mrs. Boudreaux had called insisting that she had some more stories to tell me. I said I knew this, that I had gone earlier that day to record her. "No," my mother pointed out, "she just called to say that she wants you to go back tomorrow because she has a few more tales that she forgot to tell you today." I returned the next day and she told me eight more stories. Over the years, she dredged up dozens of stories from her memory to tell me, because she had learned that I found them valuable and interesting. Similarly, I first met Ben Guiné while tracking down leads on storytellers, the old way, in Parks. After several visits, during which I met many interesting people, but no one to tell the kind of stories I thought I was looking for, I reached the last name on my list. Not knowing where this person lived, I asked some children playing outside for directions. The little boy who won the footrace to my truck climbed in and directed me to the house. That visit turned up dry as well, but the boy who was listening to my questions about animal tales offered that his grandfather told stories like that. He took me to his grandfather's house where I met Ben Guiné, who quite literally left a plate of steaming food on his kitchen table to come into the living room to tell his tales. Over the years, he too told me dozens of stories of all sorts. His remarkable storytelling talents and wide repertoire of stories eventually attracted considerable attention, including a filming session by Louisiana Public Broadcasting on the porch of his little house in Promised Land, across the Bayou Teche from Parks, to the astonishment and delight of his neighbors. Based on a philosophy of cultural activism, I tried to find ways to integrate them into the ongoing effort to preserve Louisiana's French language and culture. Mrs. Boudreaux, Ben Guiné, and several other storytellers appeared in storytelling events at festivals and in schools, thrilling crowds and school children with their impressive repertoires and masterful styles.

PROGRAMMING CULTURAL PRESENTATION: THE EXAMPLE OF THE FIRST CAJUN MUSIC FESTIVAL

Sometimes in addition to, sometimes instead of documenting and analyzing past performances within the scholarly community, some folklorists strive to program and present one of those next performances in a setting that will communicate it to wider audiences, not on the page but on a stage. This practice brings problems of its own. For example, the most sensitively programmed cultural presentation at a folk festival is not the same as the natural performance in its own time and place. But some of these concerns can be resolved with the same sort of careful and serious study of performance and context as that produced in the academic setting.

Programming issues were directly related to the activist fieldwork and archival philosophies at the heart of the University of Louisiana's Center for Acadian and Creole Folklore. The theoretical issues underpinning the fieldwork that initially led to the production of the first Cajun Music Festival on March 26, 1974, as well as the issues that emerged and evolved as the festival became an annual event, were directly related to the establishment of the center's archives. The programming of the festival was based on a marriage or an integration of ideas that grew out of two distinct camps: on the one hand, activist folklife-based considerations as influenced by the Smithsonian

Institution's Festival of American Folklife, and on the other, linguistic-based considerations that grew out of the Council for the Development of French in Louisiana's language and cultural preservation initiatives. Fieldwork and programming practices evolved based on a desire to discover and present excellent folk performers from real-life (authentic) contexts, avoiding the more self-conscious, public purveyors of folkloric (authentic-like) culture. The fieldwork practices that grew out of the festival experience also contributed to the fieldwork practices that addressed the collection and analysis of other traditional genres in French Louisiana, including oral tradition and material culture. Selecting the collection of performers who would essentially define the moment in Cajun music and zydeco each year posed interesting problems and opportunities for festival producers, including the incorporation of young performers and the new, emerging styles that are necessarily part of a living tradition. Dewey Balfa put it best, insisting on the importance of treating tradition as a process, not a product. "I'm interested in the very life of this culture and how it continues to evolve in its own terms. I don't want to freeze-dry it or pin it to a wall like a dead butterfly." Dewey was not only a musician, but what folklorists have come to call a community scholar, that is, a member of a folk community who has learned to address the issues that are at the heart of the study and practice of folklore, such as cultural equity and the relationship between preservation and innovation within the traditional context.

Inspired by Dewey and enriched by his connections to the Smithsonian's Folklife Program staff, including especially Ralph Rinzler, we prepared the first Tribute to Cajun Music which turned out to be the first large popular rally of the Council for the Development of French in Louisiana's renaissance movement. The fieldwork we did for the festival was a natural extension of the fieldwork that had begun with John and Alan Lomax, who began collecting folksongs for the Library of Congress in the 1930s. The Lomaxes had a New Deal–style activist agenda, intending for their collection to serve as the basis for cultural recycling projects in regions throughout the country. Based on their experience in French Louisiana in 1934 and 1937, Alan had used his position on the Newport Folk Festival board to send Ralph Rinzler and Mike Seeger to Louisiana early in 1964 to identify musicians who would be invited to perform at Newport later that year. Following leads from Harry Oster, who had collected in the area a few years before, they found Gladdy Thibodeaux, Louis "Vinesse" Lejeune, and Dewey Balfa (who served as a last-minute replacement on guitar). The trio received standing ovations for their performance of old-time traditional Cajun music at Newport. Dewey

Balfa was overwhelmed by this reception for what was often dismissed as "nothing but chanky-chank" back home. He came back home determined to spread the good news that Cajun music was appreciated outside of the area. He maintained close contact with Rinzler, who in 1967 became the Director of Folklife Programs at the Smithsonian Institution. There Rinzler continued to produce folk festivals celebrating America's rich cultural diversity; these festivals often featured the Cajun and Creole music he had encountered during his early fieldwork. Through his steady contact with Rinzler and other public folklorists, Balfa learned to articulate such issues as cultural conservation and the process of tradition.

The first Cajun music festival was an overwhelming success, surprising even the most enthusiastic of its organizers. Musicians were selected according to the notions of cultural authenticity established by Rinzler and Balfa. "No crooners," Rinzler cautioned, for example. His preference for the clear, high-pitched vocals and unadorned instrumental styles of earlier Cajun music dominated the evening. The concert was structured to feature the historical development of Cajun and Creole music, ballad singers Inez Catalon and Marcus Landry, twin fiddlers Dennis McGee and Sady Courville, early stylists Marc Savoy, Lionel Leleux, and Varise Connor, Nathan Abshire, the Balfa Brothers, and the Ardoin Family, as well as the more modern sounds of Clifton Chenier and Blackie Forrestier and the Cajun Aces. Cajun country star Jimmy C. Newman, whose hit "Lache pas la patate" was in full swing, was used to anchor the concert, despite his silky smooth instrumentals and rich vocals. Even Rinzler saw the wisdom of Dewey's brilliant plan to use Newman's popularity to attract a crowd that would then be there to hear the rest of the evening's lineup. And it worked; many in attendance commented then and later that they had come to hear Newman and were in some cases reminded of and in others surprised by the power of the more traditional performers. The festival was an undeniable success, packing Lafayette's Blackham Coliseum despite lightning, thunder, and driving rain. It turned out to be the largest mass rally of what was coming to be called the Louisiana French renaissance movement.

"CULTURAL RECYCLING":
THE ARCHIVES AS A SUPPORT OF TRANSMISSION

Organizers also saw the opportunity to use the energy produced by this initial concert to fuel a long-term project. In the momentum of the moment, the University of Louisiana at Lafayette (then the University of Southwestern Louisiana) created the Center for Acadian and Creole Folklore to integrate this new field of study into the academic community. Balfa, who had seen the benefit of the archives at the Library of Congress and at the Smithsonian Institution, insisted that we needed a similar bank of information on ourselves here in Louisiana. When I pointed out that I did not have the financial resources to produce an archive, Balfa pointedly asked, "Do you have enough money to buy one tape?" I answered yes. He continued, "Then buy one and go out and record an interview, and put that tape on a shelf. Then record another one when you can afford it. And when you put that second tape next to the first one on the shelf, you have the beginnings of an archive." He was right, as usual; the beginnings of the archive were just that homemade and it worked. About the same time, the Council for the Development of French in Louisiana bought dozens of tapes and funded early recording efforts, using the fieldwork tapes in French radio programming. Soon enough, we also received critical support from the Rockefeller Foundation that paid for hundreds of tapes, which were recorded and gathered on the shelves to extend the archive. We also contacted folklorists who had worked in Louisiana in the past, such as Lomax, Oster, and Rinzler, to obtain copies of their fieldwork materials. Other collections from the past, such as those of Elizabeth Brandon, William Owen, and Corinne Saucier, were also obtained. Now, gathered in one place for the first time, the center's archives provided a sense of the evolution and development of Cajun and Creole music from unaccompanied ballad tradition to contemporary dance band styles. Fieldwork on oral tradition and material culture was added as well. The field recordings of students and colleagues continue to enrich our understanding of who we are and how we have come to be that way. But the collection is not an end in itself. Instead, it is intended to serve as a resource for cultural recycling. For example, when the center acquired copies of the 1934 Lomax's field recordings, it was not only to repatriate this important research for archival purposes. Copies were provided to the families of the original performers, and contemporary musicians were encouraged to use the collection as a source for "new" material.

In this spirit of cultural recycling, the Center for Acadian and Creole Folklore also organizes festivals and special performances, television and radio programs, and offers classes and workshops through the university's French and Francophone Studies program. The center produces books and articles that communicate new discoveries and interpretations to community members as well as scholars. There were precious few books and articles available on Cajun and Creole culture, and most of the few that there were had been done by outsiders who often misunderstood the culture. I became interested in writing so that there would be some. But books and articles do not reach the large audiences, especially of Cajuns and Creoles who needed to have access to information about themselves. So the center has explored other ways to disseminate its findings. We joined forces with record producers to release special recordings based on the fieldwork we were collecting. We joined forces with radio producers and filmmakers to produce special programs and documentaries based on the fieldwork we were collecting. We joined forces with educational institutions to have singers and storytellers perform in classes and special lecture series. Student and faculty researchers have focused on a wide range of subjects, including the traditional Mardi Gras, traiteurs, folk religion, folk justice, traditional humor, social institutions, foodways, dances, and material culture. This research typically focuses on contemporary as well as historical aspects of the issues, reflecting Dewey Balfa's concerns, considering folklore as a vital ongoing process rather than as a stagnant product. The roots and development of Cajun and Creole folklore are actively explored, taking researchers back to the regions of France (especially Poitou, Vendée, and Bretagne) that provided most of the French settlement of Louisiana, as well as the other major sources of influence, including Spain, Germany, England, Ireland, Québec, and the Acadian Maritimes, the West Indies, and Africa. Of particular interest is the process of creolization, the unique blending of cultures that occurred in Louisiana to produce the folk architecture, music, oral tradition, and cuisine of the region. Through this range of activities, we try to integrate both sides of folkloristics, the scholarly and the public, without getting caught in the perceived trap between the two.

THE NEED TO NEGOTIATE WITH FESTIVAL SITES AND AUDIENCES

Folk festivals often tend to follow the high-energy model, oriented toward large audiences, developed decades ago at such events as the National Folk Festival and the Newport Folk Festival. This method of presentation has had positive effects, not the least of which has been the providing of national-level validation for regional folk performers by having them perform on stages high off the ground with fancy electronic amplification before large enthusiastic audiences, often alongside nationally known performers. This method also has had certain limitations. Quieter, more intimate performance genres are difficult to program in such high-energy settings. In most cultures, ballad singing is a concert performance, that is, without dancing; it does not usually happen before thousands or even hundreds of people. In a large festival setting, both audience and performer must be prepared for this change in format. Smaller, more intimate, so-called workshops can provide a more familiar, intimate setting. But even these may not be enough to set a cultural event in its best performance context. By drawing on careful observation of the rules and nature of cultural performance in its natural setting, folklorists can develop better, more sensitive, more effective, and less abusive methods of presenting folklore and folklife in public settings.

The kinds of programming that folklorists produce are not the spontaneous events that occur naturally in folk communities. Folk festivals and concerts are often designed to reach an audience that could not otherwise easily experience the folk arts in question. They are thus almost invariably out of context, sometimes less so, as in the case of a festival in or near its own cultural region, such as the New Orleans Jazz & Heritage Festival, other times more so as in the case of the major national festivals or a concert of folk music at Carnegie Hall. For better or worse, folklorists and festival producers often exhibit a penchant for this sort of invasion of "foreign" territory. To be successful, such public-sector programming must be clever and calculating. It must inform and sensitize audiences while entertaining them. Careful preparation and presentation can usually get a crowd to understand enough to appreciate a folk performance in its own terms. Sometimes this can include simply enough ethnic and aesthetic background to set up a performance. Other times, sites and audiences can be renegotiated to create a more natural environment for certain types of performance.

Storytelling, for example, has been one of the most difficult cultural features to program effectively in a festival setting. Usually, storytellers are tacitly expected to perform as stand-up comics, though many do not possess the skills for entertaining the masses, nor are they necessarily interested in developing those skills. But settings can be renegotiated to work better for performer and audience as well. Storytelling is generally, by nature, an intimate performance that occurs among a small group of people who know each other and share a common language. Some storytellers can go a long way toward reaching a festival audience which may number in the hundreds, but a crowd that large will strain even the most outstanding performer. NEA National Heritage Award winner Ray Hicks told his stories well enough on stage at the 1983 Festival of American Folklife, but he seemed much more comfortable telling his stories backstage or on the grounds between performances to any crowd he was able to draw and hold on his own, a practice which more closely resembled the dynamics of his performances back home. Festival organizers soon noticed this and encouraged Ray to tell his stories in a more spontaneous way under the trees and without amplification (which imposed natural limitations on such important factors as the nature and size of the crowds).

During a performance at the University of Louisiana's French House, Creole storyteller Ben Guiné renegotiated his own audience in a similar way, but with slightly different results. A crowd of some seventy people showed up to hear this extraordinary storyteller perform. He was pleased with the show of interest, but as he began, I noticed that something was off. He was telling well, but he was not taking off as I had heard him do so often while listening to his stories in his living room or on his front porch. I realized later that he was straining to engage every person in the room. He realized this before I did. I was sitting next to him and about a third of the way through his first story, he accidentally bumped my knee during one of his expansive gestures. When he noticed I was within reach, he turned his chair to face me and proceeded to tell *me* the stories. He knew from our many long sessions that I understood his Creole and his stories. Also I was an audience that he could handle, tapping, pushing, and pinching me to make the appropriate points. He then hit full stride and the rest of the evening, the crowd watched and listened to Ben Guiné telling me stories, which was much better for everyone concerned. When I realized what happened, I began experimenting with new formats for programming storytelling based around the concept of getting storytellers to tell in a small setting and arranging a crowd around the event to witness it from outside. One of these settings involved a circular stage setting with storytellers sitting in a circle around a table or ice chest facing inward toward each other, and with the audience in a larger circle all around. The audience thus hears the storytellers tell each other tales over their shoulders.

Ironically, ballad singers used to singing for listeners can sometimes enjoy a more natural context at some festivals than dance bands who are often asked to perform as a concert band with people only listening to their music. Members of these bands can experience a range of feelings from confusion to frustration and even depression because they are used to the positive feedback of dancing crowds. While it is understandably important to some programmers to have people listen to the music, some festivals have learned to program dance parties as well as concert settings to provide these bands with a more appropriate context for their performance. Audiences sometimes take matters into their own hands when festival programmers don't provide this context. By 1974, when Dewey Balfa talked the Council for the Development of French in Louisiana into sponsoring the first Tribute to Cajun Music concert, he had already come to understand enough about the dynamics of such events from his own experiences on the folk festival circuit to invert the design on purpose. He knew that a Cajun crowd would dance if it were at all possible, as they did every Saturday night in dance halls throughout South Louisiana. But the intent of this special concert was to get Cajuns to appreciate the value of their own music by getting them to listen to it. So he encouraged programmers to hold the concert in a setting where dancing would not be possible. That evening, twelve thousand Cajuns wiggled in their seats in Lafayette's Blackham Coliseum and listened to sounds that they had heard only shortly before.

Traditional ballad singers are not used to singing before huge festival crowds, and conversely, huge festival crowds are certainly not used to listening to traditional ballad singers. Sometimes, however, unexpected programming can jar an unexpected response from a crowd. Ballad singers typically sing for small groups in intimate settings. Some have attested that they remember singing for as many as a hundred or so during wedding receptions, but the tens of thousands that show up for the Cajun Music Festival are another matter altogether. Add to the numbers, the matter of electronic amplification, and the festival stage could be thought of as a place quite alien to the performance of traditional ballads, which have been described as home music. Nevertheless, convinced that the unaccompanied human voice has a power that could carry such a moment, Cajun Music Festival organizers invited Marcie Lacouture to perform a few venerable ballads during a break between two high-energy bands at the 1985 festival. The crowd was stunned by the powerful simplicity of her beautiful voice singing songs laden with the patina of history. In 1986, she appeared in a more formal way with one of her mentors, Inez Catalon, listed in the schedule between Zachary Richard's Zack Attack and the Balfa Brothers Band. The pair once again captured the moment, focusing the huge dance crowd's attention on the earliest sounds of Cajun and Creole music. Zachary Richard instinctively knew this himself, occasionally inserting an a capella ballad into his hard-driving performances.

Some elements of traditional life, such as material culture, occupational folklife, and foodways, are not as prone to presentation as performance, as music, and even as storytelling. Some festivals have developed ingenious ways to present these to visitors. At the Smithsonian's Festival of American Folklife (FAF), the National Mall has been plowed to demonstrate traditional agricultural techniques. It has been turned into a racetrack to demonstrate traditional horsemanship. Airplanes and eighteen-wheelers have been brought in to serve as settings for the occupational folklore of pilots and truckers. The reflecting pond has been used to launch traditional boats built on-site by craftsmen.

An especially difficult aspect of folklife to program in a festival context is foodways. It is unfair to expect a traditional cook to perform à la Julia Child. Yet festivals have become increasingly adept at presenting cooking techniques with the assistance of presenters who specialize in getting people to talk about what seems second nature to them. Sometimes participants take over and provide even more than the programmers had bargained for. During 1982, a Cajun housewife was invited to demonstrate Louisiana French traditional cooking at the Smithsonian Festival of American Folklife. Fieldworker and presenter Kathy James was able to expand the presentation to include the housewife's extended family, which produced results that would not have been possible with one isolated cook. The housewife was accompanied by her husband, who offered to demonstrate some of the outdoor cooking men do in that same culture. Their four children joined them as well. Two of these were married and brought along their spouses and their own children for a vacation in Washington, D.C. This ultimately turned the foodways demonstration tent and surrounding area into a holistic family folklore experience that covered much more ground than just cooking. Mom's cooking demonstrations involved the whole family, with members taking on traditional roles and engaging in typical conversation around the stove and chopping block. Dad's barbecue effortlessly and unselfconsciously became a family storytelling session around the pit as it always did back home, with festival visitors listening in from across the rope. This wasn't home, but it was much closer than festival visitors usually experience because the extended family was enough to achieve a sort of cultural critical mass. Yet, as Robert Cantwell (1992) noted, such programming can sometimes be less than successful, ironically if it too successfully re-creates cultural dynamics. Potential visitors can be reluctant to wander into contextual spaces, intimidated by the apparently closed nature of the exhibition.

Sometimes festival organizers develop new ways of presenting culture based on their observations of performance in its own context. Sometimes participants can and do take over with their own theories about context and performance. Over the years, Dewey Balfa was visited by many folklorists and invited to many festivals. He learned from them what he needed to know to guide his own efforts to regenerate interest and respect for Cajun music in his native South Louisiana. This information also turned Balfa into quite an expert on folk festival theory, sometimes to the chagrin of festival organizers who had not always thought out the issues as well as he had, and certainly did not feel them as he did. An example of his insight was his constant struggle to perform with his own band rather than as a member of a Cajun All-Star band. He reasoned that he should be allowed to perform in a way that was current and real, not to mention comfortable. His problem was compounded by the fact that he broke onto the folk festival circuit in the 1960s performing with the legendary Cajun accordionist Nathan Abshire. The combination of Balfa and Abshire was indeed magic, and the music they made became set in the minds of audiences and festival producers alike. A number of factors, including alcohol, egos, and the stress of travel, placed a great strain on the band, and the two stopped performing together around 1970 in order to preserve their friendship. Despite their decision to avoid playing together, festival organizers continued to try to set up encounters between Balfa and Abshire. In 1976, the Balfa Brothers were invited to the Festival of American Folklife along with Nathan Abshire and his Pinegrove Boys in the hopes that the two musicians might at least be encouraged to visit each other on stage. They carefully avoided such a reunion, with Dewey finally explaining that he hoped to remain friends with Nathan long after the festival ended and the crowds went home. He added that if they ever were to perform together again for a crowd, it would probably be in the Bearcat Lounge in their native Basile, or even more likely at someone's home for a friendly jam session and supper.

Two more Balfa festival stories give an excellent example of his under-standing of culture as process rather than as product. For years he tried to convince festival organizers to allow him to come with his current band as he performed in the dance halls every Saturday night. He eventually won a partial victory, coming with most of his dance band, but he was never allowed to bring along his steel guitar players. The argument was that the steel guitar was too modern, an inappropriate and inauthentic addition to the traditional instrumentation. Never mind the fact that Dewey Balfa, long recognized as a pillar of cultural preservation in America, chose to perform weekly with a steel guitar in his band, just as dozens of other Cajun bands did. In 1978, he finally confronted Smithsonian festival personnel on the issue, asking them, "Are you trying to present Cajun music as you wish it still were, or as it really is?" He was allowed to bring along fiddler Dick Richard, who also played a few tunes on the steel guitar that year.

In 1985 Dewey delivered a brilliant extemporaneous address on the traditional process from the stage of the cultural conservation area of the Washington, D.C., festival. Invited as an outstanding example of the effort to conserve America's traditional culture, he pointed out halfway through a forty-five-minute set that he had been playing some traditional songs, songs that he and his brothers had composed just before Rodney and Will died in 1978. He went on to explain that he didn't have to turn around to know that he had just made some people backstage very nervous, because he was there to represent cultural conservation. But for him cultural conservation did not mean freeze-drying culture and preserving it under glass. For him, cultural conservation meant preserving the very life of the culture. And if this was successful, then the culture was going to be alive and well and continue to grow and evolve in its own terms. And if this effort was successful in his native Louisiana, then fifty years or so from now, some young musicians were going to need some songs that were fifty or so years old to play, and so he had made some, and he was going to play them. He did, and the stage personnel as well as the audience were delighted to hear that his new songs sounded much like the old ones from his family tradition. He capped this remarkable demonstration by pointing that out and explaining that they sounded like the old stuff because they were coming from the same tradition and through the same process.

Festival organizers should never be afraid to be surprised. The people we invite to perform at festivals are sometimes uneducated, but rarely unintelligent. In a sense, Dewey's presentation was much more successful than the one that was originally intended for the cultural presentation stage that day. The audience and festival personnel alike had the opportunity to learn a fancy lesson about culture. After years of performing in such contexts, Dewey learned precisely how to operate the machinery. In this case, he was aiming his message in two directions at once. The immediate message was aimed at the audience, but that message and its reception was obviously meant to rebound backstage.

The Smithsonian staff has learned over the years to adapt and even yield to the natural momentum of traditional cultures. In 1985, Louisiana was featured at its annual Festival of American Folklife. Along with Cajuns and Creoles, there were folk performers and craftspersons from all over

Louisiana, including Mardi Gras float builders, Mardi Gras "Indians," second-line dancers, and a jazz band from New Orleans. Participants and presenters came up with the idea to have these groups parade through the site to give the crowds something of a Mardi Gras experience. Festival organizers hesitantly agreed. As the improvised parade snaked its way through the site, it became clear that something larger than anticipated was happening on its own. The parade went outside the Louisiana area attracting crowds like a magnet. Soon there were thousands of people instinctively imitating Pork Chop and Kidney Stew as they danced and marched a second line following the floats, the jazz band, and the "Indians." Eventually the procession arrived at its planned destination, the Louisiana dance party stage. The jazz band and the "Indians" gave inspired performances before yielding the stage to Filé, a traditional Cajun band scheduled to perform that evening. Filé opened its dance party concert with the traditional Cajun Mardi Gras song as several participants and Louisiana staff members appeared in traditional costume to lead the dancing. By then, the crowd was in a near frenzy. Festival director Diana Parker came up to me and said with genuine concern in her voice, "We're very close to losing control here." She was right, but that was, after all, the point. I replied happily, "I know! It's great, isn't it?" To her credit, she immediately switched gears and celebrated the triumph of the moment. We had somehow conjured the spirit of Mardi Gras on a summer day in Washington, D.C. In the controlled chaos of the improvised events, the crowd had gotten even closer to a true Mardi Gras experience than even the most hopeful of this affair's instigators could have imagined.

When the Liberty Theater's weekly live radio show was inaugurated over a decade ago, the cultural tourism benefit of having a performance that visitors could count on finding every Saturday night was an important part of the City of Eunice's strategy, but several unanticipated factors involved in the implementation of this plan strained the production team's resources. Identifying and booking appropriate and effective cultural entertainment on a weekly basis proved to be a huge undertaking and chronically threatened to overwhelm the Liberty show's mostly volunteer staff. If the programming were to avoid depending on a limited number of known name bands from week to week, some fieldwork would be necessary. There was no provision for fieldwork built into the show's infrastructure. Consequently, programming was based essentially on the knowledge and experiences of interested and dedicated staff members. Some performers contacted the Eunice mayor's office, offering their services. Others contacted the host, the producer, the stage manager, the sound technician, or a stagehand. Many furnished their own demo recordings for consideration. Nevertheless, in this seemingly haphazard way, over the years, the program succeeded in debuting such memorable performers as Steve Riley and the Mamou Playboys; Richard Leboeuf and Two Step; Kenneth Thibodeaux and Cajun Dance; Balfa Toujours; McCauley, Reed, and Vidrine; Charivari, Felton Lejeune, and the Cajun Cowboys, Feux Follets; Keith Frank; Zydeco Force; Chris Ardoin; and Geno Delafose, among many others.

Sometimes the "fieldwork" was very close to the presentation, as in the case of Horace Trahan's debut. Helena Putnam, the stage manager, reported hearing a remarkable young accordion player and singer who was sitting in at a jam session at the Jean Lafitte Acadian Culture Center next door earlier that afternoon. During the Liberty show that night, she recognized the young man sitting in the audience and pointed him out to me. On a whim, and trusting the judgment of my colleague based on years of shared mutual observations from our backstage perspective, I went down into the audience during a song and invited him to perform a song or two on stage that night. He accepted and performed sitting on a chair all alone in the middle of the stage during a stolen moment between scheduled performances. The crowd, my mutual friend, myself, and he were all quite literally moved to tears by the experience. He eventually performed with his own full band and others many times on the same stage, and on many others.

PERFORMANCE AS A BATTLEGROUND FOR ACTIVISTS

Several programming issues were raised over the years, almost as much on the fly as the fieldwork on Horace Trahan. Based on a need and a desire to represent all of South Louisiana's musical traditions, we have programmed both Cajun music and zydeco, as well as other styles, including old-time country and bluegrass, swamp pop, gospel, and blues. Some of these forays are more successful than others for a variety of reasons. Over the years, we have noticed that the crowd prefers Cajun music to zydeco, and traditional or mainstream Cajun music to more modern Cajun fusion styles. We often lose much of the audience when zydeco or Cajun rock performances have been scheduled to close the show. Some of this undoubtedly has to do with the residue of racial intolerance. Another factor has to do with the language factor; much of contemporary zydeco and Cajun rock is in

English, clashing with the established French focus of the show. Still another factor is stylistic; much of contemporary zydeco has drifted far from their traditional roots, conflicting with the penchant among Liberty regulars for more traditional styles. Some modern Cajun bands, such as Mamou, have experienced the same lack of interest among that crowd. This has meant coming up with innovative programming to ensure cultural equity in programming. This can include opening with a zydeco or highly contemporary Cajun band and closing with a more mainstream Cajun band, or sandwiching a highly innovative band between opening and closing performances by a Cajun band. It is interesting to note that the storytellers who have been featured occasionally have not been subjected to the same sort of language filter. Though some, such as Ed Deshotels and Thelma Daigle, told many of their stories in French, others such as Ralph Begnaud, Dave Petitjean, and A. J. Smith have told theirs almost exclusively in English.

Dancing has also been a source of considerable improvisation and innovation. Many in the crowd were from another generation and may not have chosen to participate in the desegregation of a dance floor. But the Liberty, as a public institution, attracted people without regard to ethnic boundaries. Dancing naturally occurred and mixing naturally followed. After a few tense moments early on, it rather quickly became a nonissue. Additionally, traditionalists were exposed to such innovations as line dances and the newly invented complexities of fancy Cajun dancing. Despite occasional grumbling, the different elements generally tolerate each other, with more traditional two-steppers gliding around pairs engaged in the fancy passes of the so-called Cajun jig.

Because of the sometimes imperfect nature of programming at the Liberty, ironically, it has been an excellent place to do fieldwork. Due to the demands of providing weekly performances, a wide variety of style and quality has run through that stage. The poor performances are sometimes hard for staffers to endure, but the tendency toward inclusion rather than exclusion has created a venue where just about anything is possible. We have used our vantage point backstage at the Liberty in much the same way that Harry Oster and Ralph Rinzler used Fred's Lounge in the 1960s and 1970s, when a wide range of musicians regularly came out of the woods and the woodwork to perform on Revon Reed's weekly live radio show. Revon was faithfully nonjudgmental, tolerating the less-talented throngs to identify the gifted few. In the end, this has proved to be an inefficient, but remarkably effective public fieldwork technique.

THE INTERACTION BETWEEN ACADEMIC AND APPLIED FOLKLORE

Academic folklorists have spent years pondering the nature and context of traditional performance, yet much of this energy has ended up only on the pages of professional journals. Meanwhile, few of the strategies and theories developed by public sector folklorists to address the specific problems of programming and presenting culture are ever applied beyond the stage in question (for exceptions see Wilson & Udall 1982). Barbara Kirshenblatt-Gimblett (1988:140–155) suggested that it was time for folklorists "to reassess their division of labor, to reexamine the split between the academic and applied traditions, and to close it." Yet as Robert Baron and Nicholas Spitzer (1992) point out, her article "has been criticized for using language, perspectives, and examples that reify the dichotomy she sought to erase. The article was aimed at provoking critical discourse in the field, and her academically centered, dialectical style of writing often appears to show value in seemingly contradictory positions." She was attempting to calm the waters in the field because of a raging debate over the relative value of what has been called "applied folklore," "folklore in the public sector," and "public folklore" (Green 1992). There are possibilities for a working relationship between "pure" and "applied" folklore, focusing specifically on performance-centered folklore theory and folk arts programming in the public sector.

The performance-centered approach to folklore studies has given us some of the most theoretical sounding and looking scholarship in recent times. Though its practice has sometimes been dismissed as a jargon-filled academic exercise, the basic notion of considering the whole context of folklore performances has more to offer than obtuse, esoteric articles, especially in the area of presenting and programming folk performances in a variety of public settings. We set ourselves up as scholars trained to learn about people from those people. We do pretty well in many cases. Other times, we fail to apply the same theories we develop to understand cultural phenomena when we present them.

Folklorists who insisted that there is more to folklore than the texts its study generates were absolutely right. There are cultural imperatives in each natural performance of traditional culture, including setting, time, and constant negotiation between performers and audience. The consideration of these complex factors has led to highly technical studies (see Dégh 1969; Glassie 1982) and several theories concerning the documentation of performance. Many of these focus on the capturing of traditional performance for contemplation and analysis. Dennis Tedlock (1983) produced a two-hundred-plus page treatise on the importance of pause, pitch, and volume in the recording and reporting of oral performance. His study is intended to be a guide to the production of transcriptions "in which the reader coordinates vision with the properly-tuned reenactment of sounds." His ultimate goal is to produce a "performable text," a transcription with so much accurate information that a reasonably skilled reader could reproduce the performance. And since so much folklore, even in this country, is originally performed in languages other than English, Tedlock takes the process one step further to strive for the "performable translation." He eventually goes on to analyze one of his own performances of a translated Zuni text as a folklore performance in itself. He is either brutally honest or getting a little far afield here. (What happened to the original Zuni performance through all this processing?)

Elizabeth Fine (1984) also applied performance theory to the development of more complete transcriptions in *The Folklore Text*. Her transcriptions contain lots of contextual and performance information including symbols to indicate pause, pitch, and volume, as well as other nonlexical features such as gesture, position, and audience reaction. They consequently look like scientific notation or complex musical scores. I'm not quite sure about the purpose of such feats of transcription technology. If they lead to a better understanding of the cultural event, then they may be worth the effort. I would hope that they do not become ends in themselves, an exercise in esoteric complexity. I would also hope that someone studying a cultural event later would not depend solely on the notation of another scholar, no matter how meticulous, without doing original fieldwork.

I buy, to a certain extent, the need for more detailed observation and analysis of context and performance (Goldstein 1974). At the same time, I wonder why so much of this scholarship seems intent on trying to express the complexities of community and group dynamics and performance on the printed page. Ultimately, even the most complex, elaborate performance transcription is not the folklore performance. Nor for that matter is the tape recording, nor the film, or the videotape. Even if a storytelling event is shot in full color with four 70 mm. cameras simultaneously and recorded in Dolby/stereo/digital sound, the resulting documentation is not the performance. Even the performer cannot reproduce that performance. An important difference between the film and the performer, however, is that he can produce another performance the very next time he tells his stories on- or off-camera.

Folklorists espousing contextual and performance-centered approaches have insisted on the importance of studying the very life and nature of cultural performance in its most natural expression and setting. Their discoveries and subsequent theories can and do serve to adapt and improve the public presentation of the folk arts, whether within a community-based cultural presentation, in a cultural presentation destined for visitors as well as members of the community, or in a multicultural presentation outside of the community. Conversely, public sector folklorists can and do extract performance theory by observing how performers adapt themselves to unfamiliar settings and unfamiliar settings to themselves. These strategies can be identified to help refine future presentations and settings.

REFERENCES

Ancelet, Barry Jean, & Elemore Morgan Jr. 1984. *The Makers of Cajun Music*. Austin: University of Texas Press. Revised 1999; *Cajun and Creole Music Makers*. Jackson: University Press of Mississippi.

Baron, Robert, & Nicholas Spitzer, eds. 1992. *Public Folklore*. Washington, DC: Smithsonian Institution Press.

Cantwell, Robert. 1991. "Conjuring Culture: Ideology and Magic in the Festival of American Folklife." *Journal of American Folklore* 104(412), pp. 148–163.

———. 1992. "Feasts of Unnaming: Folk Festivals and the Representation of Folklife." In *Public Folklore*. Robert Baron & Nicholas Spitzer, eds. Washington, DC: Smithsonian Institution Press, pp. 263–305.

Dégh, Linda. 1969. *Folktales and Society: Storytelling in a Hungarian Peasant Community*. Bloomington: Indiana University Press.

Fine, Elizabeth. 1984. *The Folklore Text: From Performance to Print*. Bloomington: Indiana University Press.

Glassie, Henry. 1982. *Passing the Time in Ballymenone: Culture and History of an Ulster Community*. Philadelphia: University of Pennsylvania Press.

Goldstein, Kenneth. 1974. *A Guide for Fieldworkers in Folklore*. Detroit: Gale Research.

Green, Archie. 1992. "Public Folklore's Name: A Partisan's Notes." In *Public Folklore*. Robert Baron & Nicholas Spitzer, eds. Washington, DC: Smithsonian Institution Press, pp. 49–63.

Kirshenblatt-Gimblett, Barbara. 1988. "Mistaken Dichotomies." *Journal of American Folklore* 101, pp. 140–155.

Saucier, Corinne. 1962. *Folk Tales from French Louisiana*. Baton Rouge: Louisiana State University Press.

Tedlock, Dennis. 1983. *The Spoken Word and the Work of Interpretation*. Philadelphia: University of Pennsylvania Press.

Wilson, Joseph, & Lee Udall. 1982. *Folk Festival: A Handbook for Organization and Management*. Knoxville: University of Tennessee Press.

5.   (RE)TURN OF THE NATIVE

Insider Ethnography and the Politics of Fieldwork in South Louisiana

—Marc David

INTRODUCTION

Cultural practices are radically contingent and historical, dialogically constructed in and through social relations, and therefore always subject to the effects of power. What follows is an attempt to focus on a particular dimension of the social relations that divorces culture from power in our ethnographies, namely, the relationship, as classically understood and practiced from a positivist perspective, between ethnographer and "ethnographee" in the context of fieldwork.

In a remarkable set of writings, Johannes Fabian (1983, 1991, 1996) has approached these issues of ethnographic practice from a perspective that is both practical and theoretical. Fabian suggests proceeding from a processual conception of knowledge, in which knowing is understood as fundamentally social, and knowing acts are transformative of reality, and not simply reflections of it. In other words, knowledge produced through ethnography is predicated on the quality of communication in actual ethnographic encounters. At the same time, Fabian characterizes the ethnographic encounter as fundamentally agonistic, because nothing eliminates the disruption that our theoretical orientation inflects on everyday practice. A convincing claim to understand and represent something about an ethnographic Other should therefore vigorously engage with the challenges posed by and for an ethnographic presence.

Inspired by this critical assessment of field and fieldwork (cf. Castaneda 1996; Marcus & Fischer 1986) and following the implications it has for eth-nography in South Louisiana, I focus here on the dynamic of presence, that is, on how contact and rapport between the fieldworker and his or her inter-locutors forms the ground of and shapes the possibilities for the "knowledge" that emerges from encounters in the field. The chapter is a brief retelling of fieldwork done during the mid-1990s and published as a master's thesis, as a way of exploring the contours of ethnography practiced from this per-spective. In this reiteration, I position myself as ethnographer relative to a text in which, following the positivist paradigm, my ethnographic presence was largely invisible. But in doing so, I also attempt to disturb connotations of stability and security in the notion of presence by problematizing the autobiographical self. Though this narrative follows certain autobiographi-cal conventions, I complicate notions of "native" origins and ethnographic authority by illuminating the possibilities and tensions that emerge between ethnographic self, authorizing institutions, and interlocutors in "the field."

THE SOCIAL ORIGINS OF "NATIVE" QUESTIONS

How does this questioning of ethnography begin? By beginning autobiographically, I want to emphasize how my own position as a "native" and as a researcher emerges dialogically from a social context that is frac-tured and interrogated, which inevitably shapes both the possibilities of and the obstacles to a particular ethnographic project. If, as Lederman (1990:88) suggests, "'the field' is not so much a place as it is a particular relation between oneself and others, involving a difficult combination of commitment and disengagement, relationship and separation," then an adequate account of fieldwork would seem to require a description of what, in a given case, actu-ally constitutes this complex and troublesome nexus of Self and Other.

Of all the things that can and have been said about Cajuns during the middle decades of the century, I would add and underscore one more: a per-vasive but subtle sense of alienation, a kind of internal fragmentation amidst the growing affirmation of a monolithic identity. That is, while "we Cajuns" were increasingly recognized (and recognized ourselves) as the presumptive majority in the region, the social practices of everyday life were anything but homogeneous and unified. The generation born in rural South Louisiana during and after World War II clearly straddled many social boundaries, or conversely, failed to straddle them.[1] Moving off the farm, or, for that matter, staying on it, required the acquisition of new kinds of cultural and economic capital as part of an engagement with modernity. And though the analysis of "Cajun" typically begins with what was happening on the farm, this is certainly not all that is relevant to understanding South Louisiana since mid-century. In both rural and urban settings, new spatial arrangements for living and working, new and transformed kinds of livelihoods, and the shifting social relations that accompanied them shaped dynamic, fluid, and heterogeneous interactions. The emphasis on identity, with its connotations of continuity and stability, hardly seems the adequate choice of terms.

Thus, for all the recent insistence, in both the academy and the mass media, that Cajuns are the nation's most well-adjusted ethnic group (e.g., Ancelet, Edwards, & Pitre 1991; Esman 1985), seamlessly combining the continuity of tradition with the demands of modernity, I would argue that such is not entirely the case. To suggest how this played out at a local and intimate yet thoroughly political level, consider the following semiautobiographical anecdote. Folded into the ambitions and accomplishments of the men in my father's family, who, by South Louisiana standards, were relatively prosperous farmers, was a sharp sense of social inferiority. Following difficult and aborted careers as grade school students, both my father and my grandfather quietly set out to prove themselves as "modern" cultivators of the soil. Despite their professional successes—land ownership, minor political office, and local, regional, and national recognition for their skill— their achievements were haunted by their socially inscribed inferiority, their thick "accents," their "lack" of education, and their "modest origins," relative to the now highly visible norm. While they largely followed assimilationist prescriptions for national belonging, and identified with Nixon's infamous white male silent majority, they were also painfully aware that they didn't fully enjoy its supposed privileges. It occurs to me now that their strong support for Edwin Edwards, whose early (and successful) gubernatorial campaigns were unabashedly ethnic in their rhetoric and tactics, were partly due to the way Edwards addressed this experience. Fervently pro-Edwards during the seventies, they responded to the way Edwards characterized his own political ascendancy as payback for their lingering sense of exclusion from a state and national "center."

A more public display of this disquiet would be Zachary Richard's famous performance at the first Festivals Acadiens in 1974, in which he angrily demanded a demonstration of *fierté* and *solidarité* from other

Cajuns. Though he comes at this fracture from the other side (i.e., he calls for allegiance to a particular kind of social being that eschews assimilation and speaks only French) his performance suggests the same social tensions, the fragmentation of a Self that cannot easily accommodate the complexities and challenges of being "Cajun" and/or "American." This conflict is implicit in the stances of both my relatives and Richard, and it underscores not so much some flaw particular to Cajuns as it does the contested ground on which any identity, and particularly white ethnic identities, are constructed in the American context.

The autobiographical significance of this point, in addition to the anecdote about my family, lies in the way that "nativist" ethnographic tropes represent a part of my own ideological genealogy. By the time I began to read seriously the literature on South Louisiana in the early 1980s, these developments were an important intellectual component in the strategy of white ethnic affirmation described previously. At that point, I had left the farm and small town where I grew up for college in Baton Rouge and New Orleans. It was a heady experience, but also quite disconcerting, in that the superficially egalitarian and homogenizing discourses in which I had been immersed were rudely disrupted by the post-Enlightenment philosophy and social theory with which I struggled in college classrooms, and by encounters with people from different socioeconomic backgrounds. A growing sense of dislocation was exacerbated by the fact that my father had passed away when I was in high school, and there was no family farm, no "home" to return to, if a B.A. in Philosophy didn't lead somewhere else. Yet I was haunted by an abiding sense of not having what was necessary to "make it" in contexts different from those in which I'd grown up. After I finished college, I decided that to quiet my sense of estrangement, I would intensify the study of my cultural and social origins, and ground my identity and future trajectory in the recovery of a "pure" voice from a "deep" past. At twenty-three, I left for an extended stay in Belgium, intending to return to Louisiana with a cultural resource I considered essential to my project: fluency in French. Ultimately, I imagined pursuing graduate studies and achieving an academic position as an "expert" in local culture. At the time, and for a number of years afterward, this path seemed to me the best way to resolve the tension of being "Cajun" and "American," in effect by combining (though not consciously) elements of strategies for accomplishing both.

As individual and singular a trajectory as this may appear, the narrative can be complicated here by pointing out that this story of in-betweenness and not-belonging more or less corresponds to descriptions of the "personal" experiences of a group of artists and academics who are roughly ten to fifteen years my senior. Consider the following description:

> By his junior year, [Barry] Ancelet had won a scholarship to study at the University of Nice on the French Riviera. Such good fortune astonished him, but delight soon gave way to gnawing discontent. "I couldn't understand why I couldn't connect," the Lafayette college professor recalled of his uneasy days in France. "I couldn't pinpoint what was missing." One day, a poster for a concert of "French music from Louisiana" caught his eye. Intrigued, he decided to attend. From the smoky basement coffee house wafted the familiar sounds of home—the astringent tones of a Cajun accordion. "It washed over me like a wave," Ancelet said. "This was it! This was what I had been missing." (Turner 2001:25A)

Clearly, we were (are) all treading down a well-worn discursive path, one that weaves dislocation, nostalgia, and travel together with tropes of discovery, insight, and life-changing decisions.

The point here is twofold. First, this correspondence between stories reinforces the earlier argument about the existence of a socially shared space of fragmented locations. The "social mobility" that opened up in the wake of the civil rights movement and the oil boom meant an unsettling of social boundaries, which contributed to an almost collective sense of unease for those who occupied this shifting ground. This discomfort, of course, is common among the American middle classes in general, where, as Ortner (1991) points out, the fear of downward mobility is intense, and questions of education and occupation as means of reproducing one's class status are paramount. Alongside the affirmations of identity, or perhaps beneath them, it is thus interesting to note the tension that is overcome in the origin myth of ethnic self-discovery. Moreover, that this attempt at resolution should lead toward careers as professional fieldworkers is not surprising. After all, it has often been noted that ethnography can be used as a technology of self-invention, "a kind of shifted, if not inverted, and metaphoric, autobiographical study . . . by which an Other is choreographed into a position adequate for mirroring [the Self]" (Castaneda 1996:23).

Second, to recognize this is to disturb tropes of an identity that is instinctively shared by "native" South Louisiana ethnographers and their subjects (e.g., Ancelet 1989b, 1992a), and to begin to locate, in cultural, social, and political terms, the position(s) from which the "native" poses her or his ethnographic questions. When it first emerged as a possibility within the discipline, the pursuit of native ethnography was proposed as a kind of antidote to ethnocentric bias. Lately, however, the adequacy of the remedy has been questioned, as, for example, the implications and complications of occupying multiple positions of age, gender, class, race, sexual orientation, and professional rank are acknowledged and theorized (e.g., Jones 1995; Narayan 1993). Common in these accounts by natives is the discovery of the lack of any guarantee that being an "insider" secures epistemologically privileged status with respect to the production of knowledge. Rapport and understanding always emerge (or not) in and through the encounter, or, as Fabian puts it, "intersubjectivity is something that is *made, rather than given*" (1991:388, emphasis added). Certainly, if the notion of instinctive sympathy and understanding is abandoned, and we approach fieldwork as the inherently agonistic undertaking that it is, this does not mean that one's "native" status counts for nothing. Rather, the challenge is to begin to think about how one might objectify these conditions, that is, how to make our simultaneous belonging/not-belonging part of what is reflected upon in an ethnographic project, and so work back and forth along the social fissures that we occupy/straddle to produce insight. Of course, this is what many ethnographers are already doing, in both everyday encounters during fieldwork, and in the ongoing reflection that is teaching and writing. The task is to render this work as explicit as possible, and to fold its results into the project itself.

Thus, my initial question was far from being simply my own, emerging as part of one strategy among many, in response to a social challenge experienced by myself and others—that of "becoming" either, or both, "Cajun" and "American." The significance of making this explicit lies in helping to specify the social location of the question—who is asking, from which place, and with what purpose?—and thereby remove it from the realm of a pure, "scientific" objectivity. As with many other white, middle-class, (mostly) men in South Louisiana, Cajun identity was (is) for me a kind of cultural predicament (cf. Clifford 1988), a challenge that is intensely personal but also social. Like a few others, I decided as a young adult to make this question part of a personal and professional project, which, because one of its orienting questions is shared with so many, can never exist as exclusive intellectual property. The question about Cajun identity, then, is mine, and it is not mine, and this is a crucial if apparently contradictory distinction to make.

REDUCED INVISIBILITY:
RETELLING THE ETHNOGRAPHIC ENCOUNTER IN 'TIT MAMOU

After almost a decade of going back and forth between South Louisiana and francophone countries in Europe and Africa, I moved to Quebec City in the mid-1990s, and began a master's degree in anthropology at Université Laval. From the start, I intended to pursue ethnographic fieldwork in South Louisiana as part of the degree program. However, alongside the cultural theory that I absorbed from reading the literature on South Louisiana, I'd also developed an interest in Marxist anthropology during my travels. From contact with Marxian scholars in Belgium to the firsthand experience of "underdevelopment" in West Africa, I began to imagine how a more materialist analysis would help "flesh out" what I perceived to be a vague understanding of social change in South Louisiana during the twentieth century. Following the conventional wisdom that locates Cajun identity and practice among the *petits habitants*, I constructed a project to explore the relationship between, on the one hand, the rise of agrarian capitalism on the southwestern prairies since the 1930s, and, on the other, egalitarian practices of labor exchange (*coups de main*, for example), and Mardi Gras as efforts to resist that trend. Managing to incorporate Mardi Gras into the study from an original perspective was a real coup, I thought at the time, and I expected it would put me in touch with the deepest cultural logic of the Cajuns.

Despite the sometimes seamless appearance of its "finished products," ethnographic fieldwork, in both its conceptualization and its execution, is never without unexplored assumptions, contradictory formulations, and important surprises. In the project outlined here, the relationship between class and ethnicity was the basis for all three. Initially, capitalism and class were conceived of as a force and a social dynamic that remained exterior to a bounded and homogeneous Cajun "society." Since Cajuns, by (the orthodox) definition that I was using, share the same class position, the practices of labor exchange and running Mardi Gras would overlap and involve the same people, and there would be a one-to-one relationship between class and ethnic culture. So, for example, there were two exceptional characteristics about the field site, Lower Mamou Prairie, or 'Tit Mamou, in Acadia Parish, which I expected would help explain something important about the reproduction of Cajun culture.[2] According to the literature, the 'Tit Mamou Mardi Gras run was one of the only runs that has never stopped occurring, continuing through the 1960s and 1970s when all other carnival traditions on the prairies subsided. It was also the only instance where the canal irrigation system, an important means of production in rice agriculture, was owned for a long period by a group of local farmers. Was an egalitarian culture of labor exchange so strong in this area that it had led to a kind of collective ownership of property? Was Mardi Gras the symbolic expression and practical renewal of these unusually symmetrical economic relationships? The project proposal I defended before leaving Québec promised a thesis demonstrating convincing links between the material and symbolic realms, and thereby revealing profound secrets of a persistent Cajun identity amid the mounting inequalities of industrial agriculture.

Methodologically, however, the research was set up in such a way as to work against this characterization, and it made for a rude awakening. Operationalizing class as an important variable translated into seeking out interviewees from across the class spectrum, and paying close attention to the class position of each interviewee—the size of their farms, how much equipment and land they owned, the kind of crops they grew, and if they participated in Mardi Gras. It wasn't long before the responses of interlocutors to my queries called my theorization of class and ethnicity into question. In interviews with retirees, there was a clear division between those who made the transition to large-scale rice farming after World War II, and went on to farm most or all of their lives, and those who left small farms in the decades following the war, often moving on to wage labor offshore or in nearby towns. To my surprise, they all described a two-tiered system of labor exchange that existed at mid-century, one for transactions between larger farmers, and the other for exchange between large farmers and small farmers. The former system was more or less egalitarian, but the latter arrangement clearly benefited the more capital-intensive operators, and in effect contributed to the impoverishment of small-scale producers.

When the subject turned to Mardi Gras, a similar split was evident. Larger farmers (with a notable exception) rarely if ever participated in the runs, and were often bemused by or indifferent to its recent rise in popularity. The small producers, meanwhile, participated more regularly in Mardi Gras, and, in some cases, came from families who ran for generations. From these came stories about their immense enjoyment of running, but also about a certain edge to the practical joking, and, most unexpectedly, about a spike in carnivalesque theft and vandalism that briefly interrupted the event in the early 1960s. As Paul, a longtime participant and observer, put it, "Sometimes it was just a joke, but people held grudges against each other, too."

Before I was halfway through my stay in 'Tit Mamou, then, the theses orienting my fieldwork had collapsed. Slightly panicked, I faxed an update to committee members in Québec, seeking advice and reassurance. The shock was more than intellectual: instead of the idyllic agrarian bonhomie that I had expected to embrace as a font of personal and collective identity, there was a fractured and fractious collectivity, all the more puzzling given the relatively small size of the place. The latent contradictions in my understanding were brought out in what people were telling me; their differing perspectives on what it meant to exchange labor or run Mardi Gras far exceeded the culturalist notions I was using to hold them all together in a single frame. Reflecting as I continued to interview and transcribe conversations, it dawned on me that class had profoundly shaped social relations in the countryside, so much so that even Mardi Gras, the supposedly quintessential ritual of ethnic unity, had to be rethought in different terms.

Another challenge, methodological as well as ethical and political, emerged in and through the practice of "participant observation." While the debate on ethnographic method, particularly as it relates to questions of reflexivity and representation in the wake of postmodern critique, has become voluminous and can only be referenced here (e.g., Marcus & Fischer 1986), suffice it to say that engagement with such issues is crucial for the future of ethnography. For example, as Castaneda (1996) has pointed out, there is something contradictory if not "scandalous" about the way ethical and political considerations are articulated in a methodological code of conduct for ethnographic research. That is, the logic of the rules governing contact with "informants" produces a kind of myth of a simultaneous presence and absence of the fieldworker. On the one hand, techniques of neutrality, nonintervention, and objectivity are supposed to prevent fieldwork from having any immediate effect, deleterious or otherwise, on the local population. On the other hand, however, there is the more or less explicit desire that the ethnographic intervention produce a "positive aftereffect" for the good of the collectivity in the long term, typically through a copy of the study presented back to the community. What is obscured in these formulas is the inescapably political nature of ethnographic contact, how the very notion of research carries with it an ethics and a politics that cannot but influence and shape its "subject."[3]

This paradox, and the potential dilemmas that it contains and partially submerges, became very explicit issues for me in the course of fieldwork and beyond. Though I didn't understand them at the time, some of

my interlocutors recounted episodes indicating just how complicitous ethnography has been in the construction of Mardi Gras as a symbol of Cajun
identity. At a discursive level, they often explained rural carnival as classical
anthropologists might have. Uncannily reproducing much of what has been
written by local academics (e.g., Ancelet 1989a), they often spoke of carnival
as a kind of timeless Durkheimian ritual that reestablishes social unity, even
as it functions as a "safety valve" for pent-up social steam. Just as importantly, though, they described their practical experience in ways suggesting
that Mardi Gras is a very complex cultural product, co-constructed by locals
and "visitors" through a thick history of appropriation, collaboration, dispute, exchange, intervention, and subsidy. So, for example, Carson, a man in
his late fifties who was involved in promoting the 'Tit Mamou Mardi Gras
run, spoke generally to me of his experience over the last few decades:

> I was seeing more and more that people were coming, and I wasn't the
> only one, there was a bunch of folks who saw that there. There were
> people coming from Massachusetts, and, oh, California, and every
> where to hear the music. And they were telling us, a bunch of these
> people were saying to me, "You have such a fine culture here, you are
> lucky that you belong to good families, that you are still people who
> know each other. Us, we live in big cities. We have a number on our
> houses, a number on our cars, a number where we work, a number
> everywhere. We're just numbers. We're nothing else but Americans.
> We can't say that we have a family or a culture that we can identify
> with." And so, more and more, we're hearing people say that, . . . in the
> beginning, it was like, let's say, it was as if . . . it was right there in front
> of us, and we could hardly see that it was true.

Though he would perhaps not agree with this interpretation, to my ears
he is describing the dialogical, reflexive, even "postmodern" conditions
in which "Cajun culture" is currently produced, undermining notions of
culture and identity as bounded and homogeneous, even as he implicates
us—ethnographers, musicians, tourists—in this process of cultural production. Furthermore, in terms of the methodological and political issues being
raised, Carson's statement suggests that a positivist stance toward the study
of this phenomenon can be problematic, for it will obscure one of its crucial aspects—namely, effects of the interaction between ethnographer and
ethnographee.

In the articulation of ethnographic practice and text, I didn't succeed in avoiding this pitfall. Following the fundamental methodological prescription for ethnographers, I became an active participant and observer during carnival season in 1995. I was not only a masked runner on carnival day, but sought opportunities to contribute to the successful realization of Mardi Gras, such as participating in the workday when the carnival trailer was assembled. I also became involved with the folklife festival in Iota that is affiliated with the carnival, locating images for a brochure and translating festival signs into French. Yet the thesis, following the positivist paradigm prevalent in the Marxist anthropology I read, studiously avoided mentioning, much less problematizing, my presence in the field. Thus, questions of how my participation had helped produce the very event that I'd come to study, and of the effect this had on the "knowledge" it produced, were left unaddressed.

This does not mean that these questions weren't preoccupations. By the time I left 'Tit Mamou, I was somewhat conflicted about the direction my fieldwork findings were pointing. I followed early hints of discord to learn that there was a heated dispute over the inauguration of the folklife festival in the late 1980s, to the point that for a time thereafter, two Mardi Gras runs, each one claiming to be more "traditional" than the other, existed side-by-side. The conflict was the culmination of years of struggle among participants over the meaning and practice of carnival, and it broke down largely along class lines. Taken together with the deepening divisions in agricultural production described to me by contemporary farmers, it appeared that social class—not culturalist notions of community or ethnicity—needed to be foregrounded to explain the trajectory of these aspects of social life. Yet how could I write critically of these dynamics when I had contributed to their reproduction through participant observation? And since my own self-fashioning was a part of the research project, how was I to interpret this unexpected lack of cohesive and homogeneous origins suitable for grounding an identity?

As Lederman points out, ethnographic writing is a practice in which we live our sometimes conflicted links to the "two worlds" we straddle: that of our relationships with interlocutors "in the field" and the one composed of interlocutors in the academy. She refers to writing as "a tangible sign" of "our sociable connections in two directions," and "to the extent that our two worlds are distinct, our loyalties are divided, and we may feel compromised" (Lederman 1990:88). To this I would add that the solutions we construct to this dilemma—in other words, our politics of ethnographic writing—are made possible by the multiple (dis)locations that comprise our position. Writing as critically as I did was made easier by the distance between my relationships on campus in Quebec City, where I returned to draft the thesis, and those I established in 'Tit Mamou. Committee members and fellow students at Laval provided feedback on and support for the basic orientation of my analysis, which I gradually realized would not correspond to the interpretation of some interviewees. As part of a return to "my roots," everything produced at Laval was written in French, which meant, ironically, that few if any of my interlocutors would read my thesis. Despite this extra buffer, which I expected would limit the negative repercussions of my work, I was uncertain enough about the text's impact to extend to the whole community the anonymity I'd promised to individuals.

At the same time, I considered the thesis as the recovery of a forgotten and ignored social history of the prairies, one which told a more adequate and complex story about the region's past and present, and which gave voice to a group—those petits habitants and their working-class descendants—whose position has largely been misrepresented or silenced. As Patricia Sawin (n.d.) suggests, a common sense about this past has become hegemonic, through distinct yet interwoven efforts of regional academics, middle-class boosters, local and national media, and governmental agencies promoting folklore and heritage tourism. Bracketing momentarily the question of how desirable or productive my (or any other) "counter-history" might be, the decision—which means the capacity of being able to decide—to occupy multiple locations is apparently a condition for this kind of work. Taking advantage of the distance opened up by occupying a position on the margins of local life, I abandoned my quest for an authentic Cajun self, shifting my allegiance to what I saw as the "betrayed" working classes on the prairies (David 1996:148).

A strategy of movement, shifting identification, and selective linking of the two worlds of ethnographic production is not without its dilemmas and problems, however, as I experienced several years later. In 1998, I decided to participate in a public debate in 'Tit Mamou and Iota over the use of blackface by Mardi Gras runners. Though race was not a primary focus of the thesis, I had noted that local claims of blackface's innocuous character did not hold up under scrutiny.[4] For example, some carnivalesque skits reproduce stereotypes which African Americans find offensive, particularly a version of a "dead man revived" (see Ancelet, Edwards, & Pitre 1991:85), in which a reveler who feigns death is "resurrected" when the *négresse* lifts "her" dress and squats over his face. During fieldwork in 1997, I also noticed an alternative Mardi Gras festival (which, I later learned, emerged after interracial disagreement) in Iota's small black neighborhood. Some locals, maintaining that blackface represents an amusing and harmless aspect of Mardi Gras, targeted Iota's Catholic priest, who initiated the discussion of blackface among parishioners, for removal from the church parish. In the campaign to persuade the local Catholic bishop to transfer the pastor, the festival's chief organizer solicited assistance from selected ethnographers who had worked in the area, asking them to write letters explaining blackface's inoffensive traditional roots.[5] I sent an unsolicited letter to the bishop, endorsing the need for debate over blackface, and pointing out that recent public subsidies for the carnival came with conditions of inclusivity and nondiscrimination. After the letter was read from the pulpit by the embattled cleric (without my prior knowledge or consent), the perils of my approach to fieldwork and writing became manifest. Both locals and their academic supporters were understandably upset—the reference to public responsibilities implied the possibility of legal action—and I was threatened with sanction by an anthropologist colleague under the discipline's code of ethics.[6]

By the late 1990s, a spate of incidents in which blacks were excluded from participating in Cajun activities—including one at the nearby Eunice Mardi Gras—indicated that racial formation was in play at South Louisiana spectacles, and merited ethnographic attention.[7] The inauguration of a separate black Mardi Gras festival in Iota suggested that it was becoming an explicit issue there as well, and I wanted to explore how various people explained and understood what was happening. Though carnivals, festivals, and tourist spectacles have received considerable attention from ethnographers (e.g., Ancelet 1989a; Esman 1982; Le Menestrel 1999; Ware 1994), such events are yet to be explored as sites in which racial difference is performed and (re)produced. Spitzer (1986:511) alone suggests that while Cajun and Creole Mardi Gras runs, though historically segregated, are practically speaking quite similar in form, each nonetheless results in the production of distinct cultural and moral meanings, and comments on the other in the process. Mardi Gras blackface, as a carnivalesque practice in which race is made visible and performed in what amount to racially "pure" spaces, hints at this. That is, though the nègre and négresse are numerically insignificant (e.g., in 'Tit Mamou, only two Mardi Gras dressed as blacks among dozens and dozens), they are symbolically quite important (the blackface couple leads the troupe and serves as foil of much carnivalesque play). To explore these issues more fully, I continued to spend time in 'Tit Mamou and Iota during brief holiday and summer trips, in anticipation of returning there for doctoral fieldwork. Beginning in the summer of 1997, I pursued a strategy of renewing exchanges with white interlocutors and increasing my contact with local blacks, discussing questions of race and Mardi Gras with all of them.

While it may be tempting to see the letters written to the bishop (mine along with those of other academics) as "extracurricular" interventions on our parts, such a view ignores the tradition of ethnographic complicity in the construction of culture. In other words, that locals would immediately seek assistance from academics in such a dispute, and that we would quickly oblige them, speaks again to the thick history of appropriation and collaboration that can typify the relationship between us and our interlocutors in representing culture to ourselves and others. My own letter was an attempt to engage and participate in this complicity, that is, to intervene with and for some interlocutors in an exchange about the nature of culture. Noting the racializing character of carnival skits, the run and the festival's civic responsibility incurred through the acceptance of public funding, and the troubling regional trend of race-based exclusion in public events, the letter supported the need for public debate about blackface, and sought to complicate the conventional view of Mardi Gras as an apolitical space (e.g., Ancelet 1989a; n.d.; see David 1996:95, 130–144).

Though I fully intended to express my opinions "publicly" (i.e., to the bishop as he reviewed the request to remove the parish priest), I never imagined that the priest would read a copy of the letter to parishioners during Sunday Mass. As a former seminarian, I am still perplexed as to how its narration was integrated into a liturgical event. From my perspective, this represented an inappropriate use of the letter, for combining my anthropological viewpoint with theological disapproval in the context of a religious service risked "moralizing" these issues in a way that I sought (and still seek) to avoid. Those who felt interpellated by it reacted with alarm and dismay, and my attempts to explain and apologize to them have met with skepticism, if not rebuke. Called "a political correctness man run amuck" by one local, my status as "race traitor" and persona non grata has been reiterated several times since then.

In addition to alienating some of my interlocutors—people with whom I disagree, but whom I respect—I have much to regret here, particularly my poor decisions to intervene without understanding the full context (e.g., the litigious atmosphere that prevailed), and to ally myself straightforwardly with the local priest. At the same time, the general approach that I followed, in terms of its methodology and its politics (i.e., interviews and participant observation with socially diverse interlocutors, follow-up questions on points raised by different groups, and intervention in a forum where academics with similar credentials weighed in), seems sound with respect to the issue in question. Yet clearly, this was not enough to ensure that the relationships I forged through fieldwork remained intact. If this were the objective, what else would need to be taken into account?

First, as I have been arguing implicitly all along, there is a need to problematize the relationship between ethnographer and his/her "publics," including interlocutors, readers, students, and those who would use our research for overt social or political ends. Perhaps the most important way of doing this is to acknowledge both the complicities and the antagonisms that our presence in the field creates, and to modify accordingly our relationship to objectivist and positivist models of narration and research. Not that we abandon vigorous pursuit of methodological or theoretical precision, but that we seek the same vigorous precision when it comes to theorizing our own positions, our biases, the constraints and contradictions of our institutional affiliations, and our political (in the broadest sense of the term) agendas. In this particular context, I translate this to mean forgoing ethnographic descriptions that efface the relations of power in which ethnographic knowledge is produced, and avoiding an objectivist voice that obscures the partial and situated space of observation and critique. And so rewriting these encounters reflexively is an attempt to articulate this kind of accountable and situated ethnographic practice, even as I recognize the unresolved breakdown of communication and exchange which prompts it.

At the same time, there is a corresponding need to reconceptualize the context in which we operate (i.e., the field). I have quoted Lederman's characterization of the field as a conflicting set of relationships in order to evoke the nexus connecting ethnographer and interlocutors, but it is equally valid to extend it to interlocutors understood as a group. When our questions address social relations in spaces that are differentiated by class, gender, or race—as my fieldwork suggests, this is the case even in "small" places like 'Tit Mamou—the relationships that constitute them are not unified, homogeneous, or consensual in any conventional sense. This has unavoidable implications for ethnographic research, requiring fieldwork strategies that anticipate and adjust to being identified as an individual whose particular affiliations, interests, and resources can be interpreted on a scale ranging from benign to threatening. The point is that a research agenda that engages questions of social difference makes an ethnographic politics of conciliatory

presence with all interlocutors implausible, if not impossible. As Le Menestrel (1999:123—124) notes, these issues are all the more difficult to negotiate
in South Louisiana when it comes to race, since skin color and the social
characteristics attributed to it open some doors and close others. Moreover,
to discuss explicitly issues of racial difference and race relations is often to
find oneself more or less immediately engaged in discourse that has a dis-
tinctly ethical bent, as it often involves judgments of moral blame and culpa-
bility (Frankenberg 1997:18). This racial "logic of the trial" (Wacquant 1997)
makes asking questions about race difficult, and coupled with a strategy of
"studying up," it has the potential to raise the issue of the ethnographer's
"loyalty" (cf. Castaneda 1996:27). When this is the case—as it was when I
represented the views of black interlocutors—there is a need for a model of
ethnographic engagement that takes conflict and dispute into account.

Finally, I would argue that the recent episodes of exclusion referenced
above challenge ethnographers working in the region to explore the relationship between the cultural politics of representation, racial formation,
and everyday practices of exclusion and hierarchy. Such projects will
necessarily require us to diversify our contacts, and to confront the issue
of the "scandalous" ethnographic fantasy of simultaneous presence and
absence. In the context of the controversy over blackface, the need, simply
put, is to find ways to become present to interlocutors of the "other" race.
This is an important methodological and political move, but one that is
made all too infrequently. My experience suggests that there are real cultural and social barriers to making this move, yet it also seems restricted
by a model of ethnographer as engaged and sympathetic advocate for a
single group. The difficulty with this model is that it is underwritten by
a highly selective interviewing strategy, which, by limiting interaction to
those who share a taken-for-granted common sense, allows one to construct a unified ethnographic self unproblematically present to a homogeneous Other. When it comes to questions of race relations and racial
representation, the limits of this strategy, of identifying straightforwardly
with a single Other, become clear.

To use one example: Lindahl, writing recently about the troubling
effects of the blackface dispute for Cajuns in Iota and nearby Basile, suggests that folklorists offer an important tool for "find[ing] a way through
this thicket of warring perceptions." It is "to listen to, repeat, and valorize the
accounts of older [white] community members, who remember times during which Mardi Gras and daily life were both less segregated than they currently are . . . and both Cajun and Creole [i.e., black] communities achieved
mutual respect from shared experience" (2001:252). Interviewing residents

just south of Basile, I, too, encountered whites who expressed this view, for at mid-century there was a large number of black farmers and tenants in the area (see Spitzer 1986). However, when I visited the last African American farmer on Lower Mamou Prairie—a woman who'd retired a decade earlier, after her husband passed away—a decidedly different understanding of "that" past and present was articulated. On the day I showed up, the woman's younger sister was visiting from out of state. The following are excerpts from my field notes:

> [These women] belong to a black family that has lived in this area for generations. . . . They recount an episode in which their grand-father was tricked out of his land by signing papers that, contrary to the stated purpose, stripped him of ownership. They mention that a similar event occurred to their parents. It seems that someone was watching the tax records at the courthouse, seizing the opportunity to claim property when tax payments were not up to date. The family was able to hire a lawyer and avoid the chicanery when the threat of loss occurred the second time. . . . After a while, I began to ask the younger sister questions about her life in Southern California. Of the twelve siblings, only her older sister remains in Louisiana, all others having moved to Texas or the West Coast. When I asked how she found race relations in California as compared to Louisiana, she said that there was a difference, and that it pertained mostly to the enforcement of laws. If "they push it too far" in California, racist discrimination can be fought in the courts, whereas in the South, they "don't even know the laws." She made several comments to the effect that she simply could not tolerate the status quo of race relations in Louisiana, and had left the state for good at an early age. [IV 25/13 April 1995]

With respect both to blackface in particular and to issues of race in general, it is the authorized absence of this view of daily life that sanctions an uncomplicated ethnographic presence. Conversely, if one decides to take this perspective seriously, that is, to let it influence the entire breadth of research activity, from theorizing and methodology to fieldwork practice and writing, then a clear-cut and trouble-free ethics and politics of fieldwork is no longer possible. Instead, one faces the challenge of describing social contradictions, the fractures that cannot be sutured by recourse to consensual categories like that of community. To repeat the claim that blackface is offensive, as I have done here, is to attempt to represent something of the antagonism that I encountered in the field, and thereby make it available for evaluation and critique. Yet it is also an intervention that labels the social field, and, as such, attempts to transform it—just as it was when some of my interlocutors made the claim to me. In deciding to reproduce it, I take up a position—inevitably partial—in the open and ongoing contest that is racial formation in South Louisiana. At the same time, because ethnography involves presence, there is also the challenge of remaining accountable to diverse if not divergent interlocutors. Writing about adherence to ethical principles in the understated style of the English academy, Barnes (1977:39–40) suggests why this can be so difficult:

> The counsels of perfection that may be appropriate and applicable when a social scientist studies citizens similar to himself, with the same values and assumptions, and similarly placed in relation to power and resources, may be inappropriate and inapplicable when there is a great cultural gap between the parties or where there is a great disparity, one way or the other, between them in terms of power to articulate and defend their interests.

To address ethnographically differences of class, race, and gender is to attempt to negotiate the "disparities" of this "gap," to take (and perhaps to shift) positions, to abandon the security that comes with studying "citizens similar to himself [sic]," and to risk being found wanting by one or the other "party." It is to make hard and responsible decisions about which questions to ask, which people to seek out and engage, and which words to write. It is to learn and practice an ethnographic politics of alliance, assertion, and apology.

CONCLUSION

This intervention and its aftermath, along with the fieldwork and writing preceding them, have become the basis for the reconsideration of ethnographic practice that I have attempted to elaborate. For reasons I have tried to illustrate—the way in which (a partial and contested) knowledge emerges from the ethnographic encounter, the historical complicity of ethnography in the construction of culture and identity, and the irreducibly political character of the ethnographic intervention as such—a positivist voice which denies ethnographic presence no longer seems to me a viable option. Thus, in this brief reprise of my master's thesis and what followed, I have retold the story, emphasizing the critical, partial, and situated complicity and engagement of my own agency as ethnographer, which were invisible in the monograph. I offer it as a modest experiment in ethnography that is more accountable, locatable, and responsible, and as a down payment on future explorations of a "positioned rationality" (Haraway 1991:196).

In this retelling, I have emphasized the split and shifting positions occupied by this ethnographic Self, along with the emergent desire to tell a "better" story about the cultural dimensions of social life in South Louisiana. Though the experience of debating blackface may seem to suggest otherwise, these are characteristics that I share with many interlocutors, and together they provide a prompt for and a possibility of ethnography that is both collaborative and critical. This, too, is a commitment and a hope carried forward into new projects. For while the excerpt from my encounter with the sisters suggests how tightly circumscribed agency can be within the space constructed for "blacks," I would also argue that, in a way that is decidedly less insidious and pervasive, constrictions also exist in the case of "Cajuns" and their "traditions." In response to a question about how Mardi Gras has changed over the years, Paul said to me:

> Used to, we'd run, the regulars, you know, and it was all people you knew. And you'd go to places, you knew everybody out there, you knew who could pick, who to pick at. *A qui tu pourrais faire la misère et tout ça. Là*, but now, you running in front of the whole state, the United States, and some of the world. That's how it is. You running, you don't know half of the people. And you don't know if they there to have fun, or just to watch and see how stupid you are. So, there's a lot of difference. . . . If you go to one of those strangers and do something, it might offend them. You got to watch it.

Watch it, indeed.

NOTES

The research project which provided the inspiration for these reflections was funded by a Merit Scholarship from the Québec Ministry of Education. I am grateful to Catherine Lutz, Patricia Sawin, and the editors for their comments and suggestions on various versions of the text.

1. Something of what is being referred to here is captured in Gold's (e.g., 1980) detailed and underappreciated work, in which differences of age, class, and structures of feeling appear clearly within and across the neighborhoods of Mamou.

2. The summary that follows, including the citations (using pseudonyms) from interviews, is drawn from David (1996).

3. I am not suggesting that the minimalist safeguards of human subjects research protocols to "do no harm" should be abandoned. Rather, I am saying that these protocols do not and cannot secure the "nonimpact" which we sometimes claim they do. Thus, an engaged and vigorous ethnographic ethics must go well beyond the foundation that minimalist protocols provide.

4. See David (1996:101). In her dissertation, Ware (1994:21) notes that the *nègre* and *négresse* were based on the racially indeterminate *paillasses*, or Mardi Gras clowns, and only emerged in 'Tit Mamou during the 1940s and 1950s—the height of Jim Crow in South Louisiana.

5. For a view on the blackface controversy that is different from my own, see Lindahl (2001), whose introduction nevertheless suggests that professional peers of South Louisiana folklorists also have difficulty accepting this ahistorical explanation.

6. Given that both sides in this dispute had already raised the specter of litigation, I now recognize this was indeed a careless thing for me to say. My general point was (and is) that blackface is not an innocuous and momentary irruption of the past into the present, but rather a fully contemporary event, with potential social repercussions.

7. For a brief summary of these events, see Le Menestrel (1999:373–376).

REFERENCES

Ancelet, Barry Jean. 1989a. *"Capitaine, voyage ton flag": The Traditional Cajun Country Mardi Gras.* Lafayette: Center for Louisiana Studies.

———. 1989b. "Mardi Gras and the Media: Who's Fooling Whom?" *Southern Folklore* 46, pp. 211–219.

———. 1992a "Cultural Tourism in Cajun Country: Shotgun Wedding or Marriage Made in Heaven?" *Southern Folklore* 49, pp. 256—266.

———. n.d. "Playing the Other: Ritual Role Reversal in the South Louisiana Country Mardi Gras." Unpublished manuscript presented at the American Folklore Society annual meeting. Jacksonville, October 1992.

Ancelet, Barry Jean, Jay D. Edwards, & Glen Pitre. 1991. *Cajun Country.* Jackson: University Press of Mississippi.

Barnes, J. A. 1977. *The Ethics of Inquiry in Social Science: Three Lectures.* Delhi: Oxford University Press.

Castaneda, Quetzil. 1996. *In the Museum of Maya Culture: Touring Chichen Itza.* Minneapolis: University of Minnesota Press.

Clifford, James. 1988. *The Predicament of Culture: Twentieth-Century Ethnography, Literature, and Art.* Cambridge: Harvard University Press.

David, Marc. 1996. "Riziculture et Mardi Gras: L'organisation du travail et le carnaval rural dans la petite production marchande en Louisiane. Le cas de la Prairie du Chêne, 1933–1995." Master's thesis. Sainte-Foy: Université Laval.

Esman, Marjorie. 1982. "Festivals, Change and Unity: The Celebration of Ethnic Identity among Louisiana Cajuns." *Anthropological Quarterly* 55(4), pp. 199–210.

——. 1985. *Henderson, Louisiana: Cultural Adaptation in a Cajun Community*. New York: Holt, Rinehart and Winston.

Fabian, Johannes. 1983. *Time and the Other: How Anthropology Makes Its Object*. New York: Columbia University Press.

——. 1991. "Ethnographic Objectivity Revisited: From Rigor to Vigor." *Annals of Scholarship* 8, pp. 381–408.

——. 1996. *Remembering the Present: Painting and Popular History in Zaire*. Berkeley: University of California Press.

Frankenberg, Ruth. 1997. "Introduction: Local Whitenesses, Localizing Whiteness." In *Displacing Whiteness: Essays in Social and Cultural Criticism*. Ruth Frankenberg, ed. Durham, NC: Duke University Press, pp. 1–34.

Gold, Gerald. 1980. "The Changing Criteria of Social Networks in a Cajun Community." *Ethnos* 1–2, pp. 60–81.

Gutierrez, C. Paige. 1992. *Cajun Foodways*. Jackson: University Press of Mississippi.

Haraway, Donna. 1991. *Simians, Cyborgs, and Women: The Reinvention of Nature*. New York: Routledge.

Jones, Delmos. 1995. "Anthropology and the Oppressed: A Reflection on 'Native' Anthropology." In *Insider Anthropology*. E. L. Cerroni-Long, ed. Arlington, VA: American Anthropological Association, pp. 58–70.

Lederman, Rena. 1990. "Pretexts for Ethnography: On Reading Fieldnotes." In *Fieldnotes: The Making of Anthropology*. Roger Sanjek, ed. Ithaca, NY: Cornell University Press, pp. 71–91.

Le Menestrel, Sara. 1999. *La voie des Cadiens: Tourisme et identité en Louisiane*. Paris: Belin.

Lindahl, Carl. 2001. "A Note on Blackface." *Journal of American Folklore* 114(452), 248–254.

Marcus, George E., & Michael M. J. Fischer. 1986. *Anthropology as Cultural Critique: An Experimental Moment in the Human Sciences*. Chicago: University of Chicago Press.

Mire, Pat [Director]. 1993. *Dance for a Chicken: The Cajun Mardi Gras*. 57 min., 16 mm., color. Eunice, LA: Attakapas Productions.

Narayan, Kirin. 1993. "How Native is a 'Native' Anthropologist?" *American Anthropologist* 95(4), pp. 671–686.

Ortner, Sherry B. 1991. "Reading America: Preliminary Notes on Class and Culture." In *Recapturing Anthropology: Working in the Present*. Richard Fox, ed. Santa Fe, NM: School of American Research Press, pp. 163–189.

Sawin, Patricia. n.d. "Woman, Outsider, Traitor: Feminist Fieldwork in Southwest Louisiana and the Contribution of Partial Perspectives." Unpublished manuscript.

Spitzer, Nicholas R. 1986. "Zydeco and Mardi Gras: Creole Identity and Performance Genres in Rural French Louisiana." Dissertation. Austin: University of Texas.

Turner, Allan. 2001. "Once-fading Cajun Becomes All the Rage." *Houston Chronicle* 7 (October), 25A.

Wacquant, Loic. 1997. "For an Analytic of Racial Domination." *Political Power and Social Theory* 11, pp. 221–234.

Ware, Carolyn. 1994. "Reading the Rules Backward: Women and the Rural Cajun Mardi Gras." Dissertation. Philadelphia: University of Pennsylvania.

6. TOURIST AND "CAJUN FROM FRANCE"

The Shifting Identity of the Anthropologist

—Sara Le Menestrel

I had never been to the United States before discovering Louisiana, nor did I ever feel particularly attracted to it. On the contrary, the image I had was rather negative, fueled by a rough idea of North America as the symbol of imperialism, capitalism, and a consumer society. Nevertheless, frustrated by an education in dead languages which had marginalized me throughout my school years, my motivation to learn English was boundless. I had heard about the efficiency of English as a Second Language programs, and decided to go spend a summer in an American university offering one. My choice of Louisiana was pragmatic: Tulane University in New Orleans was surprisingly among the least expensive programs. Besides, a friend of mine convinced me to take this opportunity to go visit his godfather in Lafayette. After five weeks in New Orleans, nothing had prepared me to encounter a francophone culture. The French Quarter was only faintly reminiscent of a French presence, and our time out on weekends had mostly made me familiar with jazz clubs, Po'Boys, and N'awlins Yat speech pattern.

Consequently, I arrived in Lafayette without any expectations. My host generously drove me around the area, first to imposing plantation homes, then to one of Lafayette's two living history museums, Vermilionville. It made me aware of the existence of the Acadians and the society they developed in eighteenth- and nineteenth-century Louisiana. But the interpreters in period dress and the re-created houses made this visit to a journey into

A meshing of roles. Anthropologist and fiddler Sara Le Menestrel (second from left) performs with her France-based Cajun band Chicane in Erath, LA (2000) in celebration of friend and colleague Dana David's birthday and newly awarded Ph.D. degree. They are joined by acclaimed Cajun songwriter and guitar player, D. L. Menard, present in person (third from left) as a neighbor and in image as a cultural icon painted on the backdrop mural. From left to right: Serge Buisson, Sara Le Menestrel, D. L. Menard, Roger Géa, and Sophie Larribe.

the past, not a discovery of a contemporary culture. However, numerous advertisements of festivals, which claimed to offer the unique experience of Cajun joie de vivre, caught my attention. I became quite curious about these unknown French descendants, and since my graduate program in ethnology required some fieldwork, I decided to go back and study Cajun festivals for three months.

SEEKING LEGITIMACY

The first festival that I attended was the Cattle Festival in Abbeville, south of Lafayette. The selection of the queen, the school dance clubs, and the parade of cars with advertising did not seem particularly typical of the area. The alligator skin that covered one of the royalties' thrones seemed a poor touch of local color. No speech was given in French, and the typical Cajun food announced was restricted to a few local specialties along with hamburgers, waffles, and ice cream. The craft booths honored the coming of

Halloween, and a few "Cajun novelties" gave an image of the locals as happy-go-lucky, dedicating their lives to good times. I wrote a bitter postcard to my thesis adviser, warning her that my quest for authentic Cajun culture in festivals might be in vain.

Discouraged by this initial conclusion, I tried to find solace among local scholars. I had heard of Jacques Henry and thought he might have mercy on a compatriot. Hurricane Andrew had just swept through the region and I told him about the alternative of studying ways locals dealt with this natural disaster now and in the past, since previous hurricanes had severely devastated Louisiana. "Would you rather spend your days interviewing elderly people, or go out and watch festive events?" he asked, seemingly aware of the necessity to palliate my indecision with a stereotyped presentation of two possible fieldwork projects. This feedback had an immediate impact on me. Since that time, I have always felt welcome to turn to him for a productive dialogue and an attentive ear, all much needed by the outsider anthropologist, especially a novice.

I soon realized that being French, moreover Parisian, was not really an asset in this francophone region. Over the centuries Cajuns have endured the prejudiced view of French officials and visitors, its most recent expression being the ethnocentrism often shown by French teachers working for the Council for the Development of French in Louisiana (CODOFIL). I could easily imagine how I sometimes aroused suspicion. The object of my research amplified this feeling, since it might be viewed as an attempt to expose the decay of Louisiana French culture through the enhancement of its commodification. I can still picture myself mumbling I was from France, strongly wishing my interlocutors would stop asking me such questions. I have to admit I long dreaded the discovery of my Parisian origins, aware of the various corollaries of this revelation (arrogance, condescension, stuffiness), an attitude quite ironic for an anthropologist interested in the identity building process. For a long time, I tended to downplay my origins hoping to compensate for the distance that they appeared to create. I realized later on that this was neither a tenable nor a healthy stance.

The trust shown by some local scholars, students, and activists was invaluable to me because it was a recognition of my ability to develop an acceptable analysis of a culture that was not mine. They deemed my work to be legitimate despite my outsider status, my cultural background, and my lack of experience in their field. Being open to exchange ideas with a foreign scholar can be positive for both parties. In the dialogue, the former finds a relief to its loneliness and wanderings, while the latter can take this opportunity to reconsider his own reflection with the outsider gaze shedding a new light on its own society.

My feeling of loneliness was not only related to the field. In French academia, my subject was not high among the most legitimate objects of research. While tourism has progressively found favor in anthropologists' eyes since the 1970s, it was still viewed as a marginal research topic. Other than through my readings, I did not have the opportunity to get direct suggestions or assistance from anthropologists familiar with this particular area. The image of Cajuns increased this isolation. Informal conversations and even sometimes comments in academic settings revealed a perception of a "folkloric" (in a pejorative meaning commonly used in French) group whose identity was more expressed through staged performance than through actual social practices. In addition to this assumption of Cajuns as actors in a fantasized Cajunland, many researchers, including specialists of North American studies, did not consider this ethnic group as a true minority since they were not part of Affirmative Action programs. Similarly, some American researchers did not show much interest in my work since it was not based on an instrumental approach to ethnicity with a focus on political function. The futility assigned to my topic actually appeared to spill over to Cajuns themselves. As they would find out about my research, some who still dreaded stigmatization by claiming to be Cajun just laughed without making any comment. It sometimes appeared as Cajuns indeed did not deserve to be the topic of academic research.

BEYOND THE GOOD TIMES

This view proved to be shortsighted. I realized that my first impression of the Cattle Festival had to be interpreted differently. The last wagon of the parade had no other ornamentation than the sign of the "Cajun Culture Association." Hesitating for a while, I finally ran after it to ask the few individuals standing there for their phone numbers. It is telling that my first relationship with Cajuns started in a typical tourist venue.

This encounter proved to be pivotal to my fieldwork. This group of people opened their houses and shared their culture without reservation. Through them, I discovered its consistency and vitality, and understood how what is performed for tourists is not restricted to distorted reality but is invested with genuine meaning by the performers.

Since the 1970s, Cajuns have been the object of intense promotion through tourism, the result of both the rehabilitation of their culture after a long period of derision and the need to diversify a regional economy devastated by the oil crisis of the mid-1980s. The Louisiana French want to take advantage of this popularity, thus conferring on tourism a vital role in the group's self-awareness. At the state level, activists with the French Movement strove to develop tourism, perceived as an asset in the revitalization of the French language. In rural communities, individuals of French descent devoted themselves to the promotion of local culture, determined to enhance it and encourage its perpetuation.

The establishment of a tourism policy lies at the heart of conflicts of power and reveals social and racial divisions. Long overshadowed by Cajuns in the tourism market, Black Creoles have begun to mobilize in order to assert their distinct identity. The admitted existence of cultural traits common to Creoles and Cajuns is not sufficient to attenuate the racial divide that separates the two groups. Notwithstanding these conflicts, tourism also represents a way to strengthen social ties in rural communities and moreover contributes to the construction of a positive identity. By presenting the group's history and traditions, tourism reinforces its collective memory. It leads to the creation of *lieux de mémoire* (places of memory) which emphasize its tenacity, its resistance over the centuries, and its ability to adapt. While the ethnic revival feeds cultural tourism, the latter ascribes to the group an appeal and an economic value which boosts its pride and legitimizes its worth.

Overall, the stereotyped vision of tourism as inherently spurious and a threat to traditional cultures proved to be irrelevant in the context of Louisiana. The internalization of the tourist image, the divergent interpretations of the notions of authenticity and tradition within the group, the attempts of some individuals to control its attribution, the meaning assigned to touristic places, and the interaction between tourists and local residents are among the many signs of compromise that takes place between the frontstage and the backstage (Le Menestrel 1999).

INFORMANTS IN CONSTANT PUBLIC DEMAND

While the theme of my research made me realize that the distinction between the tourist stage and reality was definitely not as clear-cut as first thought, I became aware of similar overlaps between the statuses of anthropologists and other visitors. Now that the fields of anthropological work are easily accessible, we are more likely to be confused with other people willing to increase their knowledge about local culture. This is particularly the case with informants much in demand because of their public involvement, such as tourism officials and musicians. The first meeting and interview with them followed a pattern similar to that of a formal business affair. They typically received me in their offices; they used the predictable rhetoric of the public relations trade despite my efforts to avoid a conventional discourse; the discussion lacked digressions, anecdotes, personal information, and expression of feelings. Interviewees often failed to see the point of my questions and they were systematically brief about their own personal backgrounds and itineraries. This contrasted with the stance of other informants who were not used to such attention and were eager to give as many details as the tape recorder could take. Given my position as a potential intermediary for attracting visitors, the theme of tourism was too much of a stake for them to readily give up an uncritical view of the initiatives undertaken in their field. Only repeated encounters in other contexts and my assiduous attendance at tourism committee meetings and related events over a long period of time enabled me to go beyond the surface and find out about dissensions, divisions, and power struggles.

The obstacle with professional musicians was similar. Although most of them remain very accessible to the public, their hectic schedules (for those who travel out of Louisiana), their late evenings, and the flow of media requests make it difficult to get and remain in touch with them. Often on tour, extending their gigs with jam sessions until the wee hours, surrounded by fans and hangers-on, popular musicians have little time for themselves. Once they are back home, they do not particularly look forward to recounting their life histories to visiting scholars. They are actually more open to the idea of socializing by playing with amateur musicians. It is then problematic to engage in an in-depth conversation with them. Compounding the difficulty of establishing rapport, I occasionally tend to practice self-censorship out of concern for the reaction of my prospective informants. If I am lucky enough to set an appointment, I am torn between the eagerness to interview the artist immediately before he slips away and the restraint I feel necessary to build up a closer relationship.

Working with artists challenges the use of our usual methodological tools since recorded interviews and note taking inherently create a distance between interviewer and interviewees. This is particularly true when researching French Louisiana music because of the way most local artists perceive it. The emphasis by musicians on simplicity, casualness, and infor-mality does not sit well with attempts at a rigorous examination. Observa-tion in dance halls definitely forces the anthropologist to give up formality. Participant observation and informal discussions are the only possible meth-ods. But it requires a significant effort of memorization to make an exhaus-tive description of the room, its decoration, the way people are dressed, their dance style, their use of space, the interaction among themselves and with musicians, the nature of the repertoire played, its interpretation, and the flow of multiple stories and pieces of gossip that increase with each drink. I could not conceivably take field notes openly since it would instantly make me stick out. Alternative methods of note taking also crossed my mind but I soon admitted they were quite inadequate: repeatedly sneaking out to the bathroom with a hidden notebook could arouse suspicion and I was afraid people would think I either stayed there too long, or went too often.

In addition to such practical issues, there are also content issues. Musi-cians are now increasingly knowledgeable about their music. They are not only aware of its history and evolution, but they produce a scholarly dis-course concerning their practice through a definition and classification of music genres and styles. Their aesthetic judgments frequently accompany claims of authenticity, legitimized by the identification of pioneers and the elaboration of anecdotes that situate the origin of the tradition in space and time. Given their expertise and their repeated contacts with people inquir-ing about Cajun and Zydeco music, such informants tended to view my pur-posefully vague questions as signs of cultural ignorance. Therefore, I some-times could not help giving them a hint about my hypothesis in order to demonstrate the worthiness of my work and encourage them to cooperate. Although aware of the obvious pitfall in inducing statements or opinions that people would not have spontaneously expressed, I did not always find appropriate ways to avoid it.

THE INNOCENT ANTHROPOLOGIST?

Studying cultural tourism in Louisiana highlights the primacy of the outsider's gaze in the way hosts build, reshape, and manipulate their identity. Tourism initiatives foster the recognition and validation of Louisi-ana French society by outsiders. Contacts with visitors and exposure to an outsider's perspective help make local residents aware of both their specificity and their belonging to a francophone community. Out-of-state travels and experiences by Louisiana residents provide similar opportunities.

The anthropologist is not detached from this process. His impact is actually increased by status, for he constructs the local culture as an object worthy of study. My extended and repeated stays over several years and the fact that I belonged to the "University of Paris" conferred an indisputable seriousness onto my research, although I certainly never encouraged such a conclusion. By satisfying my curiosity, some Cajuns were hoping to rehabilitate their culture through my work and break the negative stereotype still present in some people's minds. I was then invested with a specific role, which consisted in giving Cajuns their dignity back and spreading a positive image of the group.

For leaders of rural tourism, the interest in my research entailed media coverage. The late Wilbert Guillory, founder of the Zydeco Festival and fervent defender of the development of cultural tourism among Creoles, made all every effort to accommodate my requests, constantly giving me a warm welcome, and always speaking openly. He spontaneously took me to two radio stations around Opelousas and had me interviewed, explicitly expressing how strongly he felt about having visitors share their impressions about Louisiana. A local journalist found it worth spreading the word about my work and his article was published in three different newspapers, Lafayette's *Daily Advertiser,* New Orleans's *Times-Picayune,* and Lake Charles's *American Press.* My work not only confirmed the attractiveness of the local culture, it enhanced and legitimized tourism policy. I deserved then to appear publicly in order to justify these efforts and to convince skeptics. In addition, my study was perceived as a potential source of publicity in France, a country particularly targeted in the promotion of international tourism.

The role ascribed to the anthropologist in Louisiana is then similar to that of the tourist. Both represent a common stake in the eyes of tourism leaders, activists, and artists. Musicians traveling on tour are particularly aware of the benefit of having fan communities around the world. The number of foreign bands playing Cajun and Zydeco music in the United States and abroad is viewed as generating a salutary impulse to local preservation and a way to reach new audiences. "The advent of Cajun music as an 'international art form' clarifies the need to live up to our reputation as that music's homeland. If Southern Louisiana is a sacred place to people in France, Holland, Seattle and Japan, it should be sacred to us as well," states journalist Josh Caffery (2001) in the conclusion of his article on international Cajun bands. This exhortation to insiders illustrates the local instrumentalization of outside attraction. Whereas several Louisiana music workshops have been organized in different regions of the United States, the Dewey Balfa Cajun and Creole Heritage Week created in April 2001 was the first Cajun and Creole music workshop organized in Louisiana. By showing evidence of the success of French Louisiana music, the organizers aimed at formally developing a local and public structure for the transmission of French Louisiana music which is mostly passed on through informal set-tings and events. Indeed most of the people who attended the workshop were non-Louisianians. Christine Balfa, daughter of famed musician Dewey Balfa and promoter of this event, stressed the importance of giving them the opportunity to experience Louisiana music in its own context. But she also expressed her wish to see more Louisianians taking advantage of this gath-ering of master artists. This strategy emphasizes the impact of an outside interest in ascribing a new status to traditions, and the impulse it can give to the renewal of their local transmission.

THE OUTSIDER INSIDE OUT

The way my hosts perceived me led me to further reevaluate the dichotomy believed to exist between anthropologists and tourists. Instead of the opposition of roles and statuses often taken for granted, a comparison appears in fact to be quite legitimate. Whether I like it or not, even after fifteen years of regular stays in Louisiana, those who do not know me have no reason not to identify me as a tourist. Although quite regular, my stays have never exceeded three months, thus never allowing me to claim I was a temporary resident. Despite my constant efforts at camouflage, I have never gotten rid of my "charming" French accent. The growth of tourism and my systematic presence at highly attended public events (Festival International, Festivals Acadiens, Mardi Gras, etc.) inevitably led to the eternal question: "Are you visiting here?"

I have been prepared for such a characterization through my research and I can even rationalize such an identification. Still, I cannot help but being annoyed by this ascribed status. The gap between scientific think-ing and personal feelings cannot be honestly denied. How dare people ask me, like any other visitor, if I have been here before, after so many trips and the development of ties that time has only strengthened? The labels I have been given resulting from these close relationships are certainly more flattering: "adopted daughter," "Cajun through the back door," or "Cajun from France." These designations acknowledge my familiarity with and immersion in the local scene. They also highlight the affective dimension of fieldwork.

I was symbolically integrated into a kinship network, a demonstration of friendship I felt very strongly about. My young age at the time I started doing fieldwork definitely helped with my integration. Some couples showed a certain pride in having taken under their wing a young student of their grandchildren's age and introduced her to Louisiana culture. The presence of my companion during my first stay also played a significant role in the relationships I developed. It facilitated dealings with a group of couples in their sixties with a rural conservative background for whom family is a central institution. My having a partner, a future husband, enabled them to ascribe me a legitimate social identity. It also made my other stays much more acceptable. Although I was traveling alone, my personal situation was in accordance with expected norms. The combination of my status as a young student and a foreigner protected me from being accused of neglecting my marital duties. Yet, once my husband and I broke up, some of these friends came to the conclusion—with true resignation and regret—that these repeated separations could not go on forever. I realized then one of the possible underlying meanings of their constant jokes about my husband's possible activities with supposedly irresistible Parisian women: while they sincerely respected my situation, they still did not find it totally legitimate.

Other initiatives also worked to reconcile my situation with this group's social norm. My friends wished to play a part in my personal life and participate in its decisive moments. They celebrated my marriage in France by organizing what they called a "wedding skit," initially supposed to be an informal party but nonetheless gathering over ninety people. It even included a fake Catholic religious ceremony with all the required parts (priest, parents, maid of honor, best man) performed by close friends and a great attention to all possible details (rosary, wedding bands, congratulations book, marriage certificate, and the ritual pinning of money on the dress). In addition to its humoristic aspect, the amount of care and the dimension of the event expressed a will to anchor my marriage locally, strongly bonding it to both our friendship and Louisiana. It also appeared to compensate for the lack of a religious ceremony at my official marriage in France. Adapting to the uncertainties of life, these same friends persisted with this strategy of integration after my divorce. They constantly tease me about the need to find me a "Cajun man" so that I can move to Louisiana.

Despite these indications of assimilation, I found out that while my immersion is real, my integration has its limits. Being called a Cajun is by no means performative. This is the very meaning of the terms sometimes added to the ethnonym: "backdoor Cajun," "half Cajun," or even "Cajun from France" are not to be confused with "frontdoor Cajun." It seems like the attribution of a Cajun identity is not easy even to a foreigner who has settled in Louisiana for good. Unlike what "the back door" suggests, a woman married to a Cajun for forty years was introduced to me as "French." While they gladly welcome a newcomer, people do not find it appropriate to maintain the illusion of integration toward a resident.

Although I am sometimes in a position where I would like to experience some kind of inside-ness, I am now more comfortable and lucid about my own irreducible identity as an outsider. Neither a tourist nor a foreign resident, I am thus not viewed as a total outsider. However, I am seen as an outsider since I am a French from abroad, a Parisian, a resident of France, and a Standard French speaker. At the same time, I have also been put in the position of an insider because of my involvement. My shifting identity is thus made up of degrees of inside-ness and outside-ness. Such an ambivalence is not always easy to deal with. However, I have now accepted the fact that outside the circle of close relationships, my familiarity and experience with the local culture are not a given, and have to be rebuilt every time I return to the Louisiana field. In a sense, it is a lesson in humility and a constant reminder of our position as intruders, inseparable from our profession whether we belong to the society studied or not.

The effort of anthropologists to assert an identity distinct from tourists' is actually another similarity they share. Much as we try to escape being categorized as tourists, visitors generate distinctions among themselves. The tourist, the holidaymaker, the day-tripper is often opposed to the visitor, the adventurer, the hiker, or the alternative tourist. The latter claim particular status as traveler, one that emphasizes open-mindedness, passion for discovery, and an ability to embrace other cultures, contrasting with the plain tourists whose experience is supposedly based exclusively on consumption (Le Menestrel 2002). Travels are therefore hierarchically classified. Some travelers make it a point to distinguish themselves from pack tourists, as adepts of cultural tourism glance condescendingly at recreational tourists. Others simply deny being tourists, as if this designation were a dishonor, and pride themselves on not being duped by "tourist traps." Tourism is then derided by tourists themselves.

Claiming not to be a tourist enhances the outsider's ability to become "rooted" in terms of residence, identity, and sometimes even genealogy when marriage takes place. Escaping this categorization entails an advancement in status. While anthropologists slide along the stranger-native continuum, tourists may also experience a changing identity. The holiday makers (themselves different depending on their modes of travel and aims of their trips) may become regular visitors, then short- or long-term residents. Tourists may become proud members of the host community, just as anthropologists take pride in their immersion. The popularity of Cajun and Zydeco music has led more and more people to make regular pilgrimages to Louisiana, sometimes several times a year. Some even make the decision to move there, attracted by a laid-back attitude toward life which they contrast to their rushed urban existence. From tourists, they turn into experts and/ or foreign residents, thus becoming hosts to other tourists. I met a middle-aged New Yorker who retired in Lafayette and spends his time learning to play the accordion and patronizing all possible musical venues. He has been particularly eager to share his indisputable dancing skills with tourists, whom he spontaneously invites. The neophytes are thrilled to be taught the basics, while more advanced visitors are shown how to improve their steps and turns. Besides subtly putting his competence forward, he seeks to bolster his credibility by mentioning the names of the numerous musicians he knows, presenting them as friends rather than acquaintances. Without doubt, his changing status and expertise have enabled him to gain social prestige among visitors.

If we turn this process upside down, natives can also experience a change of status. Many Cajuns and Creoles have temporarily or permanently moved out of state, becoming immigrants themselves and "returnees" when they come "home" for a visit. Depending on the extent of their exile, their perception by longtime residents ascribes the migrants a new identity. The concepts of inside-ness and outside-ness are once again challenged, an evolving pattern that necessitates reevaluation of the relevance of touristic terminology. Should we not use the term "visitor" or "guest" as a generic term instead of "tourist," and then be more specific? In any case, a diachronic perspective proves to have a heuristic value (Kohn 1997).

SHIFTING POSITION

For me, learning to play the smallpipes was a way of repositioning myself, a way of being closer to undefinable essences, a way of experiencing some of what I wanted to know, a way of getting beyond detachment and into the realms of feeling, emotion and experience from a vantage point many ethnographers have avoided.
—Burt Feintuch, quoted in Bendix (1996:227)

My implication did not enable me to avoid the obstacles mentioned previously, but it surely added a deeper dimension to my work. It was a way not to focus strictly on the subject of my research and to widen the scope of my vision. In some instances, our analysis can be the result of an indirect course.

My personal involvement with music in Louisiana started as an aside to my research. While doing fieldwork for my dissertation, I stayed with amateur and professional musicians with whom I developed close bonds. Immersed in music on a daily basis, I realized that playing music with them could enrich our relationship. In addition, I was convinced that my implication would improve my understanding of the importance of music in the promotion of Louisiana culture and the frequent debates about the nature of musical tradition.

The impact of my learning was almost immediate. I first started with the 'tit fer (triangle), an instrument whose playing, against all appearance, requires competence and technique. My teacher practiced with me, and we played over recordings. He quickly pushed me to join his band at jam sessions. Both musicians and spectators are very encouraging of someone who is willing to play an instrument. Still, it took me much longer to convince myself that I could pick up the fiddle. Regardless of how clumsily I played, I was always pressed to pursue my efforts. Teachers and listeners remarked on my improvement and never doubted my ability to "get it." I kept practicing in Louisiana and in France and I attended several workshops. With a considerable effort to overcome the anxietyI felt whenever I performed in public, I finally dared to play with other musicians. It took me even more time to understand the primacy of sociability over performance in the French Louisiana music scene. Conditioned by my classical training, I had difficulty overcoming my fear of being judged by others. However, I progressively realized it was useless to dread playing, since it was about sharing a pleasure, not proving skills. This is probably why playing music in Louisiana became so crucial to me and proved so rewarding. I was finally able to give, and not only receive. This process not only compensated for my position as an observer but also enabled me to become integrated into an exchange process which is fundamental to the local social life (see chapter 3 in this volume).

Very often combined with the sharing of a meal, playing music in a private setting is a strong socializing factor. It generates immediate complicity between the participants. I happened one day to join some friends who had invited me to a private jam session to be joined by an old and formerly renowned but never-recorded fiddle player. I showed up late after everybody had enjoyed the food and the conversation of a crawfish boil. But it just took a few fiddle tunes to connect with the old master, who then encouraged me to play some more tunes with him. A few days later, a friend present on that evening called me to let me know he was trying to gain this old player's confidence. Strongly involved in the promotion of local music, he eventually intended to record him so that his talent could be preserved and passed on. He asked me to join him in the visits he was planning, explaining that he had noticed how the musician obviously enjoyed playing with me. Clearly, he was mostly interested in the rapport he had witnessed, not in my musical competence.

After some time, I joined a French Cajun band and started playing regular gigs in France. This made my involvement even more valuable and serious in the eyes of my Louisiana contacts. My friends took pride in this evolution, thrilled to have nourished my interest. They also felt that they had indirectly contributed to the development of the Cajun music network in France and to the enhancement of their heritage. When my band finally took the step to travel to Louisiana, my Cajun friends were eager to provide us with opportunities to perform, although it was not our primary intention. They graciously put us in touch with dance hall owners and made sure to come see us play wherever we performed.

The development of my musical skills greatly affected the perception people had of me, and it created an additional bond with my informants. It also acted to compensate for the professional distance inherent in my position. I was always careful in expressing my opinions and I never was a key figure in activist endeavors, although I have supported some. Playing music added a valuable dimension to my situation. My position as a researcher, standing back, listening, and watching, did not after all prevent a personal implication. The resultant blurring of boundaries between my professional and personal lives gave me more credibility as a human being who could be moved and even overwhelmed by emotions. My strong feelings about the region and its culture were revealed in a nonverbal manner, which is particularly meaningful in Louisiana where music is so closely intertwined with history, identity, and daily life.

Being a musician gave me access to contexts that I was able to explore from the inside. It enabled me to attend several events as a musician, and in doing so to enrich my fieldwork experience. Attending the Dewey Balfa Cajun and Creole camp as a student and a foreigner among many others, I was not different from anybody else. Instead of being in the position in which I was initiating an encounter or an interview, my participation gave me a far sharper insight. Observation was wide-ranging and permanent. As an example, attending morning class was by no means comparable to any kind of interview, which would have been devoid of the rich combination of practice and discourse. I was not only able to experience my teacher's pedagogical methods but also to benefit from his interaction with students, his answers to their questions, his use of storytelling and humor to present Cajun music and culture. Only my position as participant-observer enabled me to gather such rich material.

My involvement also modified my own understanding and perception of music. Before I played the fiddle, I tended to be influenced by the musicians around me and by their particular interpretations. In following the steps of previous folklorists or anthropologists who have exerted their control as assessors and guarantors of authenticity, I was tempted to view some styles as more faithful to the tradition I had in mind. Once I started playing music and working on the interpretation of songs, the boundaries I had set became much more fluid and my vision correspondingly less restrictive. I learned not to confuse my personal taste with the nature of French Louisiana music which, like any other music, is extremely diversified and subject to multiple interpretations. I could now better understand the desire of some musicians to incorporate new elements—tunes, rhythms, chord successions, instruments—and to explore different facets of the musical heritage without feeling they were distorting it. Against all expectations, and despite a personal preference for a "traditional" Cajun style and old-time twin fiddle tunes, my implication led me to a less clear-cut definition of what fits within the tradition.

WHEN A DISTANT FIELD EXTENDS TO HOME

The impact of my playing and my grasp of Cajun culture extended beyond Louisiana. The discovery of the "Francadien" network in France (as local amateurs of Cajun music call themselves) made me aware of their own different representations of French Louisiana music. It allowed me to extend the scale of my research, and to better identify the values associated with it and the needs that it fulfills. Playing Cajun music in France testifies to a particular attitude toward life. Many fans have been involved in or feel close to the folk movement of the 1960s. They emphasize the preservation of a sense of community, which compensates for the reported decline of "social capital" in modern life. Cajun music is therefore closely linked to the notions of authenticity, conviviality, fraternity, and symbiosis with nature. The rural, low socioeconomic status of musical pioneers backs up the idea of simplicity. In other words, an idealized way of life is contrasted with commercial mass culture, modernity, individualism, and materialism.

This perception is also based on the characteristics of the music itself, whether in terms of structure or style. For instance, Cajun music provides leeway for improvisation, which is often associated with spontaneity and authenticity. It also utilizes a limited number of chords, primarily C, D, and G. This seemingly simple structure makes those who are not familiar with Cajun music judge it with condescension, and characterize it as strictly festive, unrefined, or repetitive. Even within folk or world music circles, some tend to underestimate the skills and talent of musicians playing Cajun music, as opposed to performers of other traditions such as Gypsy music or *musette*, for example. Amateurs of Cajun music thus confront an elitist perception. Notwithstanding my own involvement in this music, its emotional dimension, and the genuine appreciation I have for it, I am not immune to the paradox that I share with other fans. Hence I do not particularly care for some interpretations or some songs I view as bare and oversimplified; and, although I do enjoy singing Cajun music, I do not find it vocally quite as fulfilling as other styles I am practicing as well, like jazz and bossa nova. My appreciation remains conditioned by an aesthetic code whose criteria largely result from classical music and its correlate representation of cultural legitimacy.

Whereas my involvement in the "Francadien" world enabled me to add a comparative dimension to my work in studying the reinterpretation and appropriation of Cajun music in France, my position as an anthropologist and my knowledge about French Louisiana culture did not go unnoticed. At "home" as well as in Louisiana, my immersion was not complete and my status remained ill-defined. When the book resulting from my research was published, many musicians showed an interest in getting a copy. They spontaneously came to me, sharing their remarks and appreciation. To my relief, their response was very positive and I was gratified with compliments, even from people who admitted their lack of attraction for such a scholarly reading. Despite the often idealized image they kept of Louisiana and the little awareness (or acknowledgment) of social divisions and internal conflicts, they never questioned my analysis on these specific subjects.

One person extensively complimented me on enhancing a culture so admirable in his eyes; another one found interest in the uneasiness he had felt reading some sections, becoming aware of issues that had never come to his mind despite a deep familiarity with Louisiana. An elderly pioneer in the diffusion and promotion of Cajun music in France expressed his will to donate to me a set of precious interviews of deceased and renowned Louisiana artists and activists he had collected. My status and institutional affiliation led him to see me as the perfect depository of a personal heritage he thought nobody before had deserved to inherit. Although music was only a part of this work, French readers seemed to view it as a validation of their passion and their commitment to Cajun culture (or to their representation of it). Whether they received all my arguments or not, my book seemed to be a legitimization of their values and ideals.

Back in Louisiana, the book's reception by academia exposed me to new challenges and feedback. I had the unexpected opportunity to briefly present my work at a conference organized by the University of Louisiana at Lafayette (ULL) for the meeting of the 1999 Congrès Mondial Acadien. Quite unprepared, I realized at the moment I started talking how uneasy my position was: I was the only French presenter among a gathering of French Americans from Louisiana, Nova Scotia, and New Brunswick. All were members of a minority group and as such, their francophone identity was closely related to notions of resistance, survival, and challenge. Mine was not, which I felt could provide a basis for questioning my assessment and analysis. In addition, my approach to Cajun identity viewed through the lens of tourism could be seen as polemical, threatening the validity of ethnic claims and fueling accusations of folklorization.

While these thoughts were crossing my mind, I was bluntly interrupted by another participant, who loudly exhaled as a sign of protest and boredom and expressed his wish to introduce the authors of a book he had edited. Taken aback, totally stunned by this arrogance and rudeness, I chose not to respond and immediately handed the microphone over to him. Nobody uttered a single word. Once the meeting was over, a woman came to me and mentioned how sorry she felt for what had happened, and a few students from University of Louisiana at Lafayette expressed their anger. I later understood this man was known for his bad-tempered antics. Still, I did not get any feedback from the organizers, and I remain puzzled by this silence. Although I do believe this incident has a lot to do with this man's personality, I am not sure he would have allowed himself such behavior with somebody else. The occasion made me fully aware of the potential risk faced by an outsider addressing the local academia and the possibility of committing faux pas, generating misunderstandings and, in this case, outright contempt.

On the other hand, the obligation of restitution and the necessity to make the data accessible to informants generate caution. Knowing my book would be read by the francophone elite and exposed to local critics produced a constant concern to address sensitive issues in the most appropriate and tactful way possible. I believe that the careful attention paid to each formulation improved the reliability of my interpretations. The subtlety lies in the necessity of balancing this care with professional obligations, between falling into a feeling of allegiance and allowing ourselves to tackle polemic and touchy subjects in all freedom of judgment.

IN AND OUT, BACK AND FORTH

Such is the ambivalent position of any anthropologist wherever our field is located. Our work entails a reconsideration of conventional oppositions between professional and private life, which are often closely intertwined in our field. These frequent overlaps confront a specific work ethic associated with a time and space distinct from leisure. Ethnographers can actually take advantage of every moment to enrich and refine their research. The blurring of boundaries can create disturbing feelings. I remember sometimes a sensation of suffocation, an urgent wish for a new fieldwork, a lassitude and the resultant fear of falling into the taken-for-granted process, where familiarity takes over our necessary curiosity and ability to be surprised. In this sense, my regular but temporary stays in Louisiana have been salutary. I needed to get away physically to be able to look at my resources differently and resist the constant temptation of gathering more material.

At the same time, I strongly believe that anthropology depends first and foremost on a long-term process. Nothing can replace extensive and repeated fieldwork. No relevant and subtle findings can emerge when rushed and pressed by time. Only repeated observation and interviews prevent us from freezing attitudes and discourses, and they enable us to practice situational anthropology, aware of informants' conflicting identity (Mendras & Oberti

116   Sara Le Menestrel

2000). In this perspective, short-term fieldwork available to anthropologists with restricted budgets is a difficult situation to advocate for. It does not leave space for adaptation and it entails a strategy of accumulation. Because we do not have total control over fieldwork conditions, because fieldwork extends to home—both as a physical space and a locus of privacy—we must remain open to its twists and turns and take the time to make necessary and inevitable readjustments. Our ability to combine detachment and implication, our aptitude to adopt an overarching view of our own position, acts, views, and feelings is a condition and a tool for the production of knowledge. This constant need for introspection is what makes this profession both challenging and gripping. One does not emerge unscathed from doing anthropology, and it is for the best.

NOTE

I owe special thanks to Kali Argyriadis, Véronique Boyer, Stefania Capone, and Anne Monjaret for their critiques, and to John Angell for his help in editing this paper. In addition, I will always be indebted to my Louisiana friends for their confidence, their endless generosity, and their invaluable assistance during my fieldwork. Whether I am an outsider or an insider, in my eyes their status is not blurred and they will always have a special place in my heart.

REFERENCES

Abram, Simone. 1996. "Reactions to Tourism: A View from the Deep Green Heart of France." In *Coping with Tourists: European Reactions to Mass Tourism*. Jeremy Boissevain, ed. Oxford: Berghahn Books, pp. 174–204.
Abram, Simone, Jacqueline Waldren, & Donald MacLeod, eds. 1997 *Tourists and Tourism: Identifying with People and Places*. Oxford: Berg.
Bendix, Regina. 1997. *In Search of Authenticity: The Formation of Folklore Studies*. Madison: University of Wisconsin Press.
Bruner, Edward M. 1995. "The Ethnographer/Tourist in Indonesia." In *International Tourism, Identity and Change*. Marie-Françoise Lanfant, John B. Allcock, & Edward M. Bruner, eds. London: Sage Publications, pp. 224–242.
Caffery, Josh. 2001. "The Travels of Magellan Breaux." *The Times of Acadiana* (March 14), pp. 14–17.
Kohn, Tamara. 1997. "Island Involvement and the Evolving Tourist." In *Tourists and Tourism: Identifying with People and Places*. Simone Abram, Jacqueline Waldren, & Donald MacLeod, eds. Oxford: Berg, pp. 13–29.

Le Menestrel, Sara. 1999. *La voie des Cadiens. Tourisme et identité en Louisiane*. Paris: Belin.

———. 2002. "L'expérience louisianaise. Figure touristique et faux-semblants." Numéro spécial, "Touriste, autochtone, qui est l'étranger?", *Ethnologie francaise* 32(3), pp. 461-473.

Mendras, Henri, & Marco Oberti, eds. 2000. *Le sociologue et son terrain: Trente recherches exemplaires*. Paris: Colin.

7. HOMING IN ON THE FIELD

—Jacques Henry

THE INTRODUCTION TO FRENCH LOUISIANA

I had no awareness of Louisiana, French or otherwise, until a friend suggested I visit him there in the mid-1970s. A physical therapist by trade, he had nonetheless been recruited serendipitously as a French teacher while traveling in the United States and ended up spending nine months in Lafayette. My earliest memory of Louisiana is one of sitting in the back of a police cruiser and chatting in French with a sheriff's deputy. Summoned by his son, who I had encountered in downtown Crowley, he had generously offered to take me to my friend's obscure address, a numbered box on some "route" in the country. Alas, it was July and my friend had already left. The officer, whose Spanish-sounding name I forgot (Hernandez? Romero?), drove back across rice fields to the police station from where I walked to Interstate 10 to hitch a ride. Twenty miles east, I stopped in Lafayette and ate a plate of rice and gravy! It was a sumptuous departure from the boring, low-budget diet of burger-and-fries and peanut butter sandwiches I had been on since my hitchhiking coast-to-coast tour of North America had begun in Québec. I also remember a late afternoon thunderstorm, threatening then exploding over the Atchafalaya Basin. On Henderson Swamp, the sky was black with bluish hues, hanging low over the dark waters pierced by dead cypress stumps. The elevated roadway, floating, seemed to be leading straight to a liquid hell. I was relieved when the lights of Baton Rouge finally flickered through the windshield.

Jacques Henry (second from right) and his CODOFIL colleagues in 1984 volunteer to pose for a line of ethnic wear with fiddler Len Harrington. For their involvement in this venture—an unequaled combination of ethnic activism, public service, business acumen, inexpensive advertising, and crass exploitation—the amateur models got to keep their shirts along with their sense of humor.

Louisiana had made an impression on me. I did not know how much I had yet to learn.

My friend and I came back a couple of years later during the Easter break. He was curious about aspects of the local French scene he had only glimpsed at during his teaching stint. A graduate student in the anthropology program at the Université Paris Descartes, I was looking for a master's research project and an opportunity to conduct fieldwork. Cajun country looked promising. My friend had kept numerous contacts whom I started to conceive of as informants. Fluent in English, I was attracted to American culture, or at least my vision of it made of rocking musical genres, mind-numbing open spaces, nonstop activity, and gregarious people. I was also familiar with a French American culture on account of my Québécoise mother; the recollections of her upbringing, the yearly visits of her mother, and my own travels among my matrilinear relatives had contributed to form an image of Québec as a French-speaking America where the *maudits français* were simultaneously adored and derided in a charmingly accented tongue.

So, on one Easter break my friend and I made our way to Louisiana. We drove nonstop from New York City, noticing at every pit stop the increasingly warm and humid air, the blinding sunlight, and the flatness of the land. I started to jot down notes on sights, sounds, and impressions. We established our base in Lafayette mostly because free and friendly accommodation was available there. From this central location, we would radiate throughout Acadiana in search of Cajunness.

Unbeknownst to me, my understanding of fieldwork was quite contrived and my preparation rather insufficient. Schooled in the classics, I had marveled at the fieldwork accounts of Malinowski, Firth, Evans-Pritchard, Griaule, Balandier, and of course Lévi-Strauss. Teachers had also suggested James Agee and Walker Evans's *Let Us Now Praise Great Men* (Agee & Evans 1941) and Antonin Artaud's (1970) *Les Tarahumaras* as alternative ethnographic accounts, fascinating readings indeed. But somehow, as faithfully as I can recollect, I could not grasp the relevance of these works for my own practice. To begin with I was way out of these masters' league: how could my two-week, non-funded jaunt on a discount airline ticket to some corner of the New World, where even tourists and journalists had gone before, compare with the deep explorations conducted by these pillars of the discipline? Whereas they had exposed and explained entire premodern cultures, I was modestly concerned with the ethnic identity of these French-speaking Americans called Cajuns. Driving around Southwestern Louisiana in an air-conditioned rental, it became quite clear that my idea of fieldwork as village ethnography in a preliterate society might not be adequate to my situation.

Practically, my preparation for fieldwork had been limited to a handful of sessions on linguistic transcription and land surveying. Ethnology professors had provided some tips on interviewing, note taking, and participant observation, but I had never actually conducted an interview or taken ethnographic notes. To be sure, I had read everything on contemporary French Louisiana to be found on the library shelves of Paris's hallowed intellectual establishments, but it was not much. I had complemented my preparation with travel and journalistic accounts that did not amount to much either. Ultimately, I now realize, I was left with relying on my friend's familiarity with the terrain to ease my introduction to the field.

Armed with a road map, a small recorder with extra batteries and tapes, a notebook, and change for telephone calls, off I went. In Lafayette, I spoke with people at the CODOFIL office, this Council for the Development of French in Louisiana that had formerly employed my friend to assist in its official mission "to further the preservation and utilization of the French language and culture of Louisiana." I awkwardly queried young and old members of the Dugas (not their real name) family outside of Eunice about their being and living as Cajuns. On a Saturday morning, I attended Revon Reed's Cajun music program at Fred's Lounge in Mamou. I visited with renowned accordionist Nathan Abshire in his ramshackle house in Basile to little avail since age and alcohol had taken their toll. I interviewed Cajun bard Max Greig in his restaurant in Saint Martinville. I also hung out with young Cajun activists involved in teaching, Mardi Gras crews, and French-language media. Among other things, they confirmed my developing impression that their cohorts were more interested in making it in Americana than maintaining the Cajun lifestyle and language of their forebears. I also spent time in libraries poring over publications and census data unavailable in France. All the while I kept a field journal, took many pictures, and collected every relevant document visitors' bureaus and educational outfits would let me have. Overall it was a fruitful trip providing me with enough material to write my thesis and stimulating the interest of my adviser, who suggested I continue on to a doctorate. Yet, this face-to-face meeting with Cajunness had left me with more questions than answers. Cajun identity appeared to be multifaceted, highly paradoxical, and quite elusive, even to its own people. Indeed my questions to Cajuns about their ethnic particularity were mostly answered with confused stares or vague accounts of the Acadian past. While allowing me to gauge the foolishness of such queries, this inaugural field research had taught me a valuable lesson: I could not expect Cajun men and women to give me the anthropological treatment of their ethnicity. That was my job.

CONSTRUCTING THE FIELD

So, in 1981, I returned once more. This time, I was armed with the intent to engage in thorough fieldwork. More confident and better situated, I was also keenly aware of the boundaries of my confusion: French

Louisiana was an area well-marked on maps but indistinguishable on the ground; about a half million self-described Cajuns lived there but they were dispersed among different kinds of non-Cajuns, who even often outnumbered them. Cajuns were supposed to be of Acadian origin, speak French, be Catholic, live in the country, and enjoy ethnic ways and pleasures, yet I had met many who displayed none of these traits. Finally, the pervasive ethnic pride touted in the media was often overshadowed by expressions of shame, disparaging comments about one's heritage, and avoidance of conversation in French. It seemed also to be greatly challenged by the avid, and I believed, culturally destructive pursuit of consumer goods and comfort offered by American society. Before I even pondered ways to make sense of all this, I started to simply wonder what I was doing at all.

My previous stay had suggested that the various steps of traditional fieldwork may not be wholly applicable. Competent bureaucracies had already counted the population and surveyed the territory. I just had to review the numerous publications by the Bureau of the Census and visit local courthouses to avail myself of the information. In other areas, scholars had expertly retraced the people's history, recorded their oral literature and music, and described their language. Although all of these fields could be revisited to refine, complement, or challenge existing knowledge, I could rely on it in my quest to understand Cajun ethnic identity. Furthermore, puzzled by the diversity and complexity of what I had learned of Cajun ethnicity, I did not believe that a village ethnography would provide me with the appropriate big picture. Empirically, what area should I focus on: the rice-growing area to the west? Marshlands in Vermilion Parish? The sugarcane country area along bayou Tèche? An urban area? A rural *voisinage*? Could I extend the findings of a village monography to the whole area? Surely different ecosystems, economic bases, and population structures would likely yield different views and practices of Cajun ethnicity. Given the large population I was concerned with, between 1 million or 250,000 depending on the criteria retained, I also ruled out many of the elementary pursuits of classical anthropology such as compiling genealogies, making inventories of household items, or recording life stories. Large-scale data collection was out of the question since I was not part of a research team and had no budget but my own limited funds. Beyond questions of sampling and statistical significance, did I want to go quantitative at all? If I chose a small, manageable sample of informants, what kind of Cajun was I to approach: a farmer? a teacher? a sales clerk? an attorney? French-speaking or not? True Acadian or coming "directly from France"? Ethnically conscious or assimilated?

Practically, I briefly established residence in Eunice with the belief that such a location—in the prairie, close to Mamou, and near key informants—would be propitious to grasping Cajun identity. I spent the next weeks driving across Acadiana and spending many nights in Lafayette where it seemed more was going on. Faced with the unenviable prospect of daily commutes and the growing despair of my companion, I opted to move our quarters to the regional hub.

The elaboration of an approach allowing for a comprehensive treatment of my topic included some reassuring parameters. Fieldwork took place among the ubiquitous modern amenities of American culture. Cajuns I encountered were by and large most welcoming, affable, willing, and even eager to cooperate. They were also keenly aware of the expectations of inquisitive visitors in their midst be they tourists, journalists, or researchers. They would react positively to my Frenchness and quite systematically asked if I was associated with CODOFIL, assuming that I was one of these hundreds of foreign teachers who had manned the French education program during the past decade. Upon learning that I was not, the relief of some questioners suggested that the official promoter of Cajun pride did not draw universal support. I deduced that negotiating my situation vis-à-vis the organization and tailoring my discourse accordingly could be highly beneficial to my data gathering activities. I took stock in the realization that the tasks I was faced with were fairly simple: I was to go to observe something, participate in it, and interview encultured informants even if practically the what, the who, the where, and the how remained elusive.

Out of both despair and habit, I turned to theory to shape the research strategy. I hoped to compensate methodological weakness with theoretical fortitude. I drew my conceptual framework mostly from conflict and structuralist scholarship stored along the years. My teachers had prepared me well for the manipulation of such notions as structural arrangements and dialectical relationships. Class work had also familiarized me with Max Weber's insistence on the centrality of meanings and Marcel Mauss's wonderful concept of *phénomène total*. My theoretical apparatus was rounded up with topical readings on ethnicity, from assimilation theory to constructionism via Fredrik Barth, and social movements, from nativism to assessments of the *situation coloniale*, a concept designed by my adviser George Balandier. As an undergraduate I had, secretly of course, struggled with theory that seemed obscure and disembodied. Later I had developed an appreciation and guarded ease with the large vistas and penetrating issues it exposed. While juggling with them was exhilarating in the Sorbonne library, their relevance quickly melted in the immediacy of the field. Malinowski's (1961:9) rudimentary views on the relationship between fieldwork and theory—"preconceived ideas" are bad but "foreshadowed problems" are good—were helpful but limited. Levi-Strauss's structural analysis of creation myths was no handy tool and Wallerstein's world system theory seemed quite out of place in the American South.

A survey of the Cajuns' situation revealed a few essential components: a shared perception of a common cultural heritage, some observable ethnic traits (Acadian surnames, use of French, distinct, profane, and religious practices), renewed claims of a cultural difference and actions taken to maintain it, rapid acculturation, and interest of outsiders in Louisiana's ethnic experience. A skeletal conceptual outline linked the pivotal belief in ethnic membership with construction of social identity and ethnic mobilization processes. In order to understand Cajun ethnic identity, I could investigate the process of ethnic identity formation taking place throughout the various actions undertaken in the name of Louisiana's Cajun French culture. I would do the ethnography of the Louisiana French Movement.

THE EXPERIENCE OF FIELDWORK

After years of cogitation, months of anxious preparation, and moments of sheer panic, I finally had a sense of what to do. Over the next year I engaged in the following: observing and participating in the activities of CODOFIL, the central and powerful organization spearheading the movement; interviewing the movement's cadres and participants, among which were educators, politicians, administrators, foreign personnel, and artists; attending ethnic and cultural events such as festivals, associative meetings, theater plays, and music concerts; visiting tourist attractions; cataloging and keeping in touch with French-language written and audiovisual media; assessing the statewide French language program and foreign assistance coming from France, Québec, and Belgium.

The topic of inquiry and the research design I devised shaped the daily practice of fieldwork. For one I did not establish residence with a Cajun family or a Cajun activist in order to share in the everyday routine of the Cajun experience, the ethnographic key to discovering culture. After all I was not concerned with the Cajun worldview in general but more pragmatically with attempts to promote a constructed version of it. Some days my data gathering activities felt more like a day at the office or a weekend outing than what I visualized as true anthropological fieldwork. There were no obscure idioms to decipher, no arduous trekking through hostile desert or rain forest, no troubling relationship with a small group of preindustrial people, and no total immersion in culture shock. No, I drove my car to appointments in offices or homes, paid for my meals in restaurants and for my tickets to cultural events, attended meetings and classes in the comfort of air-conditioned buildings. My major informants were not "typical," "ordinary" Cajuns (I use these terms in the lay sense not as conceptual devices), but activist, culturally endowed, erudite individuals. I was studying "up," focusing on an elite group of learned, opinionated informants. In dealing with this unusual situation, I now realize that I developed an interview style that was, well, unorthodox. Instead of the ethnographic interview by an unobtrusive anthropologist, I found that challenging, arguing, and even critiquing my informants' positions yielded significant results. It helped clear formulaic answers, ready-made arguments, or propaganda-like statements from my informants' discourse. Such verbal sparring, sometimes heated but always courteous, helped unearth areas of tension and reveal paradoxes. A useful device for my research, I failed to grasp at the time how troubling and ethically questionable it may have been for my interviewees. I also neglected to systematically share with them preliminary texts in order to ensure the accuracy of the representation of their voices, an emerging practice at the time, now a standard ethnographic convention. In hindsight, these and other instances paint a quite embarrassing picture of unpreparedness, ignorance, and lack of rigor. I am relieved I was not aware of it at the time and ended up, after all, causing no irreparable harm.

I retain powerful and informative memories from this period. I paid one of my first visits to CODOFIL on a Friday afternoon. The end-of-the-week bustle engulfed the office now spaciously housed in Lafayette's former city hall. Since my first visit three years before, CODOFIL had grown from a benevolent militant outfit into a genuine bureaucratic organization. Cultural activism now appeared to be efficient and official, although this impression was tempered by tagging along in James Domengeaux's entourage. The CODOFIL chairman had invited the participants and some fellow hangers-on to a local eatery after a round of meetings with foreign officials. Serious business was actively conducted after-hours and without protocol while guests generously sampled local delicacies. The joyous occasion did not fit my idea of international negotiations.

In a different context, I vividly recall an instance where a close female informant made a racist comment directed at a group of black youth watching traffic go by in rural Evangeline Parish. It contrasted with the image of the loving mother and caring person I had developed of her. I would witness other episodes of racism but this first contact with prejudice among Cajuns came as a shock. I labored to keep my feelings in check, then and later on, but I must acknowledge that these situations blunted some of my empathy for Cajuns' cultural struggle. Pragmatically, it helped me situate the renaissance movement in its historical and social context and critically evaluate the ambient ethnic romanticism.

In the process I traveled throughout most of Southwest Louisiana. I wanted to explore my field extensively, literally covering the territory. Short of visiting every community, traveling to the boundaries seemed to be the next best move. Gone crabbing in the Rockefeller Refuge, I explored the southern fringe of Acadiana, following Highway 82 across the marshes in the parishes of Vermilion and Cameron to Grand Chenier. I drove westward to the Texas border, up the Sabine River, and went boating on the Toledo Bend Reservoir area where Acadiana residents go for various forms of aquatic recreation. I served as a counselor at a summer camp for high school students outside Bunkie, a village located at the tip of the French Louisiana triangle in Avoyelles Parish. I followed the Mississippi River from False River in Pointe Coupee Parish down to New Orleans visiting plantation homes and sites of the original Acadian settlements.

Driving down to Cocodrie, a fishing community in Terrebonne parish, was a memorable experience. Highway 56 runs along Bayou Petit Caillou with houses on piers lodged in between, their front doors facing the road and back doors looking out over the water. The road cuts through the marshes and bridges jump over the canals. Shrimp boats and other vessels occasionally appear in my rearview mirror. I must be hallucinating: boats on the road! They are just sailing. Water is everywhere. Then the paved road stops at a grouping of buildings on piers: beyond is Terrebonne Bay, the Gulf of Mexico. From the marina, I see a landscape of grass islands, sandbars, pipes, valves, and oil rigs sticking out of the shallow brownish water. And boats, all sorts of them: supply boats, tug boats pushing barges, shrimpers, a flotilla of pleasure crafts.

Most excursions from my Lafayette base had a clear purpose: attend a festival, conduct an interview, visit a radio station. But some others, especially some of the farthest ones, had no other objective but to allow me to get a feel of the space. I would listen to the French-language program on the local radio station, read the local newspaper in search of Cajun-related cultural events, perusing family names mentioned in death notices and other announcements, engage in informal chats with people met in roadside restaurants, gas stations, or tourist attractions. I would not accumulate much hard data or acquire some pivotal information, yet I felt good about these short excursions: I had been there. They were in a way a motorized variant of Malinowski's "walks" through his Trobriand field. These various encounters with people and places made me empirically grasp how rich and poor, welcoming and inhospitable, immutable and fast-changing South Louisiana could be. I marveled at how determined and ingenious Acadian settlers had to be to endure in such an environment. I appreciated how resilient and adaptive their descendants had become.

Eventually, the excitement of venturing into undiscovered corners of Cajun country wore off. Gradually I lost the impetus to get in the car and drive just to see what was out there. Country roads and little communities started to all look alike, I started to tire of listening to yet another recounting of the Acadian plight, and I was growing increasingly doubtful that I would stumble onto some person or situation that would give me the key to the whole phenomenon. Boredom, irritation seeped in accompanied with a lackadaisical attitude toward data. I would no longer pay attention to details, I would take fewer notes, and fail to pursue leads. I interpreted these signs as the end of fieldwork. Over the next few months I wrote the dissertation and returned to France to defend it.

RETURN TO THE FIELD

Sometime toward the end of my eighteen-month stay, I had decided I wanted to remain in Louisiana, although not in the field. I was well accustomed to my environment, I truly enjoyed the relaxed yet active lifestyle, and opportunities abounded in the mid-1980s. The cultural bustle fostered visions of international trade, cross-cultural exchange, and renewed pride. I returned in early 1984 and planned to establish myself as a bilingual consultant. I proceeded to offer my services to businesses, travel bureaus, and agencies in charge of economic development. It took about a month for my ill-advised hopes to succumb to plain economic logic. My contacts were all courteous and supportive, but it became clear that very few wanted to pay for translations and cultural awareness training. I reacted with genuine surprise, commensurate disappointment, and suspicion of hypocrisy. Was the ethnic renaissance so superficial that it evaporated at the cash register? True, I had mostly dealt with government bureaucracies and volunteer outfits, largely bypassing the world of private enterprise, but had I gotten it all wrong? A few translations and French lessons later, I realized I had confused the Movement and the Market, two real but distinct entities. They coexisted but did not necessarily correlate. Later I met dyed-in-the-wool Cajuns and dedicated Francophones who did not care one bit about expanding their construction business or law practice to the Acadian homeland. I also dealt with Anglo entrepreneurs who would mine the ethnic connection for all it was worth. And then there were all the possible cases in between. With a fifteen-year hindsight, this state of affairs now seems quite commonsensical, but I had failed to fully grasp it during my research.

This epiphany yielded another lesson. While my skills as a newly minted doctor in cultural anthropology were spurned by the world of business, they appeared to be wanted in another sphere. In the course of doing my rounds as a job seeker, I had stopped at CODOFIL by courtesy and for old times' sake. I was surprised when the director proposed to hire me as a communication specialist. I was familiar with Philippe Gustin, a former teacher from Belgium and now a dogged administrator, who had been a graceful and cooperative informant. I thought about the bureaucratic structure, the questionable cultural objectives, the hectic day-to-day operations, the overbearing chairman, and declined the offer. Then I thought about it some more, pondering anew the combination of life choices and making a living. Soon, CODOFIL had its man.

The transition from being a critical evaluator of CODOFIL's mission to acting as its public information officer was brutal, both practically and ideologically. I had spent much time thinking about French Louisiana and I could argue points of cultural policy at length. In fact and in retrospect, deadlines saved both my sanity and my job. Telephone queries had to be answered on the spot, press releases were to be sent to local news organizations within hours, and the printer was expecting the monthly bilingual newspaper that was thrown in my lap to write and edit. There was little time for debate and analysis. I learned to succinctly answer queries on the spelling of "Laissez les bons temps rouler" or on the history of Acadian settlement. I silently deplored the sacrifice of accuracy and exegesis to plainness and promptness. Could one really be informed on the complexity of Louisiana French cultures with such packaged bits of information?

Although scholarship and public relations work did not seem to mix very well, some situations lent themselves to an expanded treatment of information. Discussions with colleagues, visiting tourists, students, or courthouse personnel from across the street would grow from questions or comments about the accomplishments of French education programs, the worthiness of Cajun speech compared to academic French, or discrimination against Black Creoles. I relished these occasions especially if they happened on a slow day. I could draw from my academic and practical knowledge to address the issue, and look up documents if needed. I could ask questions, and elicit views and opinions. Occasionally we would engage in a popular sport at the time, criticism of CODOFIL, its endeavors, its personnel, and its ambitions. Outsiders, associates, and even the leadership willingly participated in these vigorous assessments of the insufficiencies of the agency, a never-ending debate which would remain largely internal and private and overall quite civil.

In this context I occupied an awkward position, one of my own doing. As a spokesperson for CODOFIL I was expected to disseminate information that presented the organization and its activities in a favorable light. Thus it was clear that the arrival of a new contingent of foreign French teachers or the establishment of a Cajun organization should be lauded, while the flimsiness of some proposed international trade venture or the meager results of French education programs were to be ignored. My eagerness to provide, when asked, a full picture of the Louisiana French phenomenon conflicted with such a one-sided position. The relation of one particular incident will illustrate how such a divergence could play out.

By 1983, the U.S. Bureau of the Census had released detailed data about ethnic identification and language gathered during the 1980 census. I was very interested in the figures since they were unavailable when I had completed my dissertation and I was curious to see if recent data would support my doctoral assessment. More ambitiously, an analysis of this trove of information still untapped could inform and help shape the cultural policy of CODOFIL. By the time I finished the compilation of the figures, I knew there was trouble ahead. The data on ancestry and location of French speakers were acceptable: about 930,000 Louisianians mostly located in the traditionally Acadian parishes declared some form of French descent, less than the 1.5 million (Jammes, n.d.) claimed but still a robust 22 percent of the state's population. The rest of the statistical picture was more somber: the number of French speakers was put at 291,000 (7 percent of the state population), much less than the symbolic million claimed, and about half the 572,000 which had listed French as their mother tongue in 1970. There were only about 26,000 young French speakers age five to seventeen, a mere 10 percent of the francophone population. In short, after a decade of bilingual educational programs, there were fewer and older French-speaking Louisianians.

When informed of these preliminary findings, chairman Domengeaux first contested their reliability and then forbade their diffusion. It was clear why such a bleak assessment was not welcome. For over ten years, legislators had funded statewide French cultural programs and supported the ethnic renaissance; foreign governments had assisted with teachers and scholarships. All were likely to reassess their involvement in the light of such information. For their part, Cajun activists who had for years criticized CODOFIL's educational policy were certain to be comforted in their approach.

I developed a dual strategy to reconcile my obligations as an employee and a scholar. I proposed an analysis of the figures which could help understand if not explain away the dire statistical situation. There were obvious methodological issues. One dealt with the question the census takers had used. In 1970, it read: "Was a language other than English used in your home when you were young?" In 1980, the question was more precise, immediate, and personal: "Do you speak a language other than English?" I argued that both questions did not measure the same phenomenon, familiarity by one, usage by the other, and thus answers could not be compared. It was also generally accepted that bilingual Cajuns tended to downplay their French-language ability because of the shame attached to their heritage. Then there were analytical issues. These aggregate figures did not lend themselves to far-reaching interpretations. They just measured a situation; they did not yield any detailed information on the efficiency of CODOFIL programs, for instance. In addition, they reflected demographic patterns out of the range of the ethnic movement. If anything, they could show how necessary and urgent actions to support Louisiana French culture were. None of these arguments and none of the positive spin swayed my hierarchy.

Since analysis was ineffective in obtaining the release of public information and violating a direct order did not appear as a constructive option, I opted for the truth. Simply, when I was asked about statistics, I replied that I was not authorized to release current figures and that my chairman or director would address the question. To the best of my recollection aided by notes I took at the times, this went on for several weeks in 1985. The ridicule, disrespect, and self-servingness attached to this maneuver did not, and still do not, escape me. After all, no crime was committed, no public funds were being squandered, no person was in danger. What was I whistle-blowing about? Who had promoted me from Information Specialist to Grand Redresser of the Truth? Did my academic credentials—which, by the way, did not include any advanced training in statistical analysis—give me the right to challenge a popular endeavor? As dubious as it was, the strategy nevertheless proved successful. I believe my boss grew tired of fielding demographic questions. I soon received word that I could release the figures, preferably with adequate explanations, which I did. To my relief, it had no adverse consequences on the organization's funding or status. It did not do it any good either.

The whole episode made me aware that beyond issues of personal and organizational sensibility, CODOFIL had never sought to acquire a sound knowledge of the Cajun experience it looked to change. The organization relied mostly on an impressionistic view of Louisiana's ethnic mosaic, gathered from an upper-class, white, well-educated, and cosmopolitan perspective. Internal debates and public statements, as well as its few publications, suggested no detailed knowledge of language use, socioeconomic characteristics, and cultural expectations among Cajuns and Creoles. Regrettably, it is also useful to point out that no assessment of the racial dimension of the enterprise had been conducted or even considered. Instead flawed estimates served propaganda objectives and reportedly helped gain political support. The urgency of proactive endeavors and the shortage of resources were strong arguments in support of bypassing a scientific assessment of the ethnic situation. In this sense the content and timing of the 1980 census data was counterproductive. However, the handicap of attempting to transform a social situation without the most basic knowledge of its parameters seemed to be even greater. CODOFIL was depriving itself of the information necessary to the understanding of the cultural context and the successful realization of its stated objectives. It is now well documented that CODOFIL's strategy of teaching Standard French and gaining international recognition alienated working-class Cajuns, the movement's main target (Gold 1979; Larouche 1982). Subsequent research has shown that Cajuns' attitudes toward the French language, formal education, and state programs were more complex and ambivalent than the enthusiasm assumed by social and political elite in charge at the time (Ancelet 1988). Buoyed by the outcome of the numbers' game, I proposed to conduct a modest research project, but in vain.

In 1989, the position of director at CODOFIL became open. Encouraged by several colleagues and activists, I submitted my application. Over the course of several interviews, I presented my vision of CODOFIL's mission. It was shaped by both my academic endeavors and my work experience. Much to my surprise, the board of directors hired me although with some reservations, particularly about my French citizenship and lack of leadership experience.

Although I was daunted by the enormity of the task, I relished the opportunity to act in the field I had been involved in for a decade. My previous involvement, as a student and as a spokesperson, had been marginal to the decision-making process since it consisted mostly of critically assessing and publicizing the actions taken. As executive director, I now had the chance to shape and influence the movement. Comments on what "they should do" could now become directives on what "we will do." The feeling of boundless freedom and opportunity was short-lived, though. It quickly succumbed under the weight of politics and bureaucracy (terms taken in their sociological acceptance as organization of power and formal structure of a complex organization). An organization needs people, money, and power, and in the early 1990s, CODOFIL had little of such resources. Personnel consisted of six full-time staffed positions including a secretary and an accountant, toiling alongside a handful of occasional volunteers and contract workers whose availability was limited. The state-funded budget hovered around $300,000, with 85 percent of it dedicated to salaries and operating expenses, the balance being earmarked for scholarships and information expenses. In addition, the dire state of Louisiana's economy and public finances at the time precluded any hopes of additional funding and for a time even threatened the existence of the agency. Finally, as a small outfit, CODOFIL yielded little power. It had no active or powerful constituency akin to the business lobby or the Black Caucus. Its educational and cultural functions were dwarfed by that of the Department of Education or the Office of Tourism; and the urgency of its mission did not compare with that imparted to social services or the criminal justice system. The political profile and savvy of James Domengeaux, a powerful attorney and former congressman, had been instrumental in the establishment and prominence of the agency. However, his death in 1988 and two decades of cultural renaissance significantly eroded CODOFIL's enduring ability to promote its agenda. In short, I could launch any action I deemed necessary as long as it required little personnel involvement and minimal funding! Ambitious plans to revamp the statewide French education program or produce French- language television shows were quickly shelved.

The limits placed on ethnic activism by scarce resources were compounded by a network of obligations contracted over the years. For two decades, the agency had been mandated to manage scholarship programs for Louisiana students, coordinate teacher-training programs, and negotiate cultural agreements with a variety of international partners. As I took office in September of 1989, my able staff lost no time in making me aware of impending deadlines. One I remember vividly dealt with propositions for the 1990–1991 budget due in December. Not only did I have little time to plan a strategy and come up with worthy projects, my accountant convincingly impressed upon me that we could neither count on additional revenues, nor modify personnel positions, nor shift funds between budget line items, nor change the agency's modus operandi without calling on the unwanted attention of auditors and legislators! His advice was to stay put for the time being and conduct business as usual. I sensed that such a move would also suit my board of directors. I went along and waited for my chance.

Clearly, the institutionalization of the French Movement was both a blessing and a serious handicap. It guaranteed predictable resources and a respectable status but it also greatly limited innovation and rapid response. I started to sympathize with my predecessors who, faced with conditions similar to mine, had been able to implement programs, and run them for two decades in the face of much criticism (including mine!) and declining resources. I developed a renewed appreciation for the vision and acumen of James Domengeaux. Alongside his image as an autocratic, yet generous, operator meddling in ethnic affairs appeared another one made of shrewd political skills, cultural foresight, and unshakable resolve. The question was asked with ever more urgency: would I be able to stand up to the task?

Again I drew my resolve from knowledge. A non-Cajun, not prone to emotional involvement, a Francophone *certes* but a cultural relativist at heart, I relied on scholarship to chart my course. I had learned from research that Cajun identity was a process more than a state, a matter of ongoing negotiation more than ineluctable tradition, and a locus of contested options more than a field of unanimity. My work experience had taught me the importance of compromise, the necessity of dealing with a multiplicity of levels (political reality, ethnic emotions, cultural values, economic imperative, and the intangible), and the primacy of practical results.

I had argued in my dissertation that the French language, Acadian past, and international connection with the *francophonie* were the fundamental themes developed by the Louisiana French Movement (Henry 1982:346). I had also proposed that they had been developed in education, the media, and cultural productions "as autonomous phenomenons, independent from one another, disengaged from their social context.

They are reduced to ideological constructions with little basis in social reality" (Henry 1982:376). I listed the disappearance of ethnic shame as the major successful accomplishment and the ambiguous status of the French education program as the most problematic failure; a solid educational structure had been established statewide but it did not teach the language to students. These themes provided me with basic strategic principles and tactical guidelines. What had been done need not be prioritized. By 1990 Louisianians were widely accepting of the state's French heritage; Cajuns and, on a smaller scale, Creoles had acquired some degree of ethnic pride; and the world, especially the French-speaking one, was aware of Louisiana as a tropically exotic part of the United States of America. Exhortations of the Acadian heritage and benefits of bilingualism had been efficient tools to mobilize ethnic consciousness, but propaganda was no longer needed. Similarly, the involvement of the state, local tourist commissions, civic organizations, and a dynamic industry in touristic endeavors called for a disengagement of CODOFIL from this field. On another front, the decline of foreign assistance and the shortcoming of language programs had to be addressed.

I identified three priorities to pursue in the traditional domains of CODOFIL's action: development of French immersion programs, development of French-language media, and development of relations with the Acadian provinces. Implementation had to be possible, rapid, and cost-effective. I also decided to revisit the research project on the linguistic and cultural behavior of Cajuns I had been unable to realize. In cooperation with several organizations, a short questionnaire was designed, a couple of thousand dollars were scrounged, and a handful of investigators were recruited. The telephone survey asked a thousand residents of Southwestern Louisiana brief questions about their language use, ethnic identification, participation in cultural events, and opinion on the bilingual education program. The results were a mixed bag. Some findings—an aging and shrinking French-speaking population—were predictably disappointing. Others—such as the overwhelming support for French language programs in schools—were encouraging or original; for instance, respondents told us they were more likely to use French with family members not living with them than with their immediate relatives. This type of information was not contained in census data and confirmed the much-reported use of French with grandparents and collaterals (Henry 1990). It was not the definitive study I had envisioned but it was all we could afford time- and money-wise.

LESSONS FROM THE FIELD

With hindsight I can make a similarly mitigated assessment of my multifaceted involvement with the Louisiana French Movement. Even as I continue to learn about the Cajun experience, I have already absorbed a handful of lessons. They deal with the limited vistas of agency bounded by social arrangements, the importance of individual adjustments such as impression management and emotion work, and the puzzling situational relevance of the insider-outsider distinction.

I view my tenure at CODOFIL as an exercise in applied anthropology. Framed by the enriching interplay between knowledge and action, it also involved combining structural forces with daily expedience and pursuing grand designs with contrived means. It revealed both the power and power-lessness of human agency. Practically, some of the objectives pursued were met and others were not. On the international front, the formalization of ties with the Acadian provinces of Canada aimed at resolving a paradox. While the Acadian connection was much extolled, Louisiana had no formal rela-tions with either New Brunswick or Nova Scotia. Cultural agreements were signed with and assistance was received from France, Québec, and Belgium but no such mechanism existed with Acadian provinces despite the pro-found emotional affinity and cultural closeness. In 1992, a multilateral agree-ment was signed. In addition to establishing a position of Acadian delegate in Louisiana, it organized the presence of Acadian teachers in Louisiana and the linguistic training of Louisiana teachers and residents in Nova Scotia. A limited administrative endeavor, it was part of a larger movement. A greater awareness of Cajuns' history, the increasing importance of Acadian ancestry in shaping Cajun ethnicity, and practically the disengagement of the govern-ments of France and Québec who shut their Lafayette offices in 1990 and 1992, all contributed to heighten the Acadian dimension. Development of tourism between the Acadie du Nord and Acadie du Sud and the meeting of the World Acadian Congress in Louisiana in 1999 contribute to demonstrate its continued relevance (Henry 1999).

Louisiana's limited but continued presence on the global scene of French culture has resulted in one enduring benefit. In 1990, an agreement was signed with TV5-Québec Canada to allow the transmission of their sig-nal in Louisiana free of charge. The programs of the consortium of French-language public television remain available on Lafayette and New Orleans cable systems. An attempt to keep a French-language publication was not as successful. *LA Gazette de Louisiane*, a monthly newsletter launched the same year, ceased publication in 2002. Advances in computer technology and the Internet (CODOFIL's website was launched in 1995) arguably render ethnic printed material somehow obsolete.

The limited vistas of agency are most obvious in the field of education. In 1992 and 1993, French language immersion programs started to operate in Lafayette, Saint Martin, and Acadia. Located in the core of French Louisiana, they represented an important addition to the two decade-old programs in New Orleans and Lake Charles. Since then, three other programs have been launched and the support for French immersion had been further mobilized by associations such as Action Cadienne and local support groups. Despite their limited scope (about three thousand students in twenty-seven schools as of 2008), these programs succeed where the statewide mandate had failed: they create French speakers.

However, I realized that pursuing further goals would necessitate a political capital I did not have and did not want to acquire. I did consider engaging in a thorough reform of French education and expanding immersion programs. It would also have necessitated the abandonment of the twenty-year-old statewide program. Although largely inefficient and resource-hungry, it still represented the cornerstone of CODOFIL's existence, its raison d'être. I did not believe I could successfully challenge the various parties involved. My board of directors included creators and managers of the said program, the state Department of Education oversaw its operation, and local school boards were allotted teacher positions to run it. I had no constituency, no support network, and little power of persuasion to face these formidable foes. In addition, interruption of one state program did not guarantee its replacement. The risk was just too great to students, teachers, and the ethnic movement in general for such a step to be taken. I backed down.

Unlike my first forays in ethnic activism, in these endeavors I had no theory I could call on to forge ahead. The combined role of global phenomena, technological advances, and local politics would not be harnessed and folded into a neat model. Conceptually, I knew of their impact on the situation of Louisiana French culture, as well as that of history and American social structure. Plotting new operations from my directorial office on Main Street, surrounded by a handful of PCs and collaborators, I practically grasped how truly overwhelming these forces were because they directly interfered with my plans. Human agency may be boundless but I had met my limits. With little inclination toward spinning my wheels and managing programs I doubted, I tended my resignation and looked for another challenge. So, in the fall of 1992, I left activism for academia. Accepting a position in the department of sociology and anthropology at the University of Louisiana at Lafayette, I was greatly pleased to be relieved of the burden of administrative tasks and setting cultural priorities. I planned to expand my doctoral research and draw from my rich work experience to propose a social scientific analysis of the Louisiana French phenomenon. Once again the transition was not as smooth as I had hoped. As I set out to write an updated account of the ethnic movement, I noticed I was struggling to put facts into a scientific perspective. Attempts at a rigorous analysis turned into press releases in defense of the cause. It eventually took about a year, many rewrites, colleagues' advice, and much fierce self-criticism to remove ethnic advocacy from my perspective. Ten years in the field, and still nothing came easy.

The realization of the continued and paradoxical importance of individual characteristics was another lesson. If dealing with structural forces was not enough, one also had to cope with impression management and emotion work. It had started during fieldwork. My efforts to be as unobtrusive as possible were regularly countered by the curiosity and assumptions of people I met. I would be quizzed on my religion, marital status, appreciation of the local cuisine and climate, on French politics, health care in Europe, or nudity on Mediterranean beaches. I would be tested on my familiarity with Cajun vernacular expressions and Louisiana personalities. I was even less prepared for that type of situation than I was for fieldwork methods. I answered these queries with variable degrees of truth to meet both the assumed expectations of my hosts and my professional needs. For a time, my companion and I lied about our unmarried cohabitation, believing that the truth would not sit well with conservative-minded middle-aged Cajuns. I would murk answers on religion ("I am baptized"), politics, and moral stances, change the subject or crack a joke as an awkward compromise between my ideas and what I thought were those of my hosts. I would play up my Canadian connection, familiarity with Louisiana trivia, and Cajun ways in the hope of gaining acceptance. My companion's amiable and cooperative disposition—much appreciated by Cajun males looking for dancing partners—also helped. It was usually a spur-of-the-moment reaction and I seriously doubt I fooled anybody. I didn't care one bit for this conscious impression management and emotion work, but I submitted to these adjustments called for by fieldwork situations.

I experienced many other emotions in the course of fieldwork and employment: puzzlement when told I was speaking Parisian French (for me, it is the sharp-edged slang of cab drivers and shopkeepers), anger when it was suggested I could not understand Cajun culture, chagrin as I shelved cultural activism for the sake of political exigency, confusion in the face of prejudice, humility, frustration, and boredom too. I also admit feeling some satisfaction every time I come across a French-speaking child enrolled in an immersion program, or when I tune in to a French-language program on television. I know I had something to do with the outcome, an unfamiliar position for an anonymous academic. Such perceptions not only impacted the quality of the work, they were part of it.

They certainly were a factor in my positioning in the fields of research and work. The insider-outsider distinction has been declared obsolete by postmodern anthropologists because it is inherently situational. Yet boundaries remain strangely present and active on the ground. Although I was and felt like an outsider when I entered the field, a combination of both familiarity and alienation emerged over the years. Initially, an intensive immersion during an uninterrupted eighteen-month period allowed for a serious socialization to life in Southwest Louisiana. Then, establishing residence in Lafayette, being employed, raising a family there, and getting involved in community activities contributed to my insertion. The field has now become my familiar surrounding. Instead of navigating between contacts and informants, I am now located within networks of friends, acquaintances, and fellow Louisianians. My involvement in cultural activism even brought me deep inside at least one dimension of Louisiana French culture. I saw the French Movement from the outside, the inside, and now the fringe. Occasionally, on my way to my CODOFIL office, I reflected on the irony of my itinerary: the intern becoming the boss, a Parisian academic espousing the Cajun cause. Yet although symbolically located at the heart of the movement, I remained an outsider. While my situation within the agency was unremarkable (none of my predecessors had been natives, some of them and at least one of my Cajun successors holds a Ph.D.), the combination of my personal characteristics and organizational duties kept me aside from a perceived Cajun mainstream. I spoke "real French," was not much of an outdoors enthusiast, had not married a local girl, lived within city limits, and worked for bureaucratic outfits more associated with Baton Rouge politics than with life on the bayou. Cajun colleagues and contacts would often note my un-Cajunness, usually quite amicably and without any hint of xenophobia. I figured I was responsible for such a state of affairs because I knew other expatriates who seemed to have espoused Cajun ways more than I had. However I took solace in the fact that native Cajuns also reported some degree of estrangement from their roots after spending time abroad, attending graduate school, or conversing in academic French.

Interestingly, Louisianians with no Acadian background look to the very same characteristics of mine and remark on their fitting into the cultural environment. I willingly answer questions on aspects of French Louisiana many non-Cajun residents know little about: yes, I can understand "their" Cajun French, I am interested in "their" culture, and indeed, I have connections to traiteurs, musicians, and ethnic activists. I do not mind taking neighbors, acquaintances, and more recently college students on a tour of their native social environment. In fact, I view such instances as fitting combinations of anthropological training with cultural activism. The presentation of information and the exposition of unsuspected patterns can elicit surprise and interest. Similarly, during my stint with CODOFIL, some foreign officials were unsettled at the sight of a nonnative representing the state of Louisiana. It sometimes required some explanation, especially when discussions took place abroad. On occasion it would also elicit the unfounded hope that my native Frenchness would deter me from vigorously defending Louisiana's positions. In such cases, there was no shared meaning of "they" and "we." My counterparts expected me to be "among ourselves," but I gladly remained "one of them." I gradually realized I could be both insider and outsider. The boundary depends on the situation. Never a native but an outsider no more, I occasionally play with the confusion or use its edge. When asked out-of-state where I am from, I answer "Lafayette Louisiana," a statement generally accepted even if the other party reacts to my accented English. Except once in Orlando, Florida, where the Wal-Mart cashier bluntly told me "No, you're not!" She hailed from Crowley, Louisiana, and noted that my accent was French, not Cajun. In a couple of sentences I gave her the short version of my American life to satisfy her curiosity and reassure her I was not a fibber. Our brief encounter ended with her saying she was pleased to meet someone from "back home." I had managed my way back in. That local people still ask about my origins is indicative of my perennial outsider status. When in a playful mood, I answer "the Saint Streets," the unofficial name of the old central neighborhood where I have lived since 1985. That usually is not enough: "But you're not originally from here, are you?" "You're not from France?" Still, considering the confusing origins and migrations of a great number of people, the length of my residence in Louisiana usually suffices to establish my claim to membership in this community.

I have continued to research and write about the Cajun and Creole experience while living in its midst. As I started this journey, I was ignorant of the paradox inherent in the position of the participant-observer, the culture-bound researcher of the Other, or the detached humanist. Pushed by circumstances, prodded by exigencies, confronted with unforeseen situations, I had to adapt. In the process, the field became my home and I turned into a hybrid, a cross between a deterritorialized individual and a grounded anthropologist. Or maybe it is the other way around.

NOTE

I dedicate this text to Patricia and the late Aaron Jortner, to whom I am profoundly and forever grateful. Their gregarious hospitality made my fieldwork an enlightening and pleasurable experience, and their generosity opened the door to America for me and my family.

REFERENCES

Agee, James, & Walker Evans. 1941. *Let Us Now Praise Great Men*. Boston: Houghton Mifflin.

Ancelet, Barry. 1988. "A Perspective on Teaching the 'Problem Language' in Louisiana." *The French Review* 61(3), pp. 345–356.

Artaud, Antonin. 1970 [1956]. *Les Tarahumaras*. In *Oeuvres Complètes*. Paris: Gallimard.

Gold, Gerald. 1979. *The Role of France, Québec and Belgium in the Revival of French in Louisiana Schools*. Projet Louisiane, 7. Downsview, Ontario: York University.

Henry, Jacques. 1982. "Le mouvement louisianais de renouveau francophone: Vers une nouvelle identité cadjine." Dissertation. Paris: Université Paris Descartes.

———. 1990. "Le français nouveau arrive?" *LA Gazette de Louisiane* 1(3), pp. 1, 4, 5; 1(4), pp. 7–8. Lafayette, LA: Fondation CODOFIL.

———. 1999. "Réalignement francophone: Les relations Louisiane-Québec-Acadie." *Francophonies d'Amérique* 9, pp. 63–72.

Jammes, Jean-Marie. n.d. "Le français en Louisiane." Pamphlet on file.

Larouche, Alain. 1982. *Ethnicité, pêche et pétrole: les Cadjins du Bayou Lafourche en Louisiane francophone*. Projet Louisiane, Monograph 1. Toronto: York University.

Malinowski, Bronislaw. 1961 [1922]. *Argonauts of the Western Pacific*. New York: E. P. Dutton.

8. FIELDWORK IN FRENCH LOUISIANA

A Québec Experience

—Cécyle Trépanier and Dean Louder

Our experience as researchers in French Louisiana goes back to 1978. It has been a love affair lasting a quarter of a century. Few "foreign" researchers have had such a long acquaintance with the region. We were there when recognition outside the United States was still embryonic. Today, Louisiana figures prominently on the map of *La Francophonie*, participates in its summitry, and is a frequent subject of discussion or scrutiny at its numerous cultural and academic manifestations.[1] To declare ourselves foreigners may be considered an exaggeration by some. Louder is an *Américain* by birth and a *Québécois* by choice. Trépanier, a dyed-in-the-wool *Québécoise*, grew up with the knowledge that at one time Louisiana and Québec were in the same boat, the French colonial Empire, with "us" at the bow, on the St. Lawrence, and "them" at the stern, on the Mississippi.

Once in Louisiana, however, it became clear to us that despite a certain historical complicity, we were nevertheless in a foreign land. We were definitely outsiders—French-speaking North Americans from Québec. Scarcely a year before our arrival in Louisiana, the population of *la belle province*,[2] as it was called then, had elected a government dedicated to obtaining political sovereignty for Québec. This event would obviously influence our perception of French Louisiana. Louisiana has changed dramatically in recent years; the same can be said of Québec which, while acquiring the economic leverage and institutional maturity necessary for the realization of its sovereignist

Dean Louder's research on French America leaves a wide trail of scholarship on land or at sea.

dream, has not yet succeeded in convincing 50 percent of its people.[3] Hence, the dream of the 1970s remains just that for the moment, a dream.

Given the rapidly evolving nature of Québec and Louisiana societies and cultures, it is useful to divide our Louisiana research experience into three distinct periods, each with its own context, raison d'être, approach, and results. The late 1970s marked the excitement and emotion of "initial discovery." The 1980s dampened our enthusiasm and sowed seeds of doubt with regard to the future of French Louisiana. In the 1990s, our worst fears were confirmed in a phase best described as one of desertion and dismay, but also of renewed solidarity. This chapter relates the vicissitudes of our fieldwork during each period.

THE LATE 1970s: YEARS OF DISCOVERY

Our curiosity about French Louisiana was piqued in the early 1970s as word filtered out of the creation of CODOFIL (Council for the Development of French in Louisiana) in 1968 and the almost immediate departure to the bayou state of relatively young Québécois. Their mission, as negotiated through meetings between James Domengeaux and then Québec premier,

Jean-Jacques Bertrand, appeared to be the preservation of the French language by teaching in the Louisiana school system. Further, the second Festival de musique traditionnelle du Québec organized in Montréal in 1974 by André Gladu and Jean-Luc Moisan brought into the public eye the richness of French Louisiana culture through the music of special guests Dennis McGee and Sadie Courville. Shortly thereafter, Revon Reed's *Lâche pas la patate* (1976) was published in Cajun French in Montréal. Almost simultaneously, the young Zachary Richard burst onto the Québec scene. It was becoming impossible to ignore French Louisiana. The thick layers of decades of collective amnesia were being peeled away. In a recent interview, Gladu (2001), currently a producer at the National Film board and author of the series *Le Son des Français d'Amérique*, which includes a half dozen films on French Louisiana, reflected upon the importance of the emergence or rediscovery of Louisiana in the mid-1970s:

> For us, Louisiana is at once a window on this continent, and a window toward the contemporary United States. . . . More than in any other community—even Québec and Acadie—the drama of the French in America has never been so well demonstrated as in Cajun music. That drama and the reason for which Cajuns are particularly expressive is that they haven't suffered the fate described so accurately by the ethnographer Robert-Lionel Séguin, that of having been domesticated rather than colonized.
>
> The drama of French Canadians, Québécois, Acadiens is that they have learned to live with violence of their disappearance. The example which comes to mind is that of the Acadian Deportation, which is seen here as a romantic episode, whereas everywhere else, it would be seen for what it was, an ethnic genocide coolly calculated. . . .
>
> Furthermore, Cajuns were subjected to religion to a much lesser extent than us in Québec and thus escaped the brainwashing that we received. Having remained independent in character and very Latin, Cajuns have maintained a side much closer to the French than we have, while at the same time preserving an old Acadian strain of resistance. Thus, they have not hesitated to incorporate it into their music. It is in this sense that traditional Cajun music has become much more expressive and dramatic than ours. That is why Louisiana was unavoidable. Whether we like it or not in Québec, we must agree that very important things have been said, are being said in Louisiana, with respect to our past and for our future as French speakers in America.

Our own discovery and exploration of French Louisiana was made possible through a concerted research effort called *Projet Louisiane* (1976–1979) which had, as its principal objective, the investigation of the so-called French revival in Southwestern Louisiana. The project was interdisciplinary, the creation of a group of anthropologists and geographers at three universities in Québec and Ontario (McGill, Laval, and York). It nevertheless involved and required, in its initial preparatory phase, the participation of Cajun social scientists and educators. For example, Louisiana State University sociologist Alvin Bertrand, who had cut his academic teeth under the guidance of well-known Louisiana State University scholar of the 1930s, Vernon Parenton, and Malcolm Comeaux, Cajun geographer trained at Louisiana State University under Fred Kniffen, both came to McGill University in 1976 to counsel, advise, and share their knowledge and insight. The former exhibited enthusiasm for the project throughout its duration. The latter manifested a certain skepticism because of what he considered to be an overemphasis upon language and the use of French as an ethnic marker in defining Cajun culture and French Louisiana.

Once in the field, young native speakers were selected through local and professional networks, then hired, along with several research assistants from Québec, to conduct household interviews. Their entry, knowledge of local peoples and conditions, and criticism of method proved invaluable. These included Debbie Clifton, Rose Anne Guidry, Richard Guidry, Michael LeBlanc, Glen Pitre, and Ulysses Ricard. Clifton, a researcher, writer, and community activist; Richard Guidry, an official with the State's foreign language program; and Pitre, a cinematographer, have since become dominant figures in contemporary French Louisiana. Ricard, prior to his untimely death, had carved out a significant niche in the field of Creole research. When asked in 1990 to assess the local impact of *Projet Louisiane*, Richard Guidry offered this analysis:

Debbie, Glen and I would never have met . . . I would never have gone to McGill. Glen may never have obtained the inspiration necessary to make his films. It is through *Projet Louisiane* that I was able to begin studying the different Louisiana dialects. Now many students from all over the world come see me for advice on linguistic studies of French and Creole languages in Louisiana. But . . . it seems impossible to truly measure the overall impact that your project had upon Louisianans. Despite all that one would like to say to the contrary, the population speaks more and more English and less and less French. (Louder 1990)

The research focused upon both rural and urban localities. In the case of the former, fieldworkers were sent into four widely recognized French-speaking areas (Mamou Prairie, St. Martin Parish, bayous Lafourche and Ter-rebonne), and two more peripheral areas, one within Louisiana (Avoyelles Parish) and one outside (China, Texas). In addition, three urban areas were selected, two on the margins of French Louisiana (New Orleans's Westbank and Port Neches, Texas, located in the greater Port Arthur–Beaumont con-urbation) and one at its heart, Lafayette. Interviews were carried out at two levels: (1) with local elites and educators involved in the revival and in foreign transnational ties with Québec, Belgium, and France, and (2) in households randomly selected in the areas just identified. Interviews, it should be noted, were nearly always carried out in the French language. Of the more than six hundred extended household interviews, which examined a wide range of topics touching French Louisiana culture, only a handful were done in English.[4] The vast majority of those interviewed, whether White, Black, Creole, or Indian, were able to express themselves in one of the regional variants of the French language which our researchers, Louisianans, or Québécois, were able to speak to a degree, understand, and transcribe.

Projet Louisiane brought credibility to the French Movement in Loui-siana by proving just how prevalent the language continued to be and how mutually intelligible the local variants and Québec French were. It con-firmed the desirability of saving what was left, which was considerably more than many thought. It likewise established a benchmark for the state of the French language in Louisiana at the close of the 1970s and provided archival materials for future reference. Publications deriving from *Projet Louisiane* proliferated.[5] Monographs and working papers were diffused throughout the French-speaking world. Scholarly articles dotted the academic literature both in English and French. *Projet Louisiane* researchers became authorities of note, enjoying a love-hate relationship with CODOFIL's president, who appreciated the notoriety that they brought, but resented the criticism that they frequently formulated.

Projet Louisiane would also have a marked impact upon geographic scholarship in Québec. It gave impetus to the development of a Laval model or school of cultural geography arising from the creation in 1979 of a course titled "Le Québec et l'Amérique française" at Laval University. Since its inception, this course, offered annually, has sought to remind Laval Univer-sity students of the continental dimension of French culture in America, to awaken a sensitivity to and an awareness of the challenges inherent in living in French outside Québec and to the traditional and contemporary roles played by Québec with respect to other French populations of both Canada and the United States. Given the impossibility of realizing these objectives without leaving Québec and going into the field, an obligatory excursion was instituted in the course with the result that over the past two decades *Projet Louisiane* researchers and their students have frequented nearly every island and islet of the French archipelago of North America.[6] *Projet Louisiane* contributed significantly "to renewal of l'Amérique française/French America as a legitimate field of social science endeavor."[7]

For Louder, a young professor brought to Laval University in 1971 from Seattle to teach quantitative methods, and Trépanier, a recent Laval (1977) graduate in urban geography, involvement with *Projet Louisiane* would constitute an immense learning experience and launch major changes in career orientation.[8] First, it meant working closely with a team of highly motivated people who talked constantly about Louisiana and research findings. Second, the anthropological underpinnings of *Projet Louisiane* implied several methodological adjustments by the geographers. For instance, much importance was given to participant observation. Hence, when in Rome not only does one do as the Romans do, but one writes daily, in considerable detail, what the Romans do, say, and think. Interviewing techniques were also quite different: a first visit to break the ice and request an appointment, then the follow-up and the administration of a lengthy questionnaire containing open questions—many seemingly quite indiscreet. Interviews were recorded and eventually transcribed. Once finished, it was as though we knew the people's lives and their very souls better than did their family and friends. All this was a far cry from the "number crunching" in quantitative geography and the analysis of intra-urban mobility that had up to that time characterized our research endeavor. Of course, it became clear from the beginning that research of this type must be at once objective but critical.

The learning experience went smoothly, in large part because of the warm hospitality and friendship of French Louisianans. It is fair to say, however, that the fieldwork generated a host of feelings and perceptions, not always objective, and frequently contradictory.[9] Trépanier summarizes these feelings in four words: surprise, admiration, anger, and frustration. The surprise derived from many aspects of the French Louisiana reality. First, even though she worked mostly in the urban milieu, Westwego and Lafayette, she did almost all of her interviews in French. This seemed like a miracle given the scant visibility of the French language in every public situation. Second, the fear of not being able to communicate properly in French with the people proved false. Once she had mastered a few regional terms and a few English words, she and her informants understood each other easily. She made an effort to use old French words, those of her grandmothers' generation, and to adopt as nearly as possible the local accent. Third, French speakers did not necessarily have a French name. In fact, many of them did not. A French patronym as an indication of Cajunness means relatively little. Fourth, the lack of pride in Cajun identity was striking. It was necessary to use the word "Cajun" with care. Fifth, among all the people interviewed, essentially none had any idea as to what CODOFIL was, the organization supposedly in charge of preserving their linguistic heritage. Sixth, the racial situation, particularly within the Catholic Church, astounded her. The existence of a Black and a White church even in the smallest community was difficult to fathom. At home, language had constituted the main social barrier, not race.

The admiration came from the richness of the culture she was discovering: the beauty of the language, its link with music, and its unique sounds, dancing styles, and the joie de vivre of the dancers; the food, with its emphasis on rice, the variety of exotic ingredients and the way they were blended, to say nothing of the devotion of those who ate it. Also striking was the closeness of the family and the community, the importance of nature and wildlife in daily life as expressed by the pride in vast gardens and freezers overflowing with vegetables and game. She had never known such generosity as here. The ability of the people to offer warm hospitality to strangers left her astounded.

The anger and frustration originated mainly from the behavior of such public institutions as church, government, school, as well as private business, all of which treated the French speakers as though they were not French. It seemed strange to spend the week speaking French exclusively with people and then attend Mass with them on Sunday where not a word would be uttered in their mother tongue: a revolting situation for someone impregnated with the idea of "faith as guardian of language."[10] One event stands out vividly. The priest in Westwego had promised to announce in church the visit of a Cajun theater group from the Lafayette area, the Théâtre 'Cadien, whose purpose was to provide entertainment, but also to rekindle pride in language and culture. For whatever reason, the announcement was not made. As a result, few people attended this very special event in their French-speaking area. Little respect was shown them, even by those called to serve them. They were treated as Anglo-Americans in their own community, whereas in their own eyes and conversation, *Américains* referred to "others," not to them. More appalling to us, as outsiders, was that such treatment bred no anger whatsoever on their part. To them, it was par for the course. To us, it was an unacceptable aberration, an abomination, an insult. Their acceptance of a demeaning situation lent credence to the treatment and proved them, after all, to be American in outlook. We were not!

These years of discovery provided insight into the ethnic complexity of French Louisiana and an appreciation for the diversity of contexts in which "French" culture evolves in North America. French Louisiana was much more than an exotic place. It was, in fact, the cradle of a multiplicity of lively French cultures, all changing rapidly, yet always playing second fiddle in their own orchestra.

THE 1980s: YEARS OF DOUBT

Despite the depth of knowledge about contemporary French Louisiana provided by *Projet Louisiane*, many holes remained. The project's working papers and monograph series generally focused on a single subregion. Little effort was made to integrate or compare the information and produce a more global analysis.[11] Given that the subregions studied were well-known and considered "typical," researchers and activists in the French Movement had only a vague idea of what was occurring in the more anonymous parts of the cultural region. In addition to the lack of geographical perspective, key aspects of the society and culture had received surprisingly little attention. Such was the case for religion and food. These would become the focus of Trépanier's doctoral dissertation at Pennsylvania State University.

French Louisiana at the Threshold of the 21st Century, completed in 1988, sought to define French Louisiana geographically. To do so, three sets of questions were asked: (1) Where are the boundaries of French Louisiana? How have they changed through time? Has French Louisiana grown or shrunk? Has the geographic change been systematic? (2) Within the boundaries of French Louisiana, is there more than one French subculture? Are any of these French subcultures regionalized? Has the regionalization changed? and; (3) Does the intensity of "Frenchness" vary geographically, and have patterns of intensity changed over time?

Detailed new data were necessary to answer these questions. For spatial precision, individual communities were chosen as the basic geographic unit for field research. Hence, to deal with the first question, it was necessary to find out whether residents perceived their communities to be "French" or to

have been French in the past. To answer the second question, it was necessary to determine which French identity the community assumed: Cajun,
Creole, Black Creole, or Indian. Two approaches were used to examine cultural variation. In the first, residents evaluated the "Frenchness" of their area
of the cultural region. In the second, the local change of traditional culture
was examined. It was impossible to document the change of all aspects of
traditional culture. Instead, research focused on three markers which have
been described by many researchers as being at the core of the French Louisiana culture: French language, Catholic religion, and foodways. Focusing
on these markers, the thesis follows cultural change across the region.

Two other decisions followed: the choice of the communities and the
choice of respondents. To select the former, two goals were set: cover the area
systematically while selecting enough communities to provide the needed
precision given a graduate student's time and means. Initially, communities were selected randomly by placing a thirty-by-thirty-mile grid over the
southern part of the official highway map of Louisiana and its surrounding areas. The communities chosen were the closest to the intersections of
the grid. Field adjustments made in the roster of study locations eventually
provided thirty-five full study communities within the cultural region while
many other communities, mostly at its border, were also visited.

Three principles guided the choice of respondents likely to provide the
needed information: uniformity (to ensure that data gathered were comparable from community to community, they should be obtained from the
same groups everywhere), familiarity (data should be obtained only from
residents who are knowledgeable about their community), and accessibility
(data should be obtained from residents who are easily accessible in order
to make efficient use of time in the field). Certain types of residents, because
of their roles or functions, are keys to the entire community. They are, in a
sense, public figures, and therefore accessible to outsiders. They also have
access to community information that others might not routinely receive. In
French Louisiana communities, postmasters, grocery store managers, and
priests are among such residents. Not only do these people know a great
deal about the community as a whole, but they may be able to point to other
residents with long experience in the locality. Thus, in each full study community, a postmaster or grocery store manager, as well as a priest, were
asked at the end of their interview to recommend longtime residents who
were especially knowledgeable about the community. Preferably, these older
people were at least sixty-five years old, so they had been in or had finished

school when French was banished from the public schools in 1922. They were required to be native to the community or to have lived in it most of their adult lives. These older residents had lived through several generations of community transformation. They should be married, with children and grandchildren, so that social and cultural changes from their grandparents' through their grandchildren's generations could be, hence, within the period of time covered by field research that reached back to the last quarter of the nineteenth century. Protestant ministers, when available for interview, were also considered useful respondents even though usually not French. Not only was it interesting to compare the information they provided with that given by priests, but they also were able to reveal an outsider's view of the French Catholic community.[12]

The four groups of respondents numbered 197. A special questionnaire was designed for each of them. The postmaster or grocery store manager received the shortest form, fifteen questions aimed primarily at identifying the character of the community and agents of change. The questionnaire for religious leaders also focused on the character of the community while exploring more in depth religious attitude and behavior. The longest form was conceived for the senior respondents (seventy-one questions) and sought to explore all the aspects of the research. Interviews were not taped and were much shorter than those of *Projet Louisiane*. The number of interviews in English varied markedly from group to group and community to community, but overall, fewer than half were in that language. Interviews generally took one day per community, starting at 8:00 a.m. and ending around 6:00 p.m. Trépanier worked from east to west, relying for sustenance on the hospitality of a few families spread across the length and breadth of the region.

Because interviews were almost exclusively conducted at the community level and not with *gros chiens* involved in the French Movement, as was the case with *Projet Louisiane*, the research effort left a smaller ripple. The results, geographically grounded, strengthened those of *Projet Louisiane*, and, hence, were far from encouraging from a Québécois perspective. They emphasized the triumph in Louisiana of an American style ethnic identity and model of cultural survival. By and large, this meant that even though the territory of French Louisiana was shrinking, promoters and politicians succeeded in creating an official and artificial one called Acadiana, along with a central "capital," Lafayette, to replace the fragmented and far-flung regional centers. Cajun identity emerged as the dominant regional identity overshadowing dramatically Creole identity that could have been racially inclusive. As a result, rather than attaining unity among French speakers, the opposite occurred. Black Creoles continued to be left out despite their significant contribution to the uniqueness of French Louisiana within the context of North American *francophonie*. The Caribbean connection remained obscured by the Canadian and, more specifically, the Acadian connection.

Cajun identity, which during the heyday of *Projet Louisiane* was defined primarily by cultural behavior, came in the 1980s to be determined by a particular set of perceived cultural roots, mostly Acadian. Culturally, this meant that the Catholic label, largely by default, remained an effective group marker in the conservative Protestant South. French language, per se, held little value; its renewal contributed to the establishment of a ceremonial language, not a language for use in everyday life. On the other hand, Cajun food had come into vogue, exhibiting the trappings of a national fad. From our perspective, the fact that French Louisiana constantly sought outside approval for its ethnicity in order to maintain itself was not reassuring. What would happen when ethnicity goes out of style?

Trépanier's work in the 1980s, limited in scope compared to that of *Projet Louisiane* a decade earlier and the work of a single individual, nevertheless provided, in the words of Acadian and Cajun observers, an accurate snapshot of French Louisiana at the threshold of the 1990s.[13] More importantly, however, at a personal level, her Louisiana experience changed the researcher forever. In 1976, she had voted for the *Parti Québécois*, like almost everybody in Québec, more as a reaction to a bad Liberal government than as a vote in favor of political sovereignty. Experiencing "French" Louisiana was an eye-opener, not just for us, but for the many Québécois who came to Louisiana as French teachers beginning in 1972 (Gold 1984). They perceived Louisiana "as providing a warning . . . as to what could happen to Québec if it fails to take its political destiny into its own hands" (Waddell 1979:19). Early in the 1970s, Québec's artists sang nostalgically of Louisiana: a *pays perdu*, a lost country.[14] In the 1980s, the expression "Louisianisation" of Québec became a way of expressing dissatisfaction with the political laxity apparent in Québec's linguistic matters.[15] This frustration derived from the referendum of 1980 when Québec's population rejected the sovereignty option proposed by René Lévesque's government. Herein lies a possible explanation why the 1980s can be branded as years of doubt, not just concerning French Louisiana, but with respect to all French speakers in North America.

THE 1990s: YEARS OF DESERTION, DISMAY, AND RENEWED SOLIDARITY

In the 1990s, the hope that French Louisiana would take its own destiny in hand and rally a significant part of the population into an ethnic revival movement remained utopian. Despite the unfailing commitment of many leaders and important advances in education via the immersion programs, and more modest progress in the media, the consensus of outside observers of the Louisiana scene was that it was too little, too late.

This perception had ramifications on the political front, seriously affecting official relations between Québec and Louisiana. In 1992, the Québec government pulled out of Lafayette, closing its office opened in 1969, and moved to Atlanta. In 1995, while adopting for the first time in its history an official policy toward the French communities outside Québec, it did not take into account its near and numerous neighbors, the Franco-Americans of New England or the Louisiana French. This new policy was limited to Canada. In the words of Canadian Minister of Intergovernmental Affairs Louise Beaudoin, "this struggle for survival is shared by all North American French-speakers, and more acutely by those of Canada" (Gouvernement du Québec 1995). At the heart of the policy was the French language, considered in its Canadian context: "the French-speakers [of Canada] share the strong conviction that the promotion of the French language passes by the right to express oneself in this language in all their daily activities."[16] It was the end of an era. Louisiana had lost its credibility and Québec its hope. Three years later, however, the same government invited Earlene Broussard, then director of CODOFIL, to attend, as special guest, the first triennial forum, a key element in the implementation of the new policy. Hence, Louisiana was used to depoliticize potentially explosive relations between Québec and Canada's francophone and Acadian communities,[17] while at the same time granting Louisiana attention and offering visibility.

Despite the ambiguity of the Québec-Louisiana relationship, the progressive disengagement on the Québec side is obvious. The consequences are significant, especially in light of Gold's (1984:131–132) assessment of the importance of the influence of Québec to the French Louisiana revival movement: "The Louisiana French could not have acted the way they did without transnational assistance. In fact, there may not have been a French movement in Louisiana were it not for Québec and the widespread interest in ethnic revival in the late 1960s. . . . Quebec's and France's presence provided an aura of international legitimacy to regional elites whose status had been eclipsed by the development of the petrochemical industry and the displacement of power away from regional centres." More recently, Cajun musician and activist Zachary Richard (2001), editorializing in Montréal's *La Presse*, reiterated the importance of Québec for communities such as his: "Québec is in a unique position. It is capable of assuming the defense of threatened cultures because its own experience grants it legitimacy." With time and with other priorities, desertion as opposed to rapprochement has become the rule.

Throughout the 1990s, we have revisited Louisiana periodically. The commercialization of the culture, anticipated earlier, was in full swing. The word Cajun, once invisible to the naked eye, can be observed everywhere. It is engraved on anything for sale! Even the French Quarter of New Orleans tries to be Cajun! The Cajun label is associated more than ever with its Acadian antecedent and less and less with its diverse origins. This association reached a climax in August 1999 when the Acadiens from around the world, but particularly from Canada's Maritimes Provinces, gathered in Louisiana for *Retrouvailles 2000* in order to meet their distant kin.

For us, the informal routes of discovery of the late 1970s and early 1980s have become official ones. We traveled them once again in October 2000, accompanied by fifteen students from Laval University, ranging in age from twenty to twenty-five, enrolled in the aforementioned course, "Le Québec et l'Amérique française." The rest of this chapter relates that field experience, sharing some of the thoughts of contemporary French-speaking university students from Québec. Before their departure for the weeklong stay in Louisiana, the students had listened to twelve hours of lectures, seen numerous relevant films, and visited the Musée de l'Amérique française in Quebec City. They had read abundantly, including Le Menestrel's probing analysis of tourism and identity in Louisiana. They had also participated in a joyful encounter, and heated debate, with a group of Franco-Americans from Maine who had been invited to class.

The group arrived in Lafayette in October. Because of its centrality and the availability of hospitable accommodation, the nearby town of Abbeville was selected as our home base. The five-day program accentuated the regional diversity of South Louisiana and focused upon a limited number of research themes. The first day was devoted to the culturally and racially diverse Teche environment, traditionally dependent upon sugar cane (Breaux Bridge, Parks, and St. Martinville). The second explored the Prairie milieu with its rice and soja culture and strong Cajun identity (Mamou and Eunice). The way of life in both regions is, of course, significantly marked by the petroleum industry. The third day provided a glimpse of the original Acadian settlement in St.

James Parish and of the cradle of Creole Louisiana, New Orleans. Day four was devoted to the twin themes of education and communication and day five to ethnic institutions, tourism, and economic relations.

The list of the institutions visited is long, as is that of those knowledgeable people who accepted to enlighten us.[18] Their kaleidoscopic vision of the region provided us a unique opportunity to take the pulse of contemporary French Louisiana. In addition, the students practiced what we call *flânerie savante*, loitering, listening, and talking with as many people as possible in their free time and recording their observations in their *journal de bord*. This precious document, containing observations along with daily and final syntheses, would account for 50 percent of the students' final grade for the course.

In order to best summarize these impressions, we have selected excerpts from what seemed to us the most coherent and best-written journals.[19] What do these excerpts represent? They reflect the students' views or what they retained from the whole experience. Yes, we prepared them through lectures. Yes, they had seen movies and read what others thought about French Louisiana or how they perceived it. But they also had the opportunity to confront what they had been told or had read with what they saw and what they heard in Louisiana. Do we share their views? Many of them, of course, but not all. For instance, their annoyance with the "repetitive sounds and rhythms" of Cajun music and their distaste for local cuisine, which they found, in general, to be "fatty" and high in cholesterol, clearly reveal that these were students of another generation compared to their professors, who had discovered French Louisiana twenty-five years earlier! What did not change, though, was the interest of our hosts in knowing our students' perceptions.

After introductory comments to provide background, we present the excerpts organized around three leading and recurrent themes: (1) the fragility of the culture as evidenced by the place to which French is relegated despite the official discourse; (2) the delicate and complex relationship between Cajuns and Creoles; and (3) the courage of the region's cultural warriors, in contrast with the passivity of the population at large, and the need for francophone solidarity throughout North America.

The Fragility of the Culture

The fragility of the culture, as evidenced by the place to which French is relegated despite official discourse to the contrary, was one of

Trépanier's conclusions in the 1980s. The insistence of the students on French language may be considered a Québécois characteristic (some might say bias). In Canadian society language, not race, is the most significant social divide, whereas in the United States it is the other way around. The numerous comments on language underline the invisibility of French and its secondary status within Cajun culture. The students viewed as hypocritical the use of French to enhance tourism while at the same time limiting efforts and budgets for teaching it to youngsters in school. They observed that French remains marginal within the society and that teachers are frustrated by the limited pedagogical resources available for its propagation. The students' comparison of CODOFIL's budget with that of the Office of Tourism in Lafayette speaks for itself. They are the ones who made the connection. Nevertheless, they close on a happy note in pointing out the interest that out-of-state people have for French and the opportunities it may provide. This is an aspect we had never considered. Beside language, the importance of music as an ethnic marker is recognized. Here again, the link with tourism is very much in evidence.

The Invisibility of French

> French, despite its importance, remains hidden; French speakers are invisible. [C.-R.C]

> French in Louisiana is a rather hidden French. It is so well hidden that Cajun French speakers speak to each other in English unless there is some specific reason to pursue a discussion in French. [M.G.]

> When one arrives at Lafayette [airport], only a few words in French testify to the long-past French colonization. A few well-meaning slogans of an exotic nature relate what Americans have done with Francos. They make use of this "foreign" language, this exoticism to attract the curiosity of the tourists. They make good use of a few linguistic gyrations to feed the ultimate American concern: making money (*faire du fric*). [F.C.]

The Place of French within the Culture and the Tourist Industry

> Life is difficult in Louisiana. It's difficult for a Cajun to live in French in Louisiana. Even though French immersion courses are available in

many parishes, it's always necessary to struggle to maintain the small gains that are achieved. At Lafayette's Prairie Elementary School, where around two-thirds of the courses are given in French, the number of youngsters has increased. The pupils, whose parents or grandparents speak French or are of French origins, are in a minority. Most students are sent to these institutions to learn a new language. The teachers are Louisianan, French, Acadian, Québécois, or Belgian. . . . Even though textbooks and teaching materials [in French] are rare in Louisiana, the teachers are resourceful and succeed in collaborating with other immersion schools' teachers. The results of these schools are fantastic. The youngsters are motivated and encouraged. The workforce is dynamic. . . . The teachers are rewarded by their pupils' success: they excel in French and other academic subjects. However, secondary French immersion schools are rare and children have to struggle if they wish to continue to live in French daily. Sure, some families are supportive of language learning. Nevertheless, many children will lose the use of French when immersed in the American pool. All that surrounds the youth contributes to assimilation. [F.C.]

[In Cajun Country], we have seen many things and met many people who work for the preservation and continuation of the French language and its culture. The culture is maintained through the availability of French radio, museums, the Jean Lafitte national parks, and programs like *Le rendez-vous des Cajuns* at the Liberty Theater in Eunice, which highlights Cajun music. Despite all of this, it does not seem that the [French] language is directly associated with the Cajun identity. Many people understand French but do not speak it. Nevertheless, they consider themselves "Cajuns," in the same way that Franco-Americans from New England consider themselves "French" despite the fact they do not speak French. [M.G.]

French, which from a tourist point of view is not necessary, is not encouraged in many places despite CODOFIL's efforts. But is it for that that "French" is threatened to disappear in Louisiana? Some optimists will say no, that it will survive and occupy a certain place in this society. Others, seeing those who live in French, will say that it's something for the elderly, and that in spite of immersion schools, French is bound to disappear with this generation, especially given that most immersion students are not Cajuns. I believe that if the current infrastructure had stronger financial support from the State, as well as more support for development of the culture, that French would have a chance to flourish in places other than daycare centers, immersion schools, and the offices of CODOFIL. [M.G.]

What are Cajuns without the French language? A bowl of spiced gumbo that you eat to the sound of a folkloric waltz? For some, French is necessary to Cajun identity. For others, the promotion of gastronomy and music is vital for Cajuns and their survival. It is true that good food and special music are characteristics of the Cajun community, but they are not cultural objects; the Cajun language cements them. However, promoters of tourism don't give a damn about the language question. It's not what fills the coffers of the State. . . . The Office of Tourism [of Lafayette] does very well with several grants and a budget of 1.5 million dollars. . . . CODOFIL must accomplish its mission with a budget of 215,000 dollars. [F.C.]

French as Perceived by Outsiders

From the beginning of the trip, I thought that French was above all something for Cajuns and Creoles. But, the things we did today demonstrated that this is not necessarily the case. The fact that young adults from Texas who have no French roots whatsoever come to study at University of Louisiana–Lafayette and decide to study French for personal gain and the opportunities that it offers, was a pleasant discovery. A question: are non-Cajuns more interested in the French language than those whose ancestors spoke it? [M.G.]

A Passion for a Music and International Recognition

As we have noticed today, folk music is much loved by contemporary Cajuns. However, it is the elderly who seem to enjoy dancing the most to the sound of a "One Step" waltz or a "Two Step." The numerous foreigners or tourists are not left out, swaying hips to the sound of the violin or the accordion. I know now that this music is internationally recognized and that those who like it show their appreciation of its rhythm by dancing. Many Cajuns play a musical instrument, many others "swing." Furthermore, it is this joie de vivre that the tourists come to see. Hence, Cajun music has become a "tourist trap," a highly promoted attraction within the United States and the whole world. In most of the dance halls visited, the number of outsiders was greater than the number of local people. This folk music culture is a source of revenue for many musicians, instrument makers, dance professors, and radio broadcasters. Is Cajun music only a business question or an authentic cultural manifestation? I believe that the Louisiana French—even though most of them communicate in English—are authentic musicians and the Cajun sound a true revelation. Nevertheless, the young "traditionalists" are rather rare but they exist; we saw it at the Liberty Theater. They have lightly modified the sound of Cajun music by the addition of certain instruments, the influence of rock and jazz, hence a new generation of Cajun music. Besides, the fact that the group *Charivari* favors French is very encouraging, considering the precarious situation of this language in the Anglo-Saxon sea. [F.C.]

"Bourbon Street" radiated with the horrible smell of "the day after," a residue of the numerous revelers wandering through the noisy streets, alleys, and bars. New Orleans does not deny its French origins. The French Quarter has made its own French frivolity, individualism, and joie de vivre. To do so, it promotes the continuous party—twenty-four hours round the clock—and all the craziness. Furthermore, the metropolis has acquired all the up-to-date cultural characteristics of the surrounding Cajun and Creole communities. One can hear jazz, blues, but also Cajun and Zydeco music. Hence, the superficial tourists don't have to cross the scary bayous to dance in the parish halls of Lafayette, Eunice, or Mamou. The Cajun population does not identify itself with *la ville*. . . . People who go to New Orleans have little interest in Acadiana's cultural specificity; they come to party. Nevertheless, the city is interesting for its ethnic diversity. . . . In the streets of the old French Quarter . . . one can see exhibitionists and proud gays; punks chased by police; tourists from Georgia and Alabama in tight shorts with camera around their neck; musicians of blues and jazz offering great performance. Rare are the places in the United States where madness is not a reason to be locked up! [F.C.]

The Relationship between Cajuns and Creoles

The students' thoughts on the relationship between Cajuns and Black Creoles may have been motivated by the fact that for us, the professors, the originality of French Louisiana, within French America, is its *créolité*. In our view, French Louisiana is not *L'Acadie du sud* but a colonial hearth in its own right, where, very early, cultures merged and influenced each other (Louder, Trépanier, & Waddell 1994, 1999). The excursion provided the students a first personal encounter with "Black Creoles" who spoke for themselves, not through us, and not through Cajuns. Even though these encounters were few, they seem to have marked the students. There were two important discoveries, facts that we, the professors did not know, before the excursions, that may have colored their perceptions. The first was revealed during our visit to St. Martinville, where we visited both the Acadien Memorial and the site of the future "African American Museum" in the company of two young Black Creoles, who resented that such a name be given to the new museum celebrating their culture. The second came as a result of learning of the relatively new relationship between CODOFIL and Haïti, and a similar relationship with a few French-speaking countries of Africa, in the quest for French teachers for the Black Creole community of Louisiana. What follows are the students' comments pertaining to the delicate and complex relationship between Cajuns and Creoles.

> Today, the relations between the two communities are tense. In the Cajun places we visited, Creoles were absent. [C.-R.C.]

> CODOFIL tries to integrate Creoles into its program. Here again, they recruit teachers outside the state, especially in countries where Creole is spoken. Can we interpret this act as an attempt to draw the two communities together? Hard to say. The example of the future museum in St. Martinville provides many potential problems. On the one hand, the museum is devoted to Cajuns, their history, beginning with the Deportation and up to the settling of Louisiana, and to the development of their culture. On the other, the museum is also for the Creole community, but its name speaks of "Afro-Americans." [M.G.]

> Thus, bearing a French name and saved from slavery, he [the Creole] grew up in freedom—contrary to the Afro-Americans—in the company of his mother. . . . It's for that reason that the name of the museum in St. Martinville, relating Creole life, is so controversial within the Creole community of Louisiana. [F.C.]

> Most people still bear French patronyms and have ancestral connections with the original Louisiana Cajuns. For example, C. Richard told me that one day (during the last World Acadian Congress) he

met a white woman named Richard. He told her that they must surely
have some common ancestors. She retorted at once that it was impossible because he was black. She left rapidly with a contemptuous look.
Why such a flagrant rejection of Black Creoles by the Cajuns when it
is widely known that the two communities shared the same misery?
[F.C.]

The Courage of the Cultural Warriors and Francophone Solidarity

This last theme, cultural warriors and francophone solidarity,
underlines two attitudes that we the professors judged essential if French
speakers are to have a future on the North American continent. The first
recognizes the importance of personal involvement in the French Louisiana
Movement. It also emphasizes the role that institutions play in any serious
cultural revival and the necessity to reach the population at large. The second is a reminder that the people of French descent in North America share
something, a heritage, a brotherhood, and hopefully a desire . . . to persevere
with others who shared a dream. What have the students retained of the
French Louisiana situation in this regard? Three observations essentially:
the existence of too few cultural warriors for an indifferent population, the
absence of militancy among traditional institutions and an overtaxed under-
financed new institution, and, finally, the need for francophone solidarity.

Courage of Cultural Warriors

Those who combat for a more regular use of French are mostly members of the elite, i.e., intellectuals. This distance between them and the
common folk has created some problems which have left a scratch on
the collective memory. [M.G.]

Further, the population has been abandoned by its institutions which
should have lent support. The Catholic Church, for instance, ceased
providing Mass in French. On school grounds, severe reprimands
were meted out to those who spoke French. English reigned royally.
The result, entire generations stopped speaking French. . . . French, an
oral tradition, could not survive in the face of English. . . . This is why
today, it is nigh impossible to find young French speakers, whereas the
majority of seniors can speak French. [M.G.]

Among the Cajuns, we have seen many things and met many people who work for the preservation and continuation of the French language and its culture. The culture is maintained through the availability of French radio, museums, the Jean Lafitte national parks, and programs like *Le rendez-vous des Cajuns* at Liberty Theater in Eunice. [M.G.]

At the University of Lafayette, the struggle for the survival of French seems to be the affair of a small group of militants, whereas at CODO-FIL, the combat seems difficult and restrained. CODOFIL . . . is responsible for hiring French-speaking teachers for the immersion courses . . . , for organizing activities which assemble French speakers (*le grand pique-nique*, for example), and for promoting innovative activities (immersion schools, for example). Their mission is at once impressive and discouraging. [F.C.]

It's true that in Québec we struggled long and hard to keep our language. Here [in Louisiana] they continue to struggle, but without adequate funding. . . . Further, when a population does not battle at the side of its militants, it is doubly hard to save the French language in Louisiana. [F.C.]

The Need for Francophone Solidarity

The trip to Louisiana was for me a period of discovery and of intense feeling. Despite the differences in climate and landscape I did not feel like a stranger in this corner of the continent as I had in Florida, for example. The people we met were so warm and curious that I quickly felt at home. Isn't it pleasant to discover another culture and the history of other cultural groups, while at the same time not having the impression that these people perceive us as foreigners? [C.-R.C.]

Creole and Cajun identities, in my book, have earned their place in North American *francophonie*. Owing to the diversity and richness of their cultures, they have attained a degree of notoriety equal to that of Québécois, who are more numerous, and Acadians, who are renowned for their history and their pride. I think that the North American *francophonie* would gain by creating stronger links between its constituent communities. I think sincerely that the French speakers of North America ought to know their own history and that of the other groups who, like them, continue to speak French in the midst of the anglophone majority. [C.-R.C.]

CONCLUSION

For us, Louisiana has been a door leading to the discovery and comprehension of contemporary French America, what Louder, Morisset, and Waddell now call Franco-Amérique (2001).[20] It initiated us to life on a far-flung island of the French archipelago in America. It has guided our steps and inspired our questions as we have explored other islands. It provided a benchmark with which to compare. It has destroyed the myths we held when we went there initially. We cringe today when we hear the term *Acadie du Sud*, which projects a false image of the ethnic complexity and linguistic diversity of this fascinating region. We have grieved at the visible loss of the French language, applauded the efforts of those who seek to save it through their Herculean efforts, and hope that our work contributes to that end. We have deplored the fact that our own government chose to pull up stakes after having played such a vital role in providing material and moral sustenance to the French Movement for over twenty years. French Louisiana has proven to be a hospitable haven to us and our students with whom we have sought to share the wonders of this complex and fragile Creole society.

NOTES

This chapter is dedicated to the three initial directors of *Projet Louisiane*: Gerry Gold, from York University, Eric Waddell, from McGill and then Laval University, and Louis-Jacques Dorais, also from Laval. Because of them, we had the opportunity to explore Louisiana, each from our own personal perspective and background.

1. *La Francophonie* is to the French-speaking world what the Commonwealth is to the English-speaking world. It is a community of interest, at the international level, sharing the French language to one degree or another. For a full account, see Têtu (1987).

2. This was the motto inscribed on Québec license plates until the mid-1970s. As Québec sought to shed the status of Canadian "province," the motto became the ambiguous and somewhat contentious, in many circles, *"Je me souviens."*

3. The Referendum of October 30, 1995, about Quebec sovereignty came within 0.5 percent of engaging the process of separating Quebec from the Canadian confederation.

4. On the average, interviews in rural areas lasted approximately three hours, in urban areas, roughly ninety minutes.

5. A bibliography of *Projet Louisiane* materials can be obtained by contacting the authors.

6. Franco-Américanie/Maine (1980, 1995), Franco-Américanie/Massachusetts (1986), Manitoba and Minnesota (1982), Ontario/Sudbury and Pentengueshene (1983), Ontario/Ottawa, Hawkesbury, and Cornwall (1989), Ontario/Sudbury and Surgeon Fall (1995), Ontario/Ottawa, Toronto, and Kingston (1998), Northern Saskatchewan (1986), Port-au-port, Newfoundland (1987), Nova Scotia/Baie-Sainte-Marie (1981, 1988), New Brunswick/Moncton and the Acadian peninsula (1990), New Brunswick/Madawaska (1993), New Brunswick/St. John River Valley (1999), Northern New Brunswick (2001), Alberta/Edmonton and the Peace River Country (1998), Prince Edward Island/Evangéline (1992), South Florida (1994), and Louisiana (2000).

7. For more on the "Laval school" and the emergence of "French America" as a legitimate field for academic inquiry see LeBlanc (1991) and Gilbert (1998:103). Louder and Waddell, actually, published in 1983 *Du continent perdu à l'archipel retrouvé: Le Québec et l'Amérique française*, which would appear in 1992 in Louisiana, slightly revised and in translation, as *French America: Mobility, Identity and Minority Experience across the Continent*.

8. For a description of Louder's transformation (conversion) from "quantitative" to "qualitative" geography, see Louder (1996, 2001).

9. Trépanier expresses these feelings in detail in Louder, Morisset, & Waddell (2001). They are briefly summarized here.

10. A dominant theme in the French Canadian ideology of *survivance: la foi gardienne de la langue*.

11. However, there are some notable exceptions, such as an article by E. Waddell (1979) published in *Les Cahiers de géographie du Québec* in French and in English as a Working Paper of Projet Louisiane (No. 4).

12. Interviews were likewise conducted with twenty-one high school graduates in four communities: Lafayette, Marksville, Mathews, and Rayne; the representatives of the Catholic dioceses of Louisiana, the bishop of the Methodist Church, and the French Mission's representative of the Louisiana Baptist Convention.

13. See, for example, 1989 correspondence with an anonymous columnist of the *Mamou Acadian Press* who wrote, "I was born in 1924 . . . and your study is certainly accurate and factual." He followed up with: "Revon Reed appreciate it very much. Now everyone want to borrow your book."

14. For instance, it was the case of Gilles Vigneault (1974) in his song "Je vous entends rêver" (I hear you dreaming): *"Puis quand nous vivrons Dans la Louisiane Anne ma soeur Anne Nous nous parlerons De ces grands pays perdus ici Anne ma soeur Anne Adieu mes amis Adieu mes pays"* (in Waddell, 1979:19). (When we will live in Louisiana Ann, sister Ann / We will talk about these great lost countries / Ann, sister Ann / Farewell my friends, farewell my countries.)

15. The first such occurrence dates probably from 1987 in a column called "Point de vue" of *La Presse*, where Rodrigue Tremblay, an economist and former Québec Government minister, stated the following: "La machine est peut-être en marche pour la 'Louisianisation' graduelle et irréversible du Québec, lequel deviendrait avec le temps un 'French Quarter' de l'Amérique du Nord" (30 janvier, 2 février: B–3). (The operation was launched toward a gradual and irreversible "Louisianization" of Quebec, which would progressively become a "French Quarter" of North America.)

16. "Les francophones [du Canada] partagent la ferme conviction que la promotion de la langue française passe par le droit de s'exprimer dans cette langue dans toutes leurs activités

quotidiennes" (p. 3). (French speakers [from Canada] share the firm belief that the promotion of the French language depends on the right to speak in that language in all activities of everyday life.)

17. In Canada, Francophones outside Québec, from all provinces by means of their provincial associations, are joined in a political lobby called *La Fédération des communautés francophones et acadiennes du Canada*.

18. Among the institutions visited: Acadian Memorial, Jean-Laffite National Park and Liberty Theater in Eunice, Fred's Lounge, CODOFIL, Louisiana Convention and Visitor Commission, Le Centre International, Prairie Elementary School (French language immersion), Jennings Museum, Retrouvailles 1999, and Organization Seeking a Queen's Pardon for Acts Committed against the Acadian People. Among the people encountered, in the order that we met them: Marc David, Etienne Dugas, Christophe Landry, Thérèse Bienvenue, Jolene Adam, Danielle Fontenette, Warren Perrin, Kirby Jambon, teachers at Prairie Elementary School too numerous to mention, Richard Guidry, Barry Ancelet, Jacques Henry, Debbie Clifton, David Marcantel, Mayor of Abbeville Brady Broussard, three senior volunteer guides in Abbeville, David Cheramie, Brian Comeaux, Gérard Breaux, Peggy Matt, and Philippe Gustin. We are grateful for their friendship and willingness to share.

19. We rely on the journals of three students: Cybèle-Rébecca Cloutier, François Cou't, and Mireille Gagnon. We thank them for allowing us to translate and use their words.

20. The term "Amérique française" or "French America" conjures up an antiquated vision of European empire, whereas "Franco-Amérique" is contemporary, inclusive, and rooted in the North American continent.

REFERENCES

Brown, Becky. 1997. "The Development of a Louisiana French Norm." In *French and Creole in Louisiana*. Albert Valdman, ed. New York: Plenum Press, pp. 215–235.

Gilbert, Anne. 1998. "A propos du concept d'Amérique française." *Recherches sociographiques* 39, pp. 103–120.

Gladu, André. 2001. "*La Franco-Amérique: Une maison sans adresse civique: Un entretien avec André Gladu*." In *Vision et visages de la Franco-Amérique*. Dean Louder, Jean Morisset, & Eric Waddell, eds. Sillery: Editions du Septentrion.

Gold, Gerald. 1984. "The Mission of Québec in Louisiana." In *Minorities and Mother Country Imagery*. Gerald Gold, ed. St. John's: Institute of Economic and Social Research, pp. 112–135.

Gouvernement du Québec. 1995. *Politique du Québec à l'égard des communautés francophones et acadiennes du Canada: Un dialogue, une solidarité agissante*. Québec: Ministère du Conseil exécutif, Secrétariat aux affaires intergouvernementales canadiennes.

LeBlanc, Robert. 1991. "A Critical Survey of Recent Geographical Research on la Franco-Américanie." In *Le Québec et les francophones de la Nouvelle-Angleterre*. Dean Louder, ed. Québec: P.U.L., pp. 107–125.

Louder, Dean. 1990. "Projet Louisiane: Ten Years Later." Communication to the Annual Meeting of Association of American Geographers, Toronto, April 19–22.

——. 1996. "*L'archipel: Un commentaire personnel sur deux cultures fortes mais marginales*." *Géographie et cultures* (Spring 1996), pp. 107–122.

———. 2001. "*A la découverte de l'Archipel: Odyssée en dehors du 'Mainstream*.'" In *Vision et visages de la Franco-Amérique*. Dean Louder, Jean Morisset, & Eric Waddell, eds. Sillery: Editions du Septentrion.

Louder, Dean, Jean Morisset, & Eric Waddell. 2001. *Vision et visages de la Franco-Amérique*. Sillery: Editions du Septentrion.

Louder, Dean, Cécyle Trépanier, & Eric Waddell. 1994. "*La francophonie nord-américaine, mise en place et diffusion*." In *Langue, espace, société: Les variétés du français en Amérique du nord*. Claude Poirier, ed. Québec: P.U.L, pp. 187–202.

———. 1999. "*La francophonie canadienne minoritaire: d'une géographie difficile à une géographie d'espoir*." In *Francophonies minoritaires au Canada: l'état des lieux*. Yvon Thériault et al., eds. Moncton: Editions de l'Acadie, pp. 19–39.

Louder, Dean, & Eric Waddell. 1983. *Du continent perdu à l'archipel retrouvé: Le Québec et l'Amérique française*. Québec: P.U.L.

———. 1992. *French America: Mobility, Identity and Minority Experience across the Continent*. Baton Rouge: Louisiana State University Press.

Reed, Revon. 1976. *Lâche pas la patate, portrait des Acadiens de la Louisiane*. Montréal: Editions parti pris.

Richard, Zachary. 2001. "*Plus qu'un grand 'French Club*.'" Montréal: *La Presse*, July 14.

Têtu, Michel. 1987. *La Francophonie: Histoire, problématique, perspectives*. Montréal: Guérin littérature.

Tremblay, Rodrigue. 1987. "*La 'Louisianisation' du Québec*." *La Presse* (30 janvier, 2 février), B–3.

Trépanier, Cécyle. 1986. "The Catholic Church in French Louisiana: An Ethnic Institution?" *Journal of Cultural Geography* 7(1), pp. 59–75.

———. 1989. *French Louisiana at the Threshold of the 21st Century*. Quebec: Projet Louisiane, Monograph 3.

———. 1991. "The Cajunisation of French Louisiana: Forging a Regional Identity." *The Geographical Journal* 157(2), pp. 161–171.

———. 1993. "*La Louisiane française au seuil du XXIe siècle: La commercialisation de la culture*." In *La construction d'une culture: Le Québec et l'Amérique française*. Gérard Bouchard & Serge Courville, eds. Sainte-Foy: Les Presses de l'Université Laval, pp. 361–394.

Waddell, Eric. 1979. *French Louisiana: An Outpost of l'Amérique française, or Another Country and Another Culture?* Québec: Projet Louisiane, Working Paper No. 4.

ABOUT THE CONTRIBUTORS

Barry Jean Ancelet is Granger and Debaillon Professor of Francophone Studies and Folklore at the University of Louisiana at Lafayette. He has given papers and published articles and books on various aspects of Louisiana's Cajun and Creole cultures and languages, including *Cajun and Creole Music Makers* (1984; revised 1999), *Cajun Music: Origins and Development* (1989), *Cajun Country* (1991), and *Cajun and Creole Folktales* (1994). He is a coauthor of the upcoming *Dictionary of French as Spoken in Louisiana*. He has also contributed to numerous documentary films and radio programs on Louisiana French culture, serves as director of the annual Festival de Musique Acadienne component of Festivals Acadiens et Créoles, and hosts the "Rendez-vous des Cadiens," a weekly live radio show from the Liberty Theater in Eunice, Louisiana.

Deborah J. Clifton received her Ph.D. in Francophone Studies at the University of Louisiana at Lafayette in 2000 and her MLIS from the Louisiana State University School of Library and Information Science in 2005. She is currently curator of collections at the Lafayette Natural History Museum and Planetarium, a member of the adjunct faculty in the Department of Modern Languages at the University of Louisiana at Lafayette, and an associate research fellow at the Center for Cultural and Eco-Tourism of the University of Louisiana at Lafayette.

Dana A. David received her Ph.D. in Francophone Studies from the University of Louisiana at Lafayette in 2000. She has studied faith healing among Cadiens in her native southwest Louisiana, taking a phenomenological approach to the study of vernacular medicine practiced by Cadien treaters. She has a strong interest in health literacy and understanding issues of health through cultural influences. She has worked at the Immigration and Health Initiative at Hunter College. She is currently teaching French at Fordham University in New York City.

Marc David received his Ph.D. in Anthropology at the University of North Carolina at Chapel Hill in 2005. His dissertation dealt with history, social memory, and race in Saint Martinville, Louisiana.

Jacques Henry's interest in French culture brought him to Louisiana in 1981 to conduct fieldwork on the French renaissance movement. He received his doctorate in cultural anthropology from the Université Paris Descartes in 1983. He eventually joined Louisiana French Movement's leading organization (CODOFIL) and became its executive director. He joined the University of Louisiana at Lafayette in 1992 where he is now teaching, researching, and publishing.

Sara Le Menestrel is a researcher with the National Center for Scientific Research in France (CNRS/MASCIPO). She works at the Center for North American Studies in Paris (CENA). She holds a doctorate in ethnology from the Université Paris X Nanterre. She published *La voie des Cadiens. Tourisme et identité en Louisiane* (1999) and *Vivre la guinguette* (2003) with Kali Argyriadis. She is currently writing on musical legitimacy and social stereotypes in the construction of the French Louisiana repertoire. She is also working with Jacques Henry on the decision-making process by hurricanes Katrina and Rita's evacuees.

Carl Lindahl is a Martha Gano Houstoun Research Professor in the English Department of the University of Houston. In addition to his work on Cajun culture, he specializes in medieval folklore and in folk narrative. His publications include *Earnest Games: Folkloric Patterns in the Canterbury Tales* (1987), *Swapping Stories: Folktales from Louisiana* (1997), *Medieval Folklore: An Encyclopedia* (2000), and *American Folktales from the Collections of the Library of Congress* (2004). He currently serves as Codirector of Surviving Katrina and Rita in Houston, a project through which Katrina survivors record their fellow survivors' experiences and narratives of the hurricane.

Dean Louder was born in Utah. His interest in French derived at a young age from the reading of Longfellow's Evangeline and an extended stay in France. He received his doctorate from the University of Washington in 1971 and accepted a position as professor of geography at Laval University. For twenty-five years, he explored French America from his Québec base. After retirement in 2003, his quest continued resulting in a voluminous blog (www.septentrion.qc.ca/deanlouder/) and a new book with Eric Waddell, *Franco-Amérique* (2008). In 1997, he received the Ordre des francophones d'Amérique for his contribution to the maintenance and development of French language and culture in North America.

Cécyle Trépanier hails from the province of Québec. A research assistant with the *Projet Louisiane*, she received her Ph.D. in geography from Pennsylvania State University. She conducted research on French America with a focus on Acadians in the Maritime provinces. She retired from Laval University in 2003.

INDEX

www.ingramcontent.com/pod-product-compliance
Lightning Source LLC
Chambersburg PA
CBHW020610270326
41927CB00005B/266